Refugee from Man

Twilight of Man

Earnest Albert Hooton

PROFESSOR OF ANTHROPOLOGY, HARVARD UNI-
VERSITY, CURATOR OF SOMATOLOGY, PEABODY
MUSEUM OF HARVARD UNIVERSITY

G·P·PUTNAM'S SONS

NEW YORK

MANUFACTURED IN THE UNITED STATES OF AMERICA

Van Rees Press, New York

To

SIR ARTHUR KEITH

A student of human evolution unsurpassed in knowledge, courage, tolerance, and modesty.

PREFACE

HERE IS MORE RAUCOUS crying in the wilderness. In the two years which have elapsed since I published *Apes, Men, and Morons* human behavior has continued to deteriorate. Devolution proceeds apace. We are still trying to redeem society by the appeasement of the antisocial and the pampering of the unfit. The attitude and policy of the tycoons of social affairs who are striving to clean up this human mess are summarized by the ungrammatical title of one of the current radio whines: "Wishing Will Make It So." The prospect of the human future is so dark that I have adapted a title for this book from *Götterdämmerung*. This does not imply that the present offering is of a heroic, Wagnerian nature. I might have called it, less pretentiously, "In the Gloaming, O my Apeling." However, this book is no sentimental threnody.

In addition to the irritating facetiousness of my literary style, the present volume has to support the incubus of my drawings. Amateur illustration by an author is like profanity in conversation. It probably serves no useful purpose and certainly is shocking and objectionable to many, but the perpetrator enjoys it. I slipped accidentally into this sin against art and taste last fall when I was trying to alleviate the grimness of graphs illustrating a supposedly "popular" volume on criminal anthropology. Now I am like a little child who, having tasted once the delight of saying a naughty word, thereafter runs about shouting "damn" all over the place.

In this book there are some inconsiderable repetitions of material which I have already published. This fact does not worry me because there are nearly 130,000,000 inhabitants of these United States who have never read anything I have written. Among them are to be numbered, according to my impression, most of my unsolicited and abusive correspondents.

I am greatly indebted to *Life* magazine for allowing me to use as a symbolic frontispiece to this Jeremiad the beautiful photograph of a sodden and semisubmerged primate taken by Miss Hansel Mieth. The *Atlantic Monthly* has graciously permitted me to republish "The Wages of Biological Sin." The present version includes some passages which Mr. Weeks did not like and which I do. I am also grateful to the editors of *Mechanical Engineering* and of *Antiquity* for the privilege of republishing "The Simian Basis of Human Mechanics," which appeared in both of these meritorious but diverse periodicals.

I am grateful to my wife for making the index of this book, and I am ungrateful to her for making me delete some of my choicest indiscretions. Miss Charity Mason, my invaluable editorial assistant, has performed the other mean jobs incidental to the production of this book. I appreciate her collaboration. In the preparation of several chapters here included I have had the advice and criticism of two of my younger colleagues, Dr. Clyde Kluckhohn and Dr. Carl Seltzer. However, neither of them is responsible for any erroneous statement, specious argument, malicious innuendo, or reprehensible vulgarism which may be found in this book.

Cambridge, Massachusetts   EARNEST A. HOOTON
June 25, 1939

CONTENTS

ix

CONTENTS

ILLUSTRATIONS

xi

TWILIGHT OF MAN

PREAMBLE

IT IS well to pause and consider before one attempts to become a savior of mankind. The interfering hero who dives in and pulls out a drowning suicide has hardly performed a social service. He would have been wiser to keep dry and watch the bubbles. In some countries of the Orient the person who preserves the life of another automatically becomes responsible for the board and keep of the rescued ever after. Social service and public aid work out in a way not altogether dissimilar. The more we "rescue the perishing, care for the dying, snatch them in pity from sin and the grave," the oftener they fall in and the louder are their demands for succor. "And what did ye do with his hat?" asked the frantic mother to whom a dripping hero had restored her sodden offspring.

The markets of the world are glutted with a surplus of human material of inferior quality. Why do not paternalistic governments offer bonuses for crop restriction? Overproduction in agriculture results in unsalable excesses of stuff which, for the most part, can at least be eaten; and there is no dearth of hungry mouths. The surplus of human production has to be fed, and not even an anthropologist would dare today to echo Dean Swift's sardonic proposal for a solution of the Irish famine—that they eat their babies. As governments become weighed down more and more heavily with the obligation of supporting their indigent unemployed and infirm, they totter toward bankruptcy and resort to the desperate expedient of starting wars, hoping to divert the famished proletariat from anarchy and revolution by holding out to them the promise of wealth to be snatched from other nations in like case. The dictators do not fail to realize that wars, at any rate, reduce the population surplus.

There is scarcely any fantastic and crack-brained economic proposal which has not been seriously entertained, or even tried out, in the hope of remedying a situation which grows steadily worse. Do you remember the little story (most appropriately German in origin) of Discreet Hans? Grethel assigned him a long succession of tasks, in all of which "he behaved stupidly." So she married him. No doubt they had a very large family.

Why it is that our leading statesmen, who so incessantly and so futilely mouth platitudes about peace, prosperity, and social security, never by any chance allude to the evil which lies at the root of our vast growth of population difficulties? It is perfectly obvious that the horrible state of affairs in which "civilization" has involved itself is due to the fact that the world is overpopulated with unintelligent and dishonest human animals. The dishonest batten upon the unintelligent, and corrupt society. Unintelligent or stupid persons are not necessarily dishonest, but they fall an easy prey to the machinations of the cunning. Dishonesty in itself is not incompatible with considerable intelligence, but it certainly is associated with mental ability principally in individuals who are insane or psychotic. However, the dishonest are not the only parasites which feed upon the multitudes of morons which we are breeding and preserving. Men of mediocre intelligence, whether honest or dishonest, are able to rise to positions of power, wealth, and influence, partly because, however meager may be their personal endowment, they, at any rate, are above the ruck of morons. Thus every politician, or nearly every one, has an interest in human

classes of individuals promote criminal activities in order to
keep themselves in jobs, any more than I would suggest that
doctors try to undermine the public health in order to enlarge
their practices. But I do feel that violent and general opposition
to measures designed to extirpate from our population the criminalistic element is not completely humanitarian in its motivation.

While theoretically we hate war and are aghast at the prospect of it, it is very hard to believe that the personnel of the
professional armies and navies of the world would welcome a
universal and lasting peace which would deprive them of their
occupations. The same applies to the industries which profit
from the sale of the materials of war, the politicians or statesmen who secure for themselves power and authority in war-
time which they never could attain in times of peace, etc. In
short, there is a good deal of self-deception and sheer hypocrisy
about our social aspirations. The reformer does not desire that
society be reformed nearly so much as he wants to continue his
function of reformer. The recalcitrance of the heathen in the
matter of conversion to Christianity at any rate insures the
permanence of missionary effort.

I do not wish to be cynical, but it seems to me that civilization
is determined to commit suicide and that man does not wish
to be rescued. Certainly if his eye offends him, he does not
pluck it out, but at best puts a patch on it and convinces himself that he has improved his looks.

Now, I am quite sure that anthropology has some of the
right answers to human problems—or, at least, can work them
out. But I do not think that most men want to know the
answers. If I want to know them and go on working at them,
I should realize that I am not trying to "do good" in any vicarious and grandiose fashion, but only to have a good time myself. I must enjoy my anthropology as some perverse persons
enjoy putting together the pieces of a picture puzzle, with
a full realization that no one has any use for the job when once
it is done.

stupidity because he can capitalize upon it. Representa
government necessarily results in the election of low-gr
public officials because the suffrages which elect them are th
of the majority of extremely unintelligent populations.

Industry has a vested interest in the stupidity of the mass
because a lack of intelligence in the human animal facilitates h
enslavement to machines. Up to a point, it is highly profitab
for acquisitive and ambitious individuals to surround then
selves with a proletariat which is capable of work but not o
thought. When education filters down to this economic sub
stratum, the less feebly endowed rise out of their class or revol
against their economic subservience. Then all of the submerged,
however witless, also revolt; and the fat is in the fire. Everyone
expects to rise, regardless of his ability and merits. Charity to
the socially unfit is extended by some out of sheer philanthropy;
privileges are granted by others from motives of expediency;
doles and bonuses and pork-barrel relief projects are put
through by men who wish to consolidate themselves in positions of power. The entire social, economic, and political
system becomes infested with legal and illegal rackets. I am
very much afraid that this is the sort of social order, or rather
disorder, that the majority of our population wants.

There is plenty of information available as to the extent of
crime and the cost of crime to the nation. Both are appalling.
It is difficult to escape the conclusion that the immediate reason
why we have so much crime is that we want it and approve of
it. Persons who commit crimes and profit by them are certainly
in favor of crime. Others who regard them with indifference or
toleration must also be counted in the procriminal party. There
is no small fraction of our population which makes an honest
living out of the criminal activities of others. In this number
must be included the police, a considerable portion of the judi-
ciary, a large percentage of the members of the bar, the officers
of correctional institutions, and a good few criminologists and
social workers. Now, I do not for a moment insinuate that these

In the application of biological anthropology to problems involving the adjustment of the individual to society, we are making definite progress. In the matter of the relation of man's physical constitution to his pathology, to his physiology, and to his mentality and temperament, we are on the verge of substantial knowledge. It is now possible to envisage a program for the study of human heredity which, within a comparatively short space of time, may enable us to make positive recommendations for the improvement of the human stock by better breeding. However, I am fully convinced that these possibilities will not be realized by the development of a messianic attitude on the part of those who are working toward the ends in question. I suppose that I have tried to sell anthropology as a means of salvation, but now I realize and am reconciled to the hard fact that if accepted it will have to be like the gospel, "free to everyone, without money and without price." Of course, when I speak of "selling" anthropology I do not refer to the actual professional (commercial) practice of hanging out a shingle, opening an office, and charging fees for consultations. I simply allude to the fact that men engaged in scientific research, like those engaged in reform or in charitable enterprises, have to persuade some philanthropist or some hopeful investor to furnish the funds necessary for carrying out the experimentation or for establishing the project.

I was moderately successful in securing funds for the prosecution of scientific research before the results of the researches began to be positive, explicit, and objectionable. In fact, I am glad to say that I have received most generous treatment. However, it has dawned upon me in the past few years that, for example, the demonstration that criminals are biologically inferior, or what I think to be a demonstration of that truth, is pretty generally regarded as bad news. I assume that everyone is acquainted with the traditional fate of the bearer of evil tidings. I assert and can offer some evidence to back up the statement that a principal cause of dishonesty, stupidity, and general human wickedness is the preservation and the propagation of degenerate human organisms. I protest that we are getting nowhere with moral suasion and institutional tinkering, and that man is still an animal and the product in large part of his biological inheritance. I stress the lessons which are to be learned from human evolution and harp upon the apes. Man knows little of his origins, but resents them. He suspects the worst and abhors the candid investigator of his own family affairs.

Yet the study of apes and lower primates reveals little or nothing that should be repellent or disillusioning to the higher creature who glories in his manhood. It reveals the capacities and the limitations of a group of highly evolved animals which, in their anatomy, physiology, and even in their psychology, are miraculously close to man. Some way or other, the anthropoid apes have barely missed the boat, culturally speaking; and it is important for man to learn why. It is also good for man to realize in how many ways the great apes are really his superiors and what he has missed because his ancestors abandoned apedom. For, whether you like it or not, there now remains no reasonable doubt that men have sprung from apes of superior endowment and initiative. Our remote heritage is simian, and that is the best pedigree which the parade of the animal kingdom can exhibit.

There are pecuniary debts, cultural debts, and debts of heredity. In the case of monetary debts, the creditor can sometimes collect, unless it be the United States Government. Cultural debts, and those of heredity, are the more readily acknowledged because they do not have to be paid. They constitute sentimental rather than financial obligations. A certain type of man who considers himself successful is prone to say, "All that I am I owe to my mother." This is very hard on mothers. To say that all man is he owes to the apes would be decidedly unfair to dumb animals who are unable to refute the aspersion. Nevertheless, to learn the ways of the lower primates is not only a salutary exercise, but even an indispensable requisite for understanding human nature. For their ways are to a great extent our ways in cruder and simpler forms. I am inclined to believe that the leaders of human affairs who have led the world into such dreadful chaos might have behaved more wisely had they known all about the living infra-human primates, and had they been thoroughly grounded in the history of man's physical and cultural evolution during the past half-million years. They, at any rate, would have obtained some perspective of the course of human and prehuman affairs. That corrective knowledge is sorely needed and is deplorably lacking among putatively educated men. The most important lesson which anthropology and biology can teach is that we cannot afford to neglect the organism.

Almost the greatest exemplification of man's perversity in refusing to know himself is the lack, anywhere in the world, of an adequately endowed, properly equipped, and competently staffed scientific institution for the study of human heredity. We are what we are largely through our inheritance, and that is the only human phenomenon which man is unwilling to investigate. Man's own organism is the only thing in the world of nature which he does not want to improve. I think that man can be improved, if he will only settle down to study his organism in its relation to his physical environment and the inheritance of good and bad qualities—anatomical, physiological, psychological, and what will you. For the constant reiteration of this belief—because I have shouted it from the housetops these many years—I am branded as a pessimist.

To my limited intelligence it seems that the neglect of society to found a science for the production of better human animals must be due to one or another of three reasons. The first possible explanation for this attitude is that man believes himself to be organically perfect and hence incapable of improvement. He is the finished and immutable product of evolution. Anyone who holds this opinion may be called an optimist. The second possible reason for the disregard of human heredity is that men think it to be "a bad business" about which nothing can be done, so that they must pretend that it is like syphilis—non-existent. The man who adheres to this view is the real pessimist, and not only that, but also a coward. The third alternative is that man imagines that his behavior bears no essential relationship to his organic constitution. This is the prime article of faith among all morons in high places, and the gospel of demagoguery, not of democracy.

The foregoing are some of the subjects which I shall discuss, elaborate, and embroider in this book. I can recommend this collection of my writings to aspiring young workers in the science of man, as a complete handbook of instruction in the art and method of preventing the subsidization of research. A policy of appeasement and a project of social uplift are essential for philanthropic approbation and foundational support, even if they leave you with no more self-respect than has the present British government.

For myself, I have quit sugar-coating the pills which I attempt to force down the throats of reluctant patients. When I was a youngster there used to be two kinds of doctors—homeopathic and allopathic. They represented two schools of medical thought (or lack of it); but to us youngsters the difference between a homeopathic doctor and an allopathic doctor was that the former gave you medicine which tasted nice and the latter stuff which was invariably nasty. However, homeopathy has virtually disappeared, partially, I suppose, because the "hair-of-the-dog-that-bit-you" theory is now in favor only with persons suffering from an alcoholic hangover. Yet the adage *similia similibus curantur* is still implicit in social science which operates on the theory that we can be cured of our stupidity by breeding more and more morons. On the whole, it seems that the nasty medicine was "what did us good." Nevertheless, we all disliked the allopaths.

I

THE SIMIAN BASIS OF HUMAN MECHANICS OR APE TO ENGINEER*

INTRODUCTION

MY SUBJECT should not be construed by the refined as a
malicious innuendo, nor by the vulgar (unrepresented among
my readers, of course) as a "dirty dig." The transition from
ape to engineer is from the ridiculous to the sublime—or, at any
rate, from a little short of one to a little short of the other.
This handsome statement must serve as my panegyric on
mechanical science. As an anthropologist, I am perturbed by
the fact that human invention has outstripped man's organic
development, and his control of nature his control of himself.
So I propose to discuss the organic basis of mechanical achievement and the cause of man's physical and social lag in relation
to his material progress.

THE ANATOMICAL ANTECEDENTS OF THE CULTURED ANIMAL

Man is the only cultured animal, and human culture is but
the product of a superior animal organism. We must examine

* The tenth Henry Robinson Towne Lecture. Delivered at the Annual
Meeting, New York, N. Y., Dec. 6-10, 1937, of the American Society of
Mechanical Engineers. Reprinted by permission of *Mechanical Engineering*
and *Antiquity*.

the paradox of a living being which creates inanimate things more powerful and more nearly perfect than itself, with potentialities either for the salvation or the destruction of the inventor. The human organism is no up-to-date machine. It is like a horseless buggy which has undergone a series of reconstructions. The tires are flat; the body is battered and obsolete, however much paint may be smeared on the radiator; but the engine still runs and the machine still advances as long as the steering gear works. Abandoning this simile, which is only a sort of sop to engineers, I will recall the successive stages of human evolution, beginning with the lowest members of our Primate order, which were already in existence some sixty millions of years ago. First we have a long-snouted, small-brained, tree-dwelling quadruped, about as large as a squirrel, equipped with five flat-nailed digits on hands and feet, of which the innermost—thumb or great toe—can grip one side of a bough, while the outer four digits grip the other. This is the lemuroid stage. Next we have another small animal which sits erect in the trees, having specialized its hind limbs for support and for hopping, while its grasping hands are used to feed itself and explore its surroundings. This beast has a shrunken snout with eyes which are moving from the sides of the face to the front, so that both can focus at the same time upon an object being carried to the mouth. The brain is larger; and the head, with its shorter muzzle, is less ill-balanced upon the end of the upright spine. This is the tarsioid stage.

Next we have a considerably larger animal, with hands capable of encircling thicker boughs, which tends increasingly to move by swinging from one hand-hold to another, the body suspended by the arms and the legs trailing. The snout has continued to recede; the eyes are completely frontal, and stereoscopic vision, which gives depth and perspective, has arrived. There is the rudiment of a brow, and the tail has shrunk to a vestige. The ears are no longer erect, mobile, and pointed, but crumpled to the sides of the head; the viscera are

hitched up with sheets of membrane to keep them from sag-
ging when the trunk is vertical. I have described a telescoped
supermonkey, subape stage of primate evolution. Next, this
animal, having become too large, too hungry, or too smart
for life in the trees, takes a chance on the ground. In order to
see the better and to have its hands free for fighting and feeding, it rears up and stands upon its unsteady legs. The flexible,
prehensile feet gradually become strengthened to bear the weight
of the body; the lesser toes shorten, and the great toe loses
its thumblike mobility so that the foot can no longer grasp.
The legs become longer and more powerful, the pelvic girdle
expanded and flattened as a transmitter of total body weight
and a framework for attachment of the great muscles used in
standing and walking. The spine gets a forward kink above
the pelvis, which serves to erect the trunk; the tail remnant
has sunk beneath the buttocks and forms a part of the pelvic
floor; the chest has been flattened from front to back by
altered gravitational pull; the arms have become shorter and
the hands refined by release from locomotive duties; the tip of
the thumb can now be opposed delicately to the tips of the
outer fingers. The teeth have become so reduced that the lips
are outrolled; the bony nose with its fleshy tip has grown and
bloomed; the eyes, formerly recessed under a jutting bony shelf,
now peer from beneath the base of an incipient dome; the brain
case has exceeded the size of a grapefruit and now resembles an
overgrown cantaloupe. This nearly human animal is all ready
to contrive tools and to use them, thus beginning a career as
master mechanic of the animal kingdom, which makes him,
perhaps, in the course of a million years, a member of the
American Society of Mechanical Engineers.

All of the items of organic equipment which have enabled
man to produce the marvels of mechanics are a part of his primate inheritance. The first are the sensitive mobile hands with
their opposable thumbs. The grasping extremities, hands and
feet, with their five digits, are an ancient vertebrate character,

observable in a crude form in some reptiles. In the little lemurs the great diameter of average tree branches, relative to the size of the prehensile hands and feet, forces them to plaster the palms and soles tight against the bough, with the inner digits directed at an angle of almost 180° with the outer four. Often the index finger is reduced to a stump. There is little development of manipulative skill in the users of this clinging or perching grasp. When primate animals of larger size develop, the rotation of the thumb and its opposability to the finger tips begin to come into tactile and exploratory use. In the larger monkeys and apes the hands are big enough to permit a large and heavy object to be held in one, while the animal tears at it with the other or with its teeth. But the tree animal has to sit up to have its hands free for feeding, fighting, or other purposes. Having to sit down in order to use your hands is not conducive to two-handed experimentation or to the making of tools when you are perched precariously in a tree. A sitting monkey usually holds on with both feet and one hand, and has but one free prehensile member, unless equipped with a grasping tail. On the ground some macaques and baboons may stand on three extremities and pick up objects with the free hand; but, whether in arboreal or terrestrial life, one free hand is not enough.

Sitting up develops balance and encourages the animal to use its eyes rather than its nose. It takes the eyes off the ground and enlarges the range of vision. No mechanical achievement springs from developing the primitive sense of smell. On the other hand, acuity of vision, the ability to judge distances accurately and to record impressions of form, to remark relations and generally to observe, are primary requisites for an animal which is to become a mechanic. It is at this point, possibly, that the brain begins to step in and play a preponderant role in the co-ordination between the eyes and the hands which ultimately results in the creation of a material culture. Next to the sensory and motor areas of the nervous covering of the brain,

Primate on the Fence between Apehood and
Manhood

there grow up regions in which movements are pictured; and beyond them, probably, those mysterious brain tracts which provide for association, memory, and creative thinking.

But no animal up a tree can initiate a culture. The realization of the possibilities of stereoscopic vision, emancipated hands, and an elaborate nervous organization had to await the descent to the ground. In arboreal life the animal must ever contend against gravitation, be on the alert to maintain his balance. He has no firm footing. Our ancestors, wisely or fortunately, descended from the trees and eventually stood upon their feet on the ground. The stabilized supporting foot is nearly as essential for tool-producing as are the free hands with their opposable thumbs. For no effective use of tools or weapons would have been possible for an animal which suspended itself by the arms from the trees, nor for one which stood and moved on the ground on all fours. It was quite as necessary that the foot be remade as that the hand preserve and perfect its primitively mobile digits. The adaptations undergone by the spine, the pelvis, the lower limbs, and the foot, enabled the animal to get his whole body into a single vertical axis and to poise the center of gravity over the bipedal base of support. This base of support could be widened or lengthened by shifting the feet, according to the exigencies of the ground surface or the balance required by varied movements and positions of the arms and torso, in the carrying of weights, the wielding of tools, or other manual activity. Moreover, the erect posture and biped gait, as a result of perfected arrangements of the bodily mechanics, soon became so effortless and so automatic that the animal acquired the ability to walk or run while still employing the hands in unrelated and skillful movements. The locomotor and supporting appendages were emancipated from the prehensile members.

Thus it appears that before a primate can become an engineer he has to have a series of very complicated engineering jobs done upon him by a firm of biological engineers which we may call Variation, Adaptation, and Natural Selection, Unlimited.

REFLECTIONS OF PREHUMAN MECHANICS IN ANTHROPOID APES—THE PSYCHOLOGICAL BACKGROUND

A clearer understanding of the primate background of human mechanics may be gained from the study of the use of implements in monkeys and apes. Professor Robert M. Yerkes, of Yale, an authority on primate behavior, does not think that primates below the level of monkeys make any use of movable objects as tools or implements. There is no doubt that some monkeys display considerable dexterity in the handling of objects. However, Yerkes has known intimately only one monkey which he considered had an aptitude for the use of implements, and this gifted individual merely played with human tools. De Haan, nevertheless, experimented with an American monkey which, in the use of a variety of implements, was judged to be more intelligent than any anthropoid ape except the chimpanzee. Most of the experiments of psychologists have as their object the testing of the intelligence of an animal by setting it a problem which may or may not require for solution the manipulation of objects in a purposeful way. The use of tools is usually only incidental to the problem.

Experiments with the gibbon, the small anthropoid ape, seem to indicate no more mechanical ability on the part of that animal than is displayed by monkeys. Given a rake with which food may be secured, the animal will draw in the food if the latter is in front of the rake, but will not attempt to place the rake behind it for the purpose. Dr. C. R. Carpenter states that the gibbon, which has very long fingers and a very short thumb, makes comparatively little use of the latter in handling food or other objects. The short thumb is pressed against one of the middle joints of the fingers rather than opposed to the tips; and, instead of picking things up by gripping them directly between finger tips and thumb, the gibbon uses a sidewise scooping method.

On the whole, the gibbon is narrowly specialized for tree locomotion. Its arms are so long that they reach the ground when the animal stands erect. It swings by its arms from bough to bough and from tree to tree, easily clearing spaces of twenty feet. Although the great length of the upper limb is a mechanical advantage in moving the body weight from brachiation (arm-swinging), it is decidedly the reverse in the skilled handling of objects. Such long arms require too much elbow room, and the very extension of the forearm, which is the fixed lever in arm locomotion, interferes with quickness and precision of movements when the hanging upper limbs are flexed in lifting objects and the forearm becomes the movable part of the lever. But it is mainly deficiency of brain and not excess of arm which prevents the gibbon from being an engineer.

The orangutan, a much larger and stronger animal, is also handicapped in tool-using by excessively long arms and short thumbs. However, this ape is easily taught such high human accomplishments as eating sliced bananas with a fork, lighting a cigarette, riding a bicycle, driving nails, and selecting the right Yale key with which to unlock a box. One of Hornaday's orangs used the bar of his trapeze as a lever to enlarge the opening between the end bar of his cage and the concrete partition, so that he could get his head through and look into his neighbor's house. Thus curiosity is the father of invention. Often orangs twist the straw from the cage floor into ropes, and use them for swinging from trapeze bars. Yerkes set a problem for his orangutan, Julius, in which the animal was supposed to pile up boxes beneath a banana suspended out of reach, so that he could climb the pile and get the fruit. Julius was very slow in solving the problem with boxes, but when given a pole he improvised a perch between the corner bars of the cage and reached the banana by swinging or leaping from the perch. If I understand Yerkes correctly,

Julius also got the banana by pole-vaulting for it. His brightest achievement, not mechanical, was to coax Professor Yerkes to stand under the banana so that the ape could climb the professorial ladder. Julius could not learn to unlock a padlock with a key, perhaps because he belonged to the period of Yerkes' sojourn at Harvard, so that he was not allowed to use a Yale key. Yerkes thinks that, on the whole, the orangutan is not mechanically gifted, although more intelligent and adaptable in the use of tools than the gibbon. Nevertheless, the orang is apparently profoundly uninterested in engineering.

The chimpanzee, a much more tractable and sociable animal, is the favorite ape for experiments, and the most accomplished and inventive in the field of tool-using. Köhler has pointed out that certain defects in the chimpanzee's perceptions interfere with his mechanical progress. He does not distinguish between a part and the whole if they are spacially connected. If a table is placed in the corner of the room so that its surface appears to be joined to the walls, the chimpanzee will pass it by in his search for a movable object. He generally fails also to distinguish between a cord which is tied to a basket of food outside of the cage, by which the prize may be drawn within reach, and a cord which merely touches the basket. The odds are even that he will pull the wrong string.

Köhler also finds that the chimpanzees have little idea of statics. They cannot learn to make a stable pile of boxes. A large box will be placed precariously on top of a smaller one, and the animal standing on the summit of the shaky pile may even attempt to pull out one of the bottom boxes to add it to the top. The chimpanzee will attempt to stand a ladder vertically under a suspended object and climb up. If the object is hung close to the wall of the room, the chimpanzee will set the ladder flat against the wall, or edge against the wall. The animal's understanding of statics is impeded, and at the same time compensated, by its own organic statics—i.e., those of its labyrinth and cerebellum. For the chimpanzee is a natural

"If I understand Yerkes correctly, Julius also got the banana by pole-vaulting."

equilibrist. When he piles up a wobbly and unbalanced structure of boxes, which will topple over if left to itself, he often succeeds in mounting it and balancing it by his own weight long enough to enable him to grab the banana. Again, he is able to set the ladder flat against the wall and climb up it before it falls or even hold it vertically in the middle of the cage, run up it, seize the prize, and jump. In other words, he accomplishes a physiological achievement without a mechanical solution. Nevertheless, these animals do not have an absolute lack of insight into statics: they do not try to suspend a box in thin air, and when they use a pole as a jumping stick from the top of a box, they do not attempt to rest the end *in vacuo,* but on the box—although perhaps on its very edge. Köhler thinks that visual orientation in space—the fixed idea of "above" and "below"—develops gradually in human children as a result of the habitual upright posture of the head, whereas in a chimpanzee the head is just as likely to be held upside-down, and lack of such firm orientation inhibits the development of statics. Again, the chimpanzee lacks the incentive for the development of statics because of his natural gifts as an equilibrist.*

The one gorilla investigated by Yerkes, a young female named Congo, in tackling the problems of utilizing poles, boxes, et cetera, showed a high degree of ineptitude. In fact, Yerkes calls her a "moron in mechanics," but notes that this kind of a moron may be capable, nevertheless, of various kinds of imaginative adaptation.† I gather that he is of the opinion that such mechanical morons may be accidents which happen even in the best of families—the Hominidæ—and especially in the females.

The question of handedness, footedness, and eyedness in the anthropoid apes has been insufficiently investigated. The

* Köhler, Wolfgang, *The Mentality of Apes,* pp. 139-172. N. Y., 1925.
† Yerkes, Robert M., and Yerkes, Ada W., *The Great Apes,* p. 513. New Haven, 1929.

preference for the use of one foot, one eye, and one hand, and the involved specialization of the controlling side of the brain are of enormous importance in man's mechanical achievement. But even in human beings the implications of bilateral asymmetry and specialization are little understood. Only comparatively recently, educational psychology has discovered the serious extent to which children who are not right-eyed and right-handed, nor yet left-eyed and left-handed, but unspecialized, are handicapped in most human learning processes. Yerkes thinks that preferential use of the members of one side occurs frequently in the anthropoid apes, but does not commit himself to positive statements as to handedness and eyedness in the different apes. But it is fairly clear that an animal has to decide which hand to use before he can accomplish any mechanical feat with either.

Certainly the lack of speech is an insurmountable obstacle to the transmission of culture in the ape. When each individual has to discover for himself, or to learn only by exemplification, there can be little or no diffusion of the inventions of the mechanical mind to the ungifted who are capable only of utilization. In the last analysis, however, there is but one fundamental reason for man's exclusive possession of a material culture, for his unique understanding and application of the laws of mechanics. Man has a more highly evolved central nervous system than any other animal. The primitive insectivore with an infinitesimally better brain than its kind takes to tree life. The tarsier, with a slightly superior nervous endowment, sits up and begins to emancipate its hands. The more elaborate cerebral cortex of the monkey expends its excess of nervous or electrical energy in an aimless curiosity. This becomes more purposeful in the bigger-brained anthropoid apes and not only adapts the organism but invests it with the quality probably shared only with man—insight. The brain begins to get the upper hand of the body. Even in the earliest of fossil men, this cerebral dominance has so far subordinated gross physical equipment of powerful jaws, big teeth, and strong grasping extremities, that these no longer require modification to enable the animal to survive. The earliest human forms we know were tool-users. Tools make organic adaptation obsolete.

STEPS IN MAN'S MECHANICAL PROGRESS

I have been dealing with the physical and psychological background of man's mechanical pre-eminence. But progress in any science presupposes a society in which competition stimulates the inventive brain, while mutual aid and imitation amplify and improve its achievements. Let us examine the social basis of man's engineering progress. Perpetuation of the species is secured by success in the food quest, by evasion of, or defense against, enemies, and by reproduction with the safeguarding of offspring. At the root- and fruit-collecting and hunting stage of man's existence there is a certain incompatibility between the food quest and social aggregation. To live upon natural products it is desirable that human groupings be small and widely scattered. For purposes of mutual defense it is, on the other hand, essential that bands of numerous families be formed, if we assume, as I think we must, that the earliest forms of men had already sacrificed muscular strength and organic defensive ability to high development of the nervous system. The great anthropoid apes are powerful enough to fend for themselves in scattered family groups, and at worst they can take to the trees. Man, in becoming a terrestrial biped, incurred great risks because of his slow locomotion and his puny strength. It seems probable that the necessity which first mothered invention was that of devising weapons to eke out the inadequate strength of the lone food collector. As soon as the contrivance of weapons of wood and stone had supplemented man's organic resources so that he could tackle the larger game animals and become a carnivore, large social

". . . a certain incompatibility between the food quest and
social aggregation."

groups became feasible and advantageous. For really big animals can best be hunted down and killed by groups, rather than by individuals; and, even if you can kill an elephant single-handed, you and your family cannot eat it by yourselves before its flesh becomes too "high" even for savage consumption. The antiquity of human combination into social groups is shown by the hundreds of thousands of stone implements of almost identical types which are found in widely separated parts of the Old World during the Glacial epoch. Already manifold types of stone implements exist, adapted for various uses. Imitation and diffusion of mechanical achievements had begun. The use of the lever is prehuman; stone-working is at least one million years old; the utilization of fire nearly as ancient, although its first artificial production cannot be dated. The harpoon and the spear are easily thirty thousand years old, as are also the spear-thrower and the sewing needle; pottery and the bow may not be more than half of that age.

The domestication of plants and animals, which probably began eight to ten thousands of years ago, furnished the greatest incentive to mechanical progress. Domestication enabled man to get an adequate command of food supply, to settle down, to construct permanent abodes, and to begin the division of labor whereby the craftsman bartered the products of his skill for food. The training of the ox and the horse to perform the tasks previously accomplished by man-power enormously increased the amount of energy available for work production. All of this is elementary and obvious.

AETIOLOGY OF MECHANICAL PROGRESS

I should like to discuss briefly here, however, the respective roles of the individual inventive genius and of the imitative crowd in the furthering of mechanical science in primitive society.

Possibly the outstanding characteristic of primitive or savage societies is their rock-ribbed conservatism. That is perhaps why many of them have remained primitive. Under these circumstances the progressive has hard sledding. People persist in doing things in the old, stupid ways and in using implements which are ineffective and obsolete, merely because of the ease with which motor habits are formed and the impermeability of the low-grade brain to new ideas. The innovator in the field of mechanical science is regarded with suspicion, fear, and hatred, because his inventions are misunderstood and because they seem to give him an unfair advantage and to depreciate the time-honored methods, inferior tools, and lesser ingenuity of the ordinary worker. These observations are valid in primitive societies and probably held true in civilized nations up to the last century. Only within that time have innovations become the rage because of industrialization. The primitive inventor had to overcome a far greater inertia of stupidity and conservatism than it is easy for us in our mechanical age to conceive. He had to possess not only the mental ability to formulate mechanical principles and to translate them into working models, but also the moral courage to persist in the contrivance and use of the novelties which made him suspect.

The almost incredible duration, through scores of thousands of years, of identical types of coarsely shaped and inefficient flint implements probably reflects the struggle of the human organism to accustom itself to extraorganic aids. It suggests even more forcibly the suppression of the gifted innovator by the unprogressive horde. It is almost treasonable to argue in this democratic society that social, material, and intellectual progress has never been a communal achievement—a sort of immaculate conception of the group mind—but always the result of the effort of the gifted individual. The genius, mechanical or of any other sort, seems to be due to a fortuitous combination of superior mental qualities which from time to time is dealt from the shuffled pack of hereditary units.

Civilization has advanced in my opinion, not because of any

improvement of mental quality in the masses within the last ten thousand years, but rather because the realization of the material advantages to be gained from the toleration of genius has slowly percolated into the torpid minds of the majority of our species. This very reluctance to adopt a new and better idea or device carries with it a tenacity in the retention of such material cultural improvements as have won acceptance. Consequently, little utilitarian mechanical knowledge is lost, and there is a slow, cumulative transmission of the scientific achievements of the past. Thus, when the rare genius comes along he is enabled in successive ages to take off his flight from higher and higher structures which have been painfully built up by his gifted predecessors, consolidated by subsequent utilization, and sanctified by custom.

EFFECTS OF TOOL-USING UPON THE ORGANISM AND UPON SOCIETY

Let us now consider the effects of tool-using in a complex society upon man's organism and his biological future. There can be no doubt that modern mechanical science is partly responsible for the diversion of human evolution into smoothly engineered highways upon which we are coasting recklessly downhill. Let me recapitulate for a moment. Man raised himself above the level of the brute ape by developing a superior brain which enabled him to bolster his physical weakness by the use of extraorganic tools. A succession of achievements along this line very quickly made him monarch of all he surveyed—"lord of the fowl and the brute." Unsatisfied with dominance of animate nature, he has proceeded, with some success, to attempt to harness the forces of the universe. Why should anyone carp at such a stupendous performance? In the first place, I think that we may assume that any living organism, by its metabolic processes, can convert into vital energy, for growth, for reproduction, or for the performance of work, an amount of food which is rigidly limited by various organic restrictions. By means of hormones, or chemical messengers, the secretions of the ductless glands direct varying amounts of energy to different parts of the organism, according to the insistency of their several demands. The active part receives the nutriment it requires; it enlarges. The idle organ is kept upon starvation diet and shrinks. The ascendant phase of human evolution emphasized cerebral development because the brain was actively functioning in order that the species might survive by mechanical progress. At the same time, this brain trust was robbing the rest of the body—but to some extent of ill-gotten gains accumulated during the brutish stages of higher primate development, when the giant anthropoid apes (including our ancestors) got the bulge upon the monkeys simply by becoming gigantic, formidable, and fearless. The increasing use of the brain both directly diverted nutriment from other parts of the body, and indirectly, through creation of tools, diminished the work which had to be done by the hands, arms, legs, and teeth. These less active organs decreased in size, and atrophy brought also impairment of quality and not infrequent pathology. Up to a point, the recession in muscular strength and in masticatory and digestive ability was perfectly all right. No man has need of the strength of the ape (unless he is a professional wrestler or that supreme product of higher education—a football player). But he *ought* to need the brains of a man; he should not be able to survive and to flourish with the mental equipment of a moron.

At first, mechanical science merely devised tools which would utilize more efficiently the supply of human energy convertible into work. Use of these tools required muscular exertion, manual skill and co-ordination, and a considerable mental effort. Thus a sort of organic equilibrium in evolution was maintained; the brain was not overfed; the body was not markedly atrophied. The mischief started when mechanical genius began to contrive tools which facilitated the performance of work with little or no cerebral exertion. In the conversion of raw products the individual was allowed not only to stop sweating, but also to stop thinking. While he did work with tools requiring a minimum expenditure of physical energy, his brain went on a vacation.

The industrial age involves an elaborate social structure with a minute division of labor. The object of this organization is the mass production of material culture with the supposed purpose of furnishing cheaply to most of mankind things which will make life easier and happier. The ideal of popular distribution of invented products has, to a great extent, been realized. It is unnecessary to regurgitate here the well-masticated question of the social and biological effect upon human organisms of their being transformed into units for this mechanized production. The working days of these human cogs are spent in performing with precision and rapidity a short series of skilled movements which become more or less automatic, but still require attention. The effect of such a life upon the nervous system, upon the mind, and even upon the muscular and other functions of the body, is devastating. Such an infinitesimal human unit in a production machine can scarcely realize from his labors that sense of creation and that pride of craftsmanship which are the incentives that make the engineer.

The anthropological effect of mechanization upon the users of these supertools is mainly maleficent. Primitive conditions require the individual to be physically and to some extent mentally active throughout his short span of life if he is to survive and perpetuate his kind. Demands upon his organism are symmetrical, though rigorous. Natural selection and social selection eliminate the physically inferior, the manually inept, and to some extent the mentally dull, because each man creates his own tools and survives through his ability to use them. Intelligence advances in step with mechanical ability and bodily fitness. However, when human ingenuity contrives machines which increase almost infinitely the individual's control over matter, the struggle for survival and the checks against population increase are largely nullified. The physically and mentally inferior multiply with astounding rapidity, partly because their feeble capacities for productive work are nevertheless sufficient to make them cheap but essential adjuncts to the machines which play the larger part in goods production. Mechanical conversion of natural resources into food and other human essentials permits the survival of the low-grade biological specimen on a level of adequate nutrition and comparative idleness which would have been unimaginable for the primitive being, even if he were at once a mental genius and a Hercules. A majority of the population exists parasitically upon the inventive genius of the few, with little exercise of its meager intelligence. The mechanical contrivances which eliminate the necessity of thought, judgment, and skill in the user are almost equally available for the use of the moron and the criminal, as for the intelligent and the social-minded. The vast potentialities of these tools are used more and more for evil, as they become perfected, cheaper, and more easily accessible. Machines get better and better, while man gets worse and worse. The extraorganic tools are no longer accessories; the tail now wags the dog and even thinks for him. It remains for the other end only to bark and bite.

The once erectly striding biped abandons human locomotion and whizzes through the landscape, crouched over wheels and levers worked by his still-prehensile hands and his flat, vestigial feet, less useful for this purpose than those of his simian ancestors. He breathes a mixture of gasoline fumes and carbon monoxide and reeks of evolutionary decay. A premium is put upon illiteracy by the radio and the talking moving picture. These mechanical marvels are the means of world-wide spread of vulgarity, depravity, and misinformation, since they pander to the tastes of those who are capable neither of contriving nor understanding but only of crude sensory perception, stimulated by turning a switch or pressing a button—motor performances within the capacity of a lemur. Truly, man can say to the engineer, "The zeal of thine house hath eaten me up."

CONCLUSION

Now, I have purposely painted a somewhat lurid picture, which may be thought a caricature and is not likely to win admiration or to give pleasure. As a matter of fact, I wish to do neither. When nearly all of mankind insist upon regarding themselves as godlike creatures, he who harps upon the apish basis of the human organism and the possible reversion to an apelike behavior cannot hope for popular acclaim. I do not wish to depreciate the virtually superhuman achievements of pure and applied science; in fact, I aspire to be regarded as a humble sort of scientist myself—possibly an impure practitioner of an unapplied science. It is my purpose, rather, to emphasize the possibility that man's mechanical science (the product of a few) has so far outstripped his biological status and his social ideals and behavior that it has become a menace. What are we to do about it—call a moratorium upon mechanical endeavor and progress until man catches up with his machines? I think not.

What we must do is to divert a modicum of that high intelligence and creative ability which is too nearly monopolized by mechanical science to the study of ways and means of repairing and improving the human machine. We must remember that we are still animal organisms, and that the higher animal elevates himself only by striving to exercise to the full his organic functions. Degeneration and evolutionary extinction are the fate of the living thing which becomes so dependent upon a specialized environment that it loses the power of adaptation, of initiative, and of progress—literal and figurative. It is no more profitable to man to become a slave to the mechanical contrivances of his own mind (or of others' minds) than to become a parasite upon anything else in nature.

Man made himself out of an ape, partly by becoming an engineer. The danger now is that the process will be reversed, and the engineers will make apes of all of us. We apes shall then destroy ourselves and hoist the engineer with his own petard. My firm conviction is that we must build the future of humanity, if there is to be any future, not upon mechanical science, which is up to this point the greatest human achievement, but upon man's biology, about which we know virtually nothing at all. If man can make machines which are better than himself, cannot he make himself better? We do not need more automobiles, we need fewer fools in the driving seats; we do not want mechanical robots, we want human animals who still have brains; not more jails, but fewer criminals; not perfected weapons of war, but peace. The gorilla can manipulate human tools, but he uses them destructively. There is but one way of making a man, and that is the biological way. There can be no stability of civilization when the human biped totters, and he cannot be propped effectively by law, by education, by religion, or even by mechanical inventions. Breed better animals by selection and elimination of the inferior; study the transmission of those organic capabilities stored up by our species through the millions of years of primate evolution which have culminated in man. You will then conclude that it is man who makes the tools, and that only men, not morons or apes, may use them for the betterment of humanity.

II

THE LANTERN OF DIOGENES*

WHEN DIOGENES was asked why he was carrying a lighted lantern through the streets of Athens in broad daylight, he replied that he was looking for an honest man. I would not affront the alumni of Harvard University, assembled in this virile and virtuous metropolis, by rekindling the lantern of Diogenes in a search for mere pecuniary honesty. That valued quality is perhaps as widely distributed as is the degree of Bachelor of Arts, although the distributions are not always coincident. I am not even looking for abstract intellectual honesty, which is a necessity made of a virtue to all who are astute enough to recognize the best human policy. This recognition is general among those of good cerebral endowment—although denied, apparently, to nearly all rulers of states, totalitarian or democratic. But an honest appraisal of the human species by any of its members seems even less attainable than honesty in government, because man has always identified himself with his own creator, who, according to Genesis, "saw everything that he had made, and, behold, it was very good."

Now, I am not a Cynic philosopher, but only an anthropologist—that apostate from the human species who attempts to

* Delivered at the Annual Meeting of the Associated Harvard Clubs, Chicago, Illinois, May 21, 1938.

31

examine man impartially rather than worshipfully. In full
consciousness of my own mediocrity, I venture to ape Diogenes
and to hold a candle to the sun of self-approbation which has
blinded man—a negative sort of candle with a dark beam. I
hope that this new light in the old lantern of Diogenes will
discover some still-uncorrupted minds which may yet arrest
the course of man's degeneration. And so I dare to
irritate you with my crude appraisal of man, because I am
convinced that the only way of human salvation is the hard
biological way, and that we must no longer dally in the prim-
rose paths of social horticulture, hoping to pluck flowers which
will both beautify the sickroom and cure the patient of his
cancer. Moreover, a virtually unanimous condemnation of my
view of man suggests that it may be right, since the disapprobation of the unintelligent is the hallmark of merit and of truth.

It is unnecessary to argue the need of a pitiless examination
of the status of man when we are confronted by the breakdown of economic systems, the decay of religion, the decline
of democratic institutions, wholesale reversion to autocracy,
and the complete disregard of human rights by maniac dictators. Why should we be afraid to attempt a diagnosis of the
pathological atavism of modern society? As yet we need not
fear to speak our minds under a government which, although
more and more domineering in its paternalism, still renders lip
service to freedom of speech and ideals of democracy. The
penalty for frankness in the United States is only unpopularity
—not capital punishment. It requires neither physical nor
moral courage to take man to pieces in the hope of finding out
what is the matter with him.

MAN'S BIOLOGICAL STATUS IN RELATION TO HUMAN CULTURE

Anyone who has studied the course of organic evolution
must recognize that man is the unique animal genius. The term

genius implies inborn mental capacity of a supreme order. Comparatively speaking, genius is the common possession of all of our species, even the least gifted, although some of us have to be set against the duller apes before our genius is discernible to the naked mind. In the bottom grade of the animal order to which we belong—the lemurs—we find a rudiment of the nervous covering of the brain which culminates structurally in the vast cerebral cortex of man, and functionally in human intelligence. Hands, feet, and brain are the Trinity of the human organism—and of these the brain is the Holy Ghost, mysterious, indefinable, and supreme. Confronted with the considerable array of data bearing upon the evolution of the primates, one can only conclude that its course has been controlled and directed at every stage by the development and function of that dominant organ with its accessory nervous system. An inherent superiority in quality of nervous endowment is our ultimate postulate as to the cause of the evolutionary rise of the primates. For some spark of this nervous genius is their common heritage. The lemur, a long-snouted, quadrupedal, tree-dwelling animal, already has adopted, by choice or by chance, a habitat which utilizes the possibilities of the sensitive and mobile digits which have been retained as items of a primitive vertebral equipment. This habitat demands agility, motor co-ordination, and acuteness of vision. It furnishes the maximum stimulus for the cerebral development of a small animal, but only if that animal is endowed with the potentiality of brain growth. I like to call that divine gift "cerebral initiative."

The primate next in order of development, the tiny Tarsius, an arboreal hopper of the East Indies, has already been impelled by that cerebral initiative to specialize the feet for support, to sit up and use the free hands as food conveyors and organs of exploration, with concomitant shrinking of the projecting snout, the primitive apparatus for grazing, smelling, and touching. The brain of the tarsier has expanded relative to its body bulk, and the eyes are shifting from the sides of the head to the front, because the animal is trying to focus its vision and concentrate its attention upon objects held in the hands.

At the monkey stage, stereoscopic sight has been achieved by the coincidence of the visual fields of the frontally directed eyes; the nervous covering of the brain has become wrinkled to provide additional area; the cerebral hemispheres have grown in every direction, and it seems probable that the nervous control of the animal's activity is less purely reflex and automatic than in lower forms. Impulses are not merely conveyed to the spinal cord and cerebellum and then reflected back as muscular stimuli, but there are also some delayed responses, in which the cortex of the brain participates by a deliberate sorting of impressions and a conscious or volitional control of ensuing movements. Associations and ideas have been born. My amateur descriptions of these neural mechanisms will doubtless make the professional psychologist squirm; perhaps they will even goad him into intelligibility. As a matter of fact, we do not need a psychologist to tell us that a monkey is intelligent. That intelligence, although it defies anatomical description and physiological analysis, looks out of his eyes and is manifested in his behavior, whether or not he is solving some "problem" with the aid or interference of the Bug Goldberg apparatus of the psychological laboratory.

With the development of the anthropoid apes, there comes the habit of arm suspension in the trees with consequent verticality of the trunk and the beginning of a special orientation in which heads are up and feet are down, together with many anatomical and physiological variations which parallel those which must have taken place among our own prehuman ancestors. In the chimpanzee and the orangutan, apes of a body bulk about equal to that of man, the brain has grown to less than one-third of human size, while the giant gorilla, with at least three times the body weight of man, has a brain still a scant third as large as that encased by the average human cranium. Yet these anthropoid brains are almost human in form and in the details of the intricate patterns of their cortical surfaces. "Almost Human," too, is the title of a book in which Professor Robert M. Yerkes has described the wide variety of emotional patterns of the great apes, their behavioral adaptability, their capacity for concentration and attention, their utilization of insight and foresight, and their undoubted display of memory and of creative imagination.

Yet it is just this anatomical deficiency of brain size, with its behavioral consequences, that separates the modern anthropoid apes from man by a vast and unbridgeable evolutionary void. A brain triply enlarged has made of man a very different animal, not in form and arrangement of bones, muscles, nerves, and viscera, but in the utilization of an almost identical organic equipment. For man differs functionally from the anthropoid apes in the unique creations of that very excess portion of the brain—language, material culture, and social institutions of a noninstinctive origin.

Throughout the whole primate order evolutionary activity has tended to concentrate in the central nervous system rather than to diffuse itself through the organism in a variety of narrow specializations of bodily parts. This predominantly nervous type of evolution inhibits such cramping and irreversible adaptations as the loss of digits and the development of hoofs or retractile claws, because the expanding cortex with multiplying areas in which impressions are sorted and blended and memories are stored encourages variation in muscular response to sensory stimuli by continual breaking of the automatic mechanism of the reflex. The animal overcomes obstacles by the increasing versatility of its responses, rather than by a painful series of bodily modifications such as fit its organism for survival under a single rigid set of environmental conditions. This concentration of evolution upon the central nervous system, with minimum specialization of other parts, permits survival under more diverse conditions of physical environment.

The animal that lives by its wits lives longest and most widely and abundantly.

Now, it is clear that all of the primates except the ancestors of man have developed outside of that sharp focus of cerebral evolution at which the specializations of other parts of the organism are inhibited by the dominating growth of the brain. Man alone has been the full recipient of the highest concentration of brain "drive," and in him only has operated the catalyst which has transformed the creature of instincts into a somewhat rational being capable of directing the major part of its activities by volitional cortical control. Throughout the progressive stages of human evolution the cerebral urge has been incessant, stimulating all sorts of bodily activity and gradually building up the ability to discriminate between the profitable and the useless. The crucial points in human emergence were reached when our ancestors abandoned the trees and adopted an upright posture and biped gait on the ground, thereby permanently emancipating their arms and hands from locomotor functions. I suggest that these two great evolutionary events were due to choice, and not to chance. There followed the one stupendous triumph of animal genius beside which all subsequent human creations pale into insignificance—the invention of tools. When man, after aimless wielding of sticks, first purposefully selected and used a club; when, after casually chucking stones about, he first intentionally chipped a stone for a cutting tool, he thereby transformed himself from an animal little higher than the apes to one "a little lower than the angels."

EFFECT OF CULTURE

Human culture is, then, the culminating product of the long evolution of the cortex of the brain. What has been its effect upon man himself? The consequences of culture may be classified as biological and sociological. We must differentiate between their effects upon primitive and uncivilized man and upon modern industrialized man, for initial benefits may work eventual harm.

Upon primitive man the first effects of culture, then limited to the using of extraorganic tools and implements, was enormously to increase his chances of biological survival. Firmly planted on his feet, he could stand erect with arms swinging from an axis some five feet above the ground. When the radius of the arm was extended by the use of a club, tipped perhaps with a sharp and heavy stone, he was able to deliver a terrific blow, not from the shoulders alone, but from the hips. He became a very formidable animal. Add the use of the thrusting spear, the projectile power of the resilient bow, the astounding lift of the lever, and the puny naked creature with a swollen brain and dangling arms became the lord of creation. For that cerebral initiative, exercised through the emancipated prehensile hands, enabled man to borrow or to imitate all of the defensive and offensive weapons which have been acquired singly, as painful bodily adaptations, by the entire concourse of the animal kingdom. Every one of these weapons could be adopted, used, and discarded at will by the erect and cerebrating biped. He did not sacrifice the grasping use of his hands to the development of claws, nor overbalance his head and starve his brain to maintain a massive outthrust snout with fighting teeth. He needed no carapace and no impenetrable hide, because he could interpose a moving shield between his body and a blow; he was not weighed down with organic armor.

The dominance of the brain in human evolution entailed, however, some organic sacrifices. You cannot eat your biological cake and have it. The expenditure of growth energy in any organism is limited by its capacity for assimilating food. The hypertrophy of any part of the body means an unduly large blood supply for the maintenance of that part and a diminished and possibly insufficient nutrition for other organs. Hypertrophy and atrophy are identical twins; but the former is large, sanguine, and predatory; the latter dwarfed, anemic, and submissive.

The brain is a spoiled and pampered child which has had its own way in the family of organs. It has demanded for itself the advantage of a lofty and commanding position so that the animal has been forced to rear up on his hind legs, kink his spine above the pelvis to secure verticality, overload the bony girdle to which are articulated the hind limbs by making it transmit the whole body weight to the legs, place a well-nigh unbearable burden of balance, support, and locomotor duties upon those unfortunate lower appendages, and crush the once mobile and prehensile feet into vestigial slabs with weak and makeshift arches. Consider for a moment the wrongs of the pelvis, especially exaggerated in the female of our species. Once a sturdy and efficient frame for the narrow back door of the body, closed by the shutter of the swinging tail, hitched to the substantial axis of the spine, and supported by the conveniently approximated pillars of the legs, what is it now? Forcibly bulged open beneath to permit the egress of foetuses with bloated brains, it is now bereft of a caudal door—a gaping osseous wound, scarcely able to contain its own viscera, and with its supporting pillars splayed apart to mechanically precarious positions. It is as if one built a house and tipped it upon its rear, supporting the weight of the structure upon the balustrades of the back porch. Contemplate, moreover, the vicissitudes of the long-suffering circulatory system. The hapless heart, designed to pump the blood along mainly horizontal channels, is now obliged to strain itself against the force of gravity, with the insatiate brain calling for ever-greater pressure on the topmost story, and the return lines from the legs leading upward, so that their weakening walls are bulged and distended with the sluggish stream of impure viscous blood—whence cold feet, varicose veins, hemorrhoids, and thromboses.

And what about the digestive tract? Let us start at its upper end and consider the rapine wrought by the tyrant brain. First look at the teeth—blackened and decaying tombstones, set awry in beds of putrescence—a contaminating sieve through which must pass every morsel of food. How did they get that way? The partial emancipation of the hands from locomotor duties and their new use as food-conveyers begin away down in the primate order among the tarsiers, and are accompanied by some reduction of the snout and the teeth. The latter continue, however, their vigorous function both in chewing and in fighting, until in civilized man the use of tools in the preparation of food is carried to such an extent that both mastication and biting become superfluous and obsolete. Then the vicious combination of atrophy of function and unbalanced diet of manufactured foods reinforces regressive evolution with virulent pathology. From this oral cesspool infections spread along the otiose lining membranes of the respiratory and digestive tracts into the degenerate nose, seat of an obsolescent olfactory sense and a vestigial sexual skin; into the vacant caverns of the sinuses, attacking the still indispensable organs of vision and hearing; down the trachea to the lungs, long working below capacity production, with many departments shut down and rusted out.

The human gut, of course, was evolved for the use of an animal living mainly on raw vegetable foods, and its great length of loops and occasional dilatations was disposed along a horizontal body axis. Finely chewed masses of coarse food of low energy production were leisurely moved through this elongated gut by muscular contraction while their body-building constituents were gradually extracted and absorbed, the roughage meanwhile massaging, scouring, and stimulating the lining of the alimentary canal. Tilting the animal up on its hind end produced a devastating effect upon these arrangements. As far back as the gibbon stage the suspension of the trunk in a vertical position necessitated hitching up the loops of gut and other viscera by mesenteries, or sheets of membrane, so that they might not slump into a snarl at the bottom of the body cavity, blocking the posterior orifice and cramping the reproductive organs. These contragravitational adjustments were never quite satisfactory, but they served as long as adequate masses of the proper coarse foods kept this long canal in a perpetual state of healthy exercise. But when unchewed gobbets of flesh and pasty masses of highly concentrated foods began intermittently to drop down this tortuous tube, accelerated by gravity, all sorts of refuse tended to accumulate in dead ends and unscoured corners, while various dangling empty loops became twisted and knotted, or painfully distended with the gas rising from decaying organic matter. Modern man cerebrates in a state of autointoxication. His brain, which has never learned to mind its own business, begins to interfere also with his digestive processes, and the sympathetic nervous system becomes excessively so and transmits his mental cares to his stomach.

It was the brain also which probably divested man of his hairy covering. Avid for sensation, it thrust out its millions of nerve endings to the lower layers of the skin, jostling the hair follicles and stealing their nourishment until they withered, leaving only sparsely scattered survivors, except in regions where glandular exuberance or protection for the brain itself facilitated the retention of a more generous crop.

Thus the vampire brain has sucked the life from the rest of the body, according only a grudging share of nutriment to those organs not under cortical control. It is a dictator which subjugates the body and molds it to its own purpose. It stifles all organic initiative other than its own. Of course, you must not think of the brain as a sort of malignant corporeal Stalin which liquidates all of its assistants in the false name of bodily communism. In fact, I do not want you to take my brain demon too seriously, because it is in some ways a benevolent and admirable ruler, being itself the fittest organ of the body and almost the only one in which man excels other animals. Culture, the child of the human brain, has been the instrument of human survival; and it is only in recent times that man has become a parasite upon it. Really, none of the structural modifications which the dominance of the brain entailed were of a sufficiently harmful character to endanger him, so long as his brain created tools which necessitated the vigorous use of other organs of the body. Dental regression and general physical atrophy in the savage and in the man who lives on the products raised by his own hands stop short of serious degeneration. The healthy and active body of modern man is by no means zoologically despicable, although extreme in its evolutionary specialization. We must consider the effect of culture on man's mentality and behavior before we can understand the vicious conjunction of brain-created influences which has produced so many worthless human creatures.

SOCIOLOGICAL EFFECTS

Probably the first psychological effects of tool-using upon primitive man were to give him the confidence that results from success and, in a measure, to banish fear. It transformed him from an animal, which may have been furtive and timorous, to a being of courage and self-reliance because he came to realize his ability to cope successfully with other apparently stronger beasts. He found that he could compensate by active use of his brain for his meager physical endowment. The contrivance of tools and weapons opened a limitless vista of cultural progress. It suggested that thought and invention pay. It put a premium upon intelligence because of the material benefits to be derived from using it.

The invention of material culture consolidated society. The food-collecting, toolless, prehuman animal probably existed in scattered family groups, because a natural basis of subsistence requires a large per capita acreage. Even the inefficient weapons of primitive man enabled him to kill more than he and his family could eat before it spoiled, and encouraged the formation of larger social groups, which could combine in food-gathering and for purposes of mutual defense. The idea of property and ownership became much more clearly defined when the goods were the creation of one's own hands—i.e., tools and weapons —than when they were merely natural food products collected here and there. Now, since the accumulation of wealth was the result of the exertion of individual ingenuity and skill in the devising of new tools and weapons, the successful man was the clever and brainy man, and the social differentiation of individuals according to intelligence and capability began. Here also was the beginning of division of labor, since the creative brain and the dexterous hand developed the craftsman, who bartered the products of his skill for the muscular exertion of the physically powerful but mentally ungifted. Even before he had achieved any considerable success in converting to his own use the flora and fauna of his physical environment, man began to turn his attention also to the larger phenomena of nature and to the supernatural. Clearly, he who could claim some understanding and even control of these mighty forces was a more clever and powerful fellow than the fabricator of tools, the skillful hunter, or the mere hewer of wood and drawer of water. Here began the pioneering in the undifferentiated fields of religion and science, with unlimited prestige for their practitioners.

Now, it is obvious that even at this early stage in the cultural development of man he began to be so obsessed with the products of his brain that he forgot that he was an animal, although he still behaved in a mainly animalistic fashion. Cultural evolution began to dominate organic evolution, since the measure of human success was what a man had in extraorganic property and what he was estimated by his fellows to possess in *mana*, or supernatural power, which would enable him to excel. The latter idea was not fundamentally unsound because, on the whole, it was based upon superior development of the cerebral cortex, a biological condition; but it was soon perverted by the more tangible and concrete evidence of superiority manifested in the possession of material wealth. Since it was observed that material property was associated with, and belonged to, the superior individual, it was soon conceived that accumulation of property made men superior and that all men would be alike if there were an equal distribution of wealth. Further, since intelligence was confused with knowledge and knowledge was conceived to be a species of material property, it was assumed that knowledge could be distributed like material wealth, with the result that all men would be equally wise and intelligent. Now we perceive the genesis of the great human fallacy that culture and society make the man and that education and social adjustment render him perfect or perfectly worthless. Man is mistakenly regarded as a sort of biological constant, with a value entirely determined by an array of sociological variables capable of manipulation and control.

Culture is, then, the creation of intelligence; it does not create intelligence, because the latter is a biological phenomenon and culture is inanimate. The virtue of culture lies in its creation by an active brain cortex. The mere enjoyment of culture, the mere utilization of its resources, no more implies intelligence of the user than the bicycle-riding of a chimpanzee presupposes a knowledge of mechanics on the part of that animal. As long as each primitive man, or for that matter each civilized man, is actually using his brain to create culture, he is exerting his intelligence and progressive evolution is going on. Thus, when each man makes his own tools and with those tools produces wealth, he is proceeding forward on the path which our prehuman ancestors trod. But when he merely uses the tools which others have invented to accumulate property either for himself or for them, he is not exercising his cerebral cortex. Evolution halts.

An active cerebral cortex functions in various and manifold types of intelligent behavior. Some men have mechanical aptitude and invent tools; others have a capacity for leadership and exercise their intelligence in organizing and directing their fellows; some, having no great intelligence but endowed with bodily strength, courage, and determination, are able to dominate the weaker by brute force and by skill in the use of weapons. To each of these categories of the variously capable, culture, once initiated, offers opportunity for the acquisition of power, influence, and wealth. To a certain type of intelligence it became evident in very ancient times that the accumulation of property is easier and more rapid if one is able not merely to use the actual tools, but also to use the people who use the tools. Forced labor and slavery became the lot of those individuals and groups who were easily subordinated because of mental or physical inferiority. The individuals successful in acquiring property or power through their cerebral initiative were often able to transmit their property or their authority to their descendants, so that these also dominated the ungifted drudges.

By this time the human animal was almost completely submerged in its own culture; society was thoroughly organized upon the basis of property in material possessions, and the facile transfer of culture from innovator to user eliminated the necessity of cerebral effort on the part of the latter. Mental evolution, in so far as it was actuated by increasing demands upon the brain, became limited to a few. The important distinction between the person who creates culture by cerebral initiative and the person who secures culture by commandeering the inventions and labor of others was lost. The latter became dominant, initially by force of arms, subsequently by hereditary tenure, and ultimately by capitalistic control. There remained for the great mass of the population only the stultifying task of using the tools which they did not invent in accumulating wealth for the consumption of their masters. Thus there developed a social and economic stratification in which the least capable mentally were condemned to labor incessantly for others at tasks requiring the minimum of thinking.

Man is, however, an intractable and pugnacious animal, and

does not readily bow his neck to the yoke, even when he is unintelligent. Since from the point of view of the oppressed the only difference between them and their masters was that they themselves created the wealth and the others consumed it, revolts of the masses involving wholesale destruction of life and property became widespread and frequently recurring phenomena. Every one of these periodic outbursts was attended by the breakdown of culture and the resurgence of the crude animal organism of man with manifestations of violent, unintelligent behavior. The idea of human rights, probably originating in the more intelligent minds, gradually began to percolate through the ossified brains of all classes. Even the less stupid of the dominating groups began dimly to realize that some sharing of wealth, some consideration of the comfort and welfare of their domestic human cattle, were necessary if they were to maintain their own positions. The ideal of human liberty burgeoned into many manifestations of the noble social policy which I call humanitarianism.

During all of this period of the progress of civilization and the growth of social philosophy, man seems to have been almost completely oblivious of his evolutionary origins, his biological status, and the relation of these to intelligence and to culture. Medicine slowly grew out of magic as a means of alleviating pain and an attempt to cure disease to which every animal organism is liable. The piling up of a wealth of foodstuffs, offering a sufficient variety and abundance to enable ignorant animals to starve themselves to death by eating, the congestion of large populations in squalid cities, resulted in a proliferation of diseases and marked organic deterioration in all ranks of society. It began to be apparent that some distribution of medical care, as well as of economic resources and social privilege, was essential for the maintenance of a tolerable social order. Some dim inkling of a relationship between organic pathology and social pathology began to penetrate the fog of man's cultural obsession. But the Latin tag, *mens sana in corpore sano,* had no real social significance.

Because man was so completely oriented toward culture and now thoroughly believed himself to be culture's own creation, he became convinced that cultural education would be the panacea of all human ills if intensively pursued and universally disseminated. Since irrational and haphazard dealing with natural resources had obviously caused no end of ructions in human society, man began to study economics and to teach it —similarly with government and with the applied sciences, and with medicine and hygiene. Even the ancient and profitless investigation of human history was rejuvenated, to some extent, in the hope that the study of the errors of past men would prevent those of present and future generations. The assumption implicit in all of this complete reliance upon education is that unintelligent behavior is caused by ignorance and is due to cultural deficiency. I am now going to argue that stupidity is generated by excess of culture; that civilization has accelerated not only the physical deterioration of man, but, in the mass of the population, also his mental decline. I shall point out the dependence of our sociological difficulties upon biological causes, and I shall exaggerate that dependence, quite deliberately.

DEPENDENCE OF SOCIOLOGICAL DIFFICULTIES UPON BIOLOGICAL CAUSES

Language

Articulate language, which is an exclusive creation of man's cerebral cortex, is the principal medium of the diffusion of culture and of its transmission from one generation to the next. It arises from the organism, and both its emission and reception are physiological phenomena. Count Alfred Korzybski has shown us that the over-elaboration of language according to a rigid Aristotelian system which involves artificial and specious

distinctions between thought and emotion, false definition, misleading generalization, and ambiguous abstraction, has perverted speech into an instrument for the creation of misunder-
standings. Even if one is able to say what one means, the words
have different meanings for different listeners. The actual
physiological effect of hurling at a child, or at an uneducated
person, a mass of this artificial verbiage is to create in that unfortunate hearer a state of muscular and nervous tension which
cuts out the cerebral cortex from any reception at all and re-
duces his nervous responses to reflexes from the cerebellum.
Thus a large part of the population grows up in a state of frus-
tration and mental bewilderment because the unnatural linguistic
categorization of things, actions, ideas, and all else which is
the content of speech, sets up a permanent state of psycho-
physical block. A considerable proportion of the organically
agile manage to adjust themselves to this semantic chaos, and
gradually arrive at some sort of conception of a least common
denominator of verbal meanings by which they get along in
society. Others work out their individual systems of semantics
and are consequently regarded as insane because words mean
something quite different for them than for the majority.

Because nobody really knows what any word means, it is
possible for unscrupulous propagandists to make words symbols for the evocation of a low animalistic type of conditioned
response which is associated with unintelligent mob behavior.
Thus such terms as "liberty," "evolution," "race," "democracy,"
"Aryan," "social security," "New Deal," are utilized by the
profiteers of man's semantic confusion to arouse hatred, prejudice, murder, and other undesirable manifestations of animal
behavior which they can turn to their personal profit.

Such a device as the radio extends to the uttermost parts of
the earth the range of one person's potentiality for misleading
and befuddling his fellow men, either by taking advantage of
their semantic difficulties or by broadcasting his own. I am a
frequent radio listener, and it is my considered opinion that

what comes over the air is mostly cacophony, lies, and imbecilic
nonsense. I do not believe even the time signals. The dog listening to "his master's voice" is a singularly appropriate trade-
mark for the phonograph, and upon each radio receiving set
should be engraved the warning: *Vox et praeterea nihil*
("noise and nothing more").

The naïve supposition that universal understanding and peace
are promoted by linguistic intercommunication is so obviously
contrary to fact that it requires no discussion. The spoken or
written word is quite as potent an instrument for the fomenta-
tion of human discord and for the destruction of culture as for
the promotion of harmony and the upbuilding of civilization.
Words are more easily and more frequently employed for the
former maleficent than for the latter benevolent ends.

Mechanical Transport and Mechanical Invention

Mechanical transport is an achievement of cerebral initiative
which facilitates the world-wide distribution of undesirable
persons and unwanted things. It is the principal carrier of war
and pestilence, the chief instrument for the despoiling of natural
resources and the enslaving and destruction of human and animal life. Of course, none of these evils is inherent in the rail-
road, the steamship, the airplane, and the motor car. These in
themselves are merely ingenious machines capable of utilization
for good or for evil. They are the creations of the active cerebral cortices of a very small fraction of mankind and have been
improved so rapidly that they have become virtually "fool-
proof." This term signifies that they may be used by fools, with
impunity, for the destruction of others. Here, of course, we
strike the very root of the evil of man's material cultural evolution—the fact that the brilliant products of the few intelligent human minds are easily convertible to the use of those
who have practically no intelligence at all. A handful of geniuses
has contrived a variety of devices of almost unlimited power
for destructive utilization by a billion and a half of morons.

"Their Master's Voice"

The effect of the achievements of mechanical science upon man's physical and mental evolution has been, on the whole, disastrous. Man's emergence from a lower primate status has been due principally to the expansion of his cerebral cortex and the incessant utilization of that new organ. No matter how loudly the bigots of professional biology may snort and scoff at the idea that the organism evolves partially as a result of its own striving, it has been the vital principle of human development ever since man became man. As soon as you invent machines which eliminate the necessity of mental exertion on the part of those who use them, you stultify mankind, unless you can contrive to make it use its brains for some other constructive purpose. It should be as easy to grasp this fact as it is to understand that lack of exercise atrophies the body.

Predacity and Humanitarianism

The evolution of human society and of its animal members is an incessant conflict between two social and individual attitudes which, for want of better terms, I call predacity and humanitarianism. Both arise from the animal organism. Predacity implies the disposition to take by force, to dominate, to prey upon other animals, to survive by combat. In higher mammals it is especially developed in the adult and in the male and gives rise to ferocious behavior. Humanitarianism, on the contrary, involves gentleness, tolerance, affection, and, to some extent, submissiveness. It is particularly noticeable in the young of many mammalian species and in the behavior of the adult female toward her infant and immature offspring. I should be foolish to enter into a psychological discussion of the organic bases of these attitudes, but it is obvious that neither of them is absent from the behavior of subhuman animals of low-grade intelligence; and that any animal, old or young, male or female, may at one or another time act humanely or predaciously. It is easy to see that these divergent attitudes, manifested in the individual, the family, and the social group, often complement each other in promoting the survival of the species. Evidently both are necessary.

A knowledge of the organic evolution and prehistory of man suggests that, on the whole, he has been for at least a million years an animal in which predacious behavior has dominated. Maternalistic or humanitarian behavior in primitive society is for the most part restricted to the family, with some feeble extension to the more remote kin and other members of the social group. It is an individual manifestation rather than a social attitude. The larger the number of human units in a group, the more feeble and limited is the exercise of humanitarianism and the more dominant is predacious behavior. For humanitarianism is basically a feeling of blood-relationship, which, in primitive society, exists only as far as kinship can be reckoned. It is easily stifled by competition, whether sexual or economic, and it is virtually absent in the behavior of total human groups or societies toward other human groups.

Now we have to consider the effect of an enormous and practically self-perpetuating body of material and immaterial culture upon the continuous conflict between predacity and humanitarianism in the human species. This culture accumulates without changing the organic nature of man; and, if I am correct, does not increase his intelligence, but rather diminishes it. It enhances enormously man's ability to control nature and to work good or evil toward his fellow men, but it does not alter his fundamental predacity; it merely enlarges the scope of its operations. Knowledge is power, but it is not intelligence. I shall endeavor to show that the exercise of knowledge unintelligently, whether in human manifestations of predacity or of humanitarianism, is responsible for the havoc of civilization. We shall then appreciate the significance of God's injunction to Adam: "But of the tree of the knowledge of good and evil, thou shalt not eat of it: for in the day that thou eatest thereof thou shalt surely die."

First let us consider the effect of knowledge upon the exercise of predacity in men. It operates in modern society, as in ancient society, in the institutions of property, government, warfare, religion, and social classification. The facility of property accumulation and its immensity in the mechanized industrial age have instigated the predaciously intelligent to enslave human beings under a capitalistic regime, whereby millions of men are condemned to sweat and labor on a minimum scale of living in the production of wealth to be used by the few for God knows what. Conversely, the desire for property on the part of the equally predacious but less intelligent masses who have it not arouses them to concerted violence. The general result of revolution is not sharing of property, but a fairly complete destruction of it, together with those who think that they produce wealth and those who imagine themselves to own it. "Ill fares the land to hastening ills a prey, where wealth accumulates and men decay."

In government the effect of knowledge (or, if you prefer so to call it, science) upon the predacious, is to enlarge the scope of despotisms and military dictatorships far beyond the paltry hole-in-the-corner affairs which antiquity and barbarity could contrive. Increased facilities of transportation and communication, infinitely more diabolical and efficient military equipment, can be used to degrade, deceive, and intimidate a population which has lost all cerebral initiative through the use of too-ingenious tools which have produced wealth without mental effort. The cunningly predacious begin their acquisition of despotic power by a subtle utilizing of slogans and symbols for the regimentation of the suggestible morons. They commence their insidious work, under the pretense of democracy, socialism, or communism, with appeals to the Aryan race, the heritage of Roman grandeur, the ideals of Karl Marx, or any other similar excitant. But they proceed inevitably and ruthlessly to military domination, murder, and the suppression of all of the liberties of the individual. Predacity can operate without let or hindrance only with the help of a mechanical civilization, and upon a population which has been idiotized by an uncomprehending participation in such civilization.

War is, of course, the most effective means of perpetuating dictatorships, not only because it gives free reign to the combative brute and suppresses every vestige of humanitarianism, but also because it destroys the most vigorous physically, thus getting rid of the more turbulent elements and leaving as the breeding stocks those which are weaker and more easily intimidated. It is hard indeed to judge whether a nation suffers more from the loss of its most virile stock on the battlefield, with the proliferation of the stay-at-home unfits, or, on the other hand, from the return of those scathed heroes who are eager to practice their predacity, aroused in war, upon the citizens, property, and government of their grateful countries.

Knowledge is, then, power pre-eminently utilizable for the predacious human animal. If one can set up a standard of good or evil, human predacity is evil and humanitarianism is good. But we shall now see how humanitarianism, through stupidity, utilizes knowledge to aggravate the evil evolutionary status of man and to pile Ossa upon Pelion in the social cataclysm which bids fair to destroy civilization.

While predacity is even more prominent as a social phenomenon than as an individual manifestation, humanitarianism is generally restricted to individuals; and only in modern times, perhaps, and under favorable environmental circumstances is it characteristic of a large social group. From it arise all of the loftier ideals and principles of human conduct implicit in such ideas as those of mercy, justice, liberty, equality, charity. These sentiments can originate only in societies which include individuals who combine with maternalistic feelings a high development of intelligence. For they must not only disregard the obvious selfish and material advantage of giving rein to their predatory inclinations, but must also employ cerebral initiative in the reasoning out of codes of conduct which will be of the greatest good to the greatest number. In humanitarianism we

perhaps have the most artificial manifestation of human behavior, involving the most complicated use of the cerebral cortex and the least dependence upon the automatic mechanism
of the reflex.

Humanitarianism as a group attitude manifests itself in religion, in government, in education, in organized charity, and in
public medicine, as well as in other varieties of social uplift.
When these sentiments are put into practice with a high degree
of intelligence and with an acute realization of man's organic
and mental limitations, they presumably promote human betterment, both biological and cultural. But when they are exercised
stupidly by unintelligent persons, however well-meaning the
latter may be, their effect is to make a bad matter much worse.

One of the highest codes of humanitarianism is that of
Christianity as exemplified and taught by the founder of that
religion. There can be no doubt that the adoption and actual
practice of that code by the large majority of human kind would
put an end to nearly every social ill. It is equally certain that
the attainment of such an ideal for the low-grade intelligences
which constitute the majority of all present populations is not
much more probable than it is for chimpanzees. Christ and one
or two other stupendous geniuses conceived the brilliant idea of
tacking ethical codes to the fear of the supernatural which
seems to inhere in man, and of enforcing the former by the
latter. However, the emphasis upon humanitarian standards of
individual and social conduct was quickly shifted back to a
virtually exclusive concentration upon ritual and belief. The
Church became preoccupied with the salvation of the hypothetical souls of individuals, conceived to be immortal and quite dissociated from their animal bodies. The specious distinction
between the organism and its mental functioning, between body
and soul, was here exaggerated to the extreme, so that man not
only forgot his animal nature, but strenuously denied it, making
confusion worse confounded. The more ignorant and stupid
the individual, the more completely he divorced his religious

belief from his conduct in society. Predacious men quickly
secured control of religious organization, so that it was transformed into an institution for the accumulation of property
and power, in which the ordinary social sanctions were reinforced by man's primitive superstition. The stifling of individual initiative and the suppression of independence of thought
have been the chief contribution of organized religions to the
stultification of mankind. Thus the most potent social means
of evolutionary progress was turned against humanity.

Democracy is the expression of humanitarian ideals in the
government of civilized states. Rude democracies of a sort are
found among savage societies, but they owe their existence at
these levels to the lack of development of economic systems, to
general crudity of institutions and material culture. They do
not rest upon principles and ideals thought out and formulated
by men of high intelligence. We have ample reason today to
prize our heritage of democratic principles and a democratic
form of government above everything else that civilization can
afford. There is, however, a strict prerequisite for the success
of democratic government that seems to have been overlooked.
Democracy can function satisfactorily only when the individual
citizens are intelligent enough to understand its ideals and principles and to subordinate themselves to the good of society.
Democracy in a population of stupid and predacious men is an
impossibility. Since unintelligent individuals and ignorant individuals are by virtue of these deficiencies intolerant of intelligence and knowledge, since they in fact hate those whom they
suspect to be superior to themselves, the suffrages of morons
inevitably put into office persons of similar endowment, or men
who successfully substitute for real intelligence a kind of low
cunning. We do not have to look at recent events in Germany,
Russia, and Italy to observe that deteriorated popular intelligence in nations attempting to carry on democratic forms of
government makes them the easy prey of dictators. That lesson
has been plainly printed where he who runs may read in the

histories of Latin American states for more than a century. As soon as a population sinks to a sufficiently low level of intelligence it at once becomes obvious that it cannot rule itself, but has to be dominated. Thus efficiency and the salvation of society become the excuses for the establishment of despotic governments.

Education is rightly conceived as the sole weapon whereby humanitarianism can fight the battle of democracy and can contribute to the advancement of civilization and the promotion of higher trends in human evolution. Man will survive or perish according to the success with which he employs this instrument. To my view the fundamental fallacies of educational theory and practice are two in number: The first is that all men are infinitely teachable and have only to learn in order to become perfect. The second fallacy is that all that is worth learning is man's culture and that he need know nothing at all about himself as a biological organism. In fact, I should say that education is entirely upside down, since it teaches men to do more and more of what they have already done too much—the elaboration of material culture and the fabrication of intricate social institutions. It teaches them nothing whatsoever of what they are biologically and what they ought to be, because education does not itself know anything about the biological nature of man and does not care to know. It proceeds upon the assumption that a process of stuffing factual and theoretical knowledge into a child will enable that child to make his living by producing, selling, transporting objects of material culture, or by exercising his wits in some form of skulduggery having to do with religion, science, government, or education. It further assumes that the intelligence of the individual increases as he acquires more and more of this knowledge, and that by virtue of erudition he ceases to be predatory, grows increasingly humanitarian, and eventually goes forth not only to sell bonds, but also to spread peace and good will.

THE BIO-SOCIOLOGICAL ATTACK UPON HUMAN
PROBLEMS

It is perhaps not too late for science and education to attempt to discover and to teach how man can arrest his physical and mental decline by studying his own biology. Medicine practiced with charity but without discrimination has been a calamitous contributor to the decline of intelligence in civilized states, since it has preserved millions of physically and mentally debilitated persons who would have been eliminated under the crude regime of natural selection. Medical science has reached a stage of development in which it is not sufficiently bad to kill off the chronic invalids, and not good enough to cure them. It is just skillful enough to ruin natural selection. The sorely needed knowledge of human heredity and of the relation of the human organism to its behavior will never be acquired as long as vapid pontiffs of the bedside manner control medical science, with one eye on the microscope, the other on the drug cabinet, and both hands clutching the halo of the witch doctor which wobbles on their alopecious crania. Yet the ferment of cerebral initiative is working in a few men who have the imagination and the courage to forget that they are physicians and to remember to study man.

I am not trying to persuade you that the salvation of man can be assured only by the promotion of the discipline of anthropology, the prosecution of its researches, and the capitalization of its discoveries. Human intelligence is not to be rehabilitated by the expansion of any single field of academic research and teaching, even when it includes a few persons who study the biological man, a few who study the social man, and when those few get together and try to make sense out of these inseparable activities of the social animal.

Now, in my unesteemed opinion, the predicament of humanity and a possible way out may be summarized finally as follows: Man is an animal in which the evolution of the nervous system has dominated the organism, partly to the detriment of its general physical status. Ultimately this superordinate brain brought forth culture—invented tools and contrivances whereby man compensated for his puny physique and conquered the world. He straightway forgot his animal nature and devoted all of his attention and energy to making more and more ingenious tools whereby he could accumulate more and more goods, with the expenditure of less and less physical energy and cerebral initiative. Soon thinking became obsolete for the majority of persons, since the machines did it for them. The resurgence of the ape within us, by nature and by selection predacious, has brought social chaos in spite of tools and wealth. But we have been too stupid to recognize that we are depressed biological victims of a cultural burden, and have gone on adding to that senseless weight and trying to teach the debilitated organism to lift a calf every day until it becomes a bull. We have sought to accomplish this effect solely by feeding the calf. We have felt somehow that man would grow accustomed to the task of Atlas if only we made that task heavier and heavier. But now the arches of Atlas have gone flat, his veins are varicose, his sacroiliac cogs have slipped, and not only are his shoulders bowed and bent but his cranium and his brain have been crushed by that superincumbent mass of culture.

We must not rush into rash and wholesale execution of stringent biological measures for bettering man when as yet we know virtually nothing of man's biology. We need not stultify our humanitarian consciences by sterilizing the insane and killing criminals as long as our primate gullets strain at that particular gnat and swallow with facility the camel of righteous murder which is called war. We must get to work upon that which is immediately practicable and appallingly exigent—the effort to find out how we may fit the whole range of physical and mental mankind, from dwarfs to giants and from idiots to geniuses, into appropriate niches in our social structure. We can do this by establishing institutes for the study of human biology, not as it relates to death and stomach-aches, but as it relates to life in modern society, and as it conditions the material and spiritual well-being of each of us. We must find a way of securing Korzybski's minimum achievement for human organisms of all grades, which will ensure for each some measure of success and happiness.

Next we must cast away the idea that culture makes man and knowledge creates intelligence, and begin to turn a large minority of the remaining intelligent minds to the problems of man's physical evolution and to the study of human heredity. We can build from the bottom by selecting some thousands of couples who are stepping over the verge of matrimony, studying them and their available ancestors by every accurate anthropological, psychological, medical, and sociological technique; then continuing these studies upon their children and upon their children's children, offering as compensation free medical care and social guidance. It will take two or three generations of concerted scientific observation to formulate constructive methods of breeding better men. But, in the meantime, we can at least direct the attention of the young to the need of biological knowledge, pointing like Moses the way to a promised land which we ourselves shall never enter. To make biologically minded the young who are fortuitously endowed with superior intelligence is our paramount duty. Let us redirect the course of education into paths which make for human betterment. Let us stop deluding ourselves with the fatuous notion that morality can be massaged into morons and intelligence into idiots. For true intelligence is inbred. From it alone come honesty and a suppression of brute predacity without loss of cerebral initiative and without lapse into that flaccid humanitarianism which has corrupted the practice of democracy.

Wobbly institutions cannot be patched and propped so that hospitalization and cure of that sick animal, man, can be effected by popping each patient into some corner of a noisome cultural structure and telling him to stay there and be good. If we ourselves have any feeble stirrings of cerebral initiative in our atrophied brains, let us go to work and try to develop a stock with a native fund of intelligence upon which we can rebuild civilization and the biological future of man.

III

THE MAKING AND MIXING OF HUMAN RACES:

I. THE FORMATION OF PRIMARY RACES*

RACIALISM AS a political doctrine is today the most potent catalyst wherewith evil and misguided men actuate the baser elements of the human animal to predatory and bestial behavior.
Racial persecution has supplanted religious persecution. In certain nations race has been transmogrified into the most maleficent religion which distorted human minds can contrive,
because the victims of its fanatical persecution are not merely
infidels or unbelievers through ignorance or sheer perversity,
but are predestined for destruction by virtue of their physical
inheritance. The religion of race accepts no converts, because the
heredity of the individual cannot be changed by baptism or by
confession of belief; it is an immutable biological fact. The
religion of race therefore admits of no tolerance; its doctrines
and policies are those of suppression and extermination. Now, a
religion of race has no more absolute validity than a religion
based upon belief as to the nature of God and the hereafter;
but it has a much stronger social potentiality, because it is
founded upon physical rather than upon metaphysical con-

* The following four chapters were given under the Richard B. West-
brook Free Lectureship of 1939 at the Wagner Free Institute of Science,
Philadelphia, April 6, 8, 14, and 15, 1939.

60

cepts. The objective reality of hereditary physical difference brooks no denial; and systems of belief, prejudice, and superstition built upon racial anatomical variations lay hold upon moronic minds with a grip far more tenacious than that of any spiritual dogma. Since the theology of this wholly evil religion is a pseudo-science of anthropology, it is up to the anthropologist to fight the Devil with fire; he cannot be combated successfully with the tepid Holy Water of humanitarian idealism.

There adheres to the anthropologist no stain of guilt for the actual propagation of a religion of race, except such German anthropologists as have been intimidated into subservience to doctrines which they know to be false. Actually, the theories of racial superiority and inferiority which have been inflated into the religion of racialism have been promulgated by charlatans and crackpots like Gobineau and Houston Stewart-Chamberlin, and by snobbish amateurs of aristocracy like the late Madison Grant—none of whom have had any reputation or recognized standing in the science of anthropology. Nevertheless, very serious sins of omission may be laid at the door of the professional anthropologist, since he has usually been too cowardly or too stupid to come to grips in a really scientific manner with the actual problem of race. He has preferred to concern himself with the innocuous details of primitive culture or with the fossilized question of the fossil remains of man. Certain anthropologists, such as that grand veteran Franz Boas, must be acquitted of this timorous avoidance of the subject of race, but I am afraid that they have overcompensated in their desire to lay the ax at the root of racialism as a religion. The anthropologist who denies the existence of race, or who tries to prove that human variation in behavior is attributable exclusively to environmental or historical causes, may have reason and justice and a vast weight of circumstantial evidence on his side, but to the bulk of mankind he merely eliminates himself from the position of a competent and impartial judge of the situation. However loudly he may shout that race is a myth, the layman remains unimpressed, since he observes it, or what he thinks it to be, as a fact of nature, a classification of zoological validity analogous to that of horses and zebras, or dogs and wolves.

Instead of pretending that race is a mere bogey of superstition lurking in the dark corners of ignorant minds, the anthropologist should have admitted its materialization in human society and should have gone to work to study its biological and sociological implications, which are not in themselves evil. By insisting that race is a figment of the imagination, or a meaningless combination of anatomical trivialities transmitted by heredity or impressed by physical environment, the anthropologist has merely left the house empty, swept, and garnished, so that spirits more wicked than himself enter in and dwell there, and the last state of race is worse than the first. If, instead of haggling over definitions of race and debating the relative influences of heredity and environment in producing races, the anthropologist had proceeded in a direct and efficient manner to classify human groups according to their apparent combinations of physical variations, he would have facilitated the examination of the mental and cultural characteristics of such groups by the psychologist, the sociologist, and the historian. As it is, the physical facts of race have been confused with ignorant fancies, and the whole matter of psychological and cultural correlates has been left for exploitation by unscrupulous and fanatical laymen who have not hesitated to utilize its vast potentialities for political and social injustice. Hence the malignant religion of race which has obsessed the German people and which has inspired them repeatedly to attempt the overthrow of European civilization.

Let it be understood that the physical groups of man which we call races are not evolutionary grades constituting a primate hierarchy, but rather types of organisms which have been selected for survival under varying conditions of physical environment. We shall then be in a position to study the capacities of these differently adapted human organisms for fitting into a planned world of culture in which each will utilize its special abilities so as to promote its own best interests and the welfare of the whole. Aggression and sanguinary competition can be reduced to a negligible minimum if we can educate the masses of the people to realize that racial peculiarities denote special capacities which may be developed and exploited, rather than inferiorities and superiorities which may be made the excuse for policies of domination, suppression, and extermination. But such realization can never be effected until two conditions are fulfilled. The first of these is an honest, impartial, and thorough study of race in all of its physical and cultural implications. That knowledge is indispensable to satisfactory racial adjustment. The second, and by far the more necessitous, prerequisite is that the multiplication of degenerates, mental inferiors, insane, and antisocial individuals within each race be checked, so that the mass of mankind can be rendered educable enough to profit from the findings of science in regard to the range and distribution of abilities in the human species.

So, in these lectures I propose to discuss rather briefly and quite simply the evolutionary forces which operate in the formation of human races, then to describe the existing physical groups of mankind with some commentary upon their probable origins and migrations, finally to indicate what science has learned about the anatomical, physiological, and sociological results of mixtures between radically different races, on the one hand, and between races which are physically allied, on the other. The factual material which I shall present is derived from scientific observations which I believe to be accurate, and all or nearly all of it should be correct. Some of the numerous opinions which I express ought also to be correct—by the law of averages, if for no other reason. All of what I have to say may be wrong in some of these lectures, and some of what I say may be wrong in all of these lectures; but all of what I say can scarcely be wrong in all of these lectures because I am not any sort of a totalitarian scientist. However, not even in this City of Brotherly Love can I subscribe to the sentiment that "all men are created equal," which for anthropological purposes should be amended to read "all men are created different." I am afraid that I am mixing up my metaphors, and I know that I am verging upon the offensive when I say that the Cradle of Liberty has turned out to be a manger, and that the dog in the manger is that mendacious statement about human equality in so far as it is applied to the capacities of individuals. On the other hand (or foot), I stand firmly upon the platform of racial equality, since the range and mean of individual capacity within the several human races has never been proved to differ significantly. Each has, in all probability, its own array of points of strength, offset by weaknesses; and these points do not always coincide in all of the different races. Add them all together in any single race, and I am afraid that it amounts to zero—or, in other words, it comes out even. Thus, all races are equal. The only way of beating this racial equality game is to mix races and then to select for survival those individuals in whom fortuitously or by genetic law the strong qualities of the parent races are combined, and eliminate the rest. I shall enlarge upon this matter later. It is not a matter of dialectics, but rather of genetics.

At this point I may well define race so that you will understand what I am talking about. I may refer to this definition as an accepted definition in the sense that I formulated it some seventeen years ago and have myself accepted it ever since. It has also been accepted by some of my students, at least for as long a time as they remained *in statu pupillari*. A race is a large body of mankind the members of which possess similar combinations of physical variations which they owe to their common descent. Race is, therefore, a physical classification based upon hereditary anatomical features. The term carries no necessary implications of language, nationality, or culture. Racial resemblances are nothing other than family resemblances spread more thinly over larger groups and with the degrees of blood relationship correspondingly attenuated.

Mankind has differentiated into races by subjection to the long-continued interaction of several natural forces, some of which are organic and others extraorganic. There can be no doubt that certain of the organic forces are stirred into operation as the responses to extraorganic or environmental stimuli, but some organic processes appear to be relatively or absolutely independent of such extrinsic causation. On the other hand, while the organism influences and modifies its environment, and radically so in the case of man, such operations have nothing to do with race-making, because race is a matter of organic differentiation.

The first of the intrinsic race-forming forces is variation. Neither asexual nor sexual reproduction operates with mechanical precision to give birth to identical organic forms. The germ plasm of a single parent is probably not constant in its qualities and properties over the period of sexual reproduction, and at the time of fertilization the possibilities of various combinations of genes in the make-up of the offspring are exceedingly numerous. Brothers and sisters are physically unlike, and even identical twins are not really identical. Thus, variation is the result of germinal instability, chance combination of genes, and erratic reproductive performance. Some of this variation is doubtless environmentally actuated, but probably a good deal of it is due to sheer germinal cussedness.

When the organism in development or during maturity actually modifies itself in response to environmental stimuli, direct or indirect, we call this process adaptation. Thus, when the skins of certain persons are exposed to ultra-violet light, the organism responds by laying down in the deep layers of the epidermis an extra amount of the opaque granular pigment called melanin. In other words, the skin is tanned, and tanning protects the underlying tissues. However, this process of adaptation can only be identified in the comparatively few cases where a simple and definite environmental cause produces a constant and discernible organic effect which can be experimentally checked and verified. For the most part, it seems probable that apparent adaptations or bodily modifications are merely selected variations which have arisen spontaneously from the germ plasm. That is to say, from the almost infinitely varied combinations of organic features which are genetically possible, there are selected for survival those which are best suited to get along in the world. Those organisms which are unlucky enough to inherit unfavorable or lethal combinations simply die out, unless they happen to get a fortunate environmental break, or unless, as in the case of modern civilized man, they are artificially preserved by unintelligent application of so-called humanitarian principles.

Environment is impersonal, unconscious, and unintelligent; but it nevertheless makes a better job of selection than does man, because it is impartial. "It sendeth the rain on the just and the unjust," and the fellow who keeps dry is the one who has an umbrella.

Another potent race-making factor is geographical isolation. Of course, this is not in any sense a force, either environmental or organic; it is merely a fact of position. If a group of people is cut off from intercourse with other human beings, this isolated group is likely to live within an area delimited by some natural barriers and, frequently, characterized by some measure of environmental uniformity. If the geographic and climatic factors are the same, or nearly the same, for the entire group, it is evident that organic adaptations which result from environmental stimuli will be similar for all. More important than this is the inbreeding which is a necessary consequence for the survival of the group thus isolated. This means that all of the variations inherent in the germ plasms of individuals tend to be swapped about or pooled. Of course, the number is limited because the size of isolated groups is usually small. There then ensues a selection of combinations which are favorable for survival and an exaggeration of these features thus combined, due to their presence in a large number of related parental and ancestral strains. Successful combinations become stabilized and are likely to include linked or associated specializations of indifferent features which have no survival value, but are inherited along with the essential modifications. Often these casually linked and unimportant physical variations constitute the most noticeable features of a homogeneous physical type. Undoubtedly, geographical isolation in a uniform environment which requires physical adaptations, together with subsequent inbreeding, constitute the most potent race-making complex of organic and extraorganic conditions. These are the agencies of certain physical differentiation. A related group of physically similar individuals becomes a race as soon as its numerical strength is sufficient to baffle the reckoning of blood-relationship.

There remain but two race-making factors which must be considered. These are genetic dominance and hybridization. Genetic dominance is the phenomenon in which one gene or potentiality for the development of a specific variation in the germ plasm overrides or submerges a competing gene carrying a different variation. This sort of struggle for dominance goes on from the fertilization of the egg through embryonic life and in the postnatal development of the individual. The mathematical calculation of the results of such inheritance is called Mendel's Law of Heredity. It is possible only when the genes or unit inheritance characters have been isolated, when their dominance or recessiveness is known, and when the genetic composition of interbreeding strains or individuals has been determined. Even then it is a very complicated business.

Hybridization, or race mixture, is merely the wider extension of the genetic dominance of characters and the environmental selection of types which take place when two separate and individually differentiated and stabilized races interbreed. It is a matter of pooling the contents of two distinct and in some respects antagonistic reservoirs of hereditary characters. Unlike oil and water, they always mix; but often there results the throwing down of a certain precipitate of characters which are, so to speak, lost in the shuffle, and the new blend is sometimes strangely unlike either of the original constituent fluids.

Thus far I have said nothing about the actual physical characters which, in their various combinations in individuals, enable us to delimit racial groups by assigning to the same class all persons who look alike. Since race is a broad measure of blood-relationship, it is necessary to select as the physical criteria of race characteristics which are inherited and which persist relatively unchanged throughout the life of the individual. This condition rules out of consideration bodily features which can be radically altered during one's life span through function and nutrition. For example, the possession of a protuberant belly or paunch, or the absence of that stately convexity, has no value as a criterion of race. Again, bodily structures which have been rigidly adapted for an identical function in all races of man are of little use in race classification, because the necessities of species survival permit of little variation in them. For this reason the human foot, which has been specialized from a grasping, ape prototype, displays only minor features of utility as racial criteria. Probably most of the variations in feet in different racial groups are attributable to the effects of various types of footgear as contrasted with the lack of any. The barefooted peoples naturally retain some prehensility of the toes, and in their case inherited form and function of the foot are not artificially altered by the constrictions of boots or sandals.

It follows that the most important features of the human organism have a very narrow range of variation because of the strict requirements of their function, and that inherited characters which are broadly differentiated in distinct groups of men so that they can be used readily as a basis of racial classification are, for the most part, functionally nonadaptive, trivial, and generally indifferent features which have little or no sur-

vival value for the species. Only in such unimportant variations
can heredity run riot without the intervention and sifting of
natural selection. This really means that racial variations, taken
individually, have little biological significance. They are merely
inherited marks of relationship.

There are two classes of data which the physical anthropologist uses in racial determination: metric and morphological.
Metric data include all features which can be measured with
calipers or tape, such as diameters, circumferences, and derived
indices (the ratios of one dimension to another expressed as
percentages). Indices are perhaps more important than the
former, since to some extent they express form and proportion,
whereas gross dimensions merely indicate size. Size alone is
usually of little racial significance and is often dependent upon
age, sex, and individual variations due to nutrition and other
environmental factors. Again, size varies continuously, and
consequently does not readily break down into clear-cut categories or classes unless these are arbitrarily fixed.

Morphological variations are differences in form of the soft
parts or the hard parts of the body which can easily be recognized and are capable of qualitative classification or gradation,
but do not lend themselves readily to accurate measurements.
They therefore fall into discontinuous categories. Some of the
more obvious morphological variations which are used for racial
criteria are: the form of the hair, whether straight, wavy, curly,
frizzly, or woolly; the color of the skin, hair, and eyes; the
amount and distribution of beard and body hair; the details of
eyelid, nose, lip, and ear conformation. While these morphological features are readily identifiable, it is very hard indeed to
grade them objectively, because each person's classification is
likely to be influenced by his own personal standard of judgment and experience. Actually, all individuals when recognizing
racial affinities base their determinations upon visual identifica-
tion of combinations of morphological features. They ordinarily

do not use measurements, because the eye is not equipped with a metric scale.

The physical anthropologist, however, uses combinations of measured characters and morphological features—the latter as standardized and objectified as possible. The more intricate the combination of metric and morphological characters utilized, the finer is the group classification. Combinations of the variations of three or four different characters are enough to establish the broad classification of relationship which we call race. Over-elaboration in the use of multiple criteria results in the delimiting of intra-racial groups or closer degrees of blood-relationship. It is perfectly possible to set up an anthropometric and morphological combination which will identify a single human individual out of the whole population of the world. Bertillon did this for criminals by anthropometry, and it is now done merely by utilizing the almost infinite combinations of patterns on the skin ridges of the finger tips.

Races cannot be classified by employing only the variations of some single character, because there are not enough recognizable varieties of any one feature to go around the numerous groups which are obviously physically distinctive and not closely related. Moreover, the important features for racial diagnosis are not the same in every group. Hair form is distinctive for Negroes and Mongoloids, but it is of little value in differentiating races within the White division of mankind. The folds of skin of the upper eyelids distinguish the Mongoloid from the Negroid and the White, but do not differentiate the two last named. Skin color does not permit a separation of the Negroid and the Australoid, nor the Mongoloid from many of the brunets of the races which are inaccurately called "White." Thus, in racial classification it is important to stress a number of different criteria, weighting them differently for the various physical groups. Racial classifications are based upon varied and not uniform combinations of characters.

In the array of modern types of man certain primary divisions may be recognized which have a somewhat broader and more general significance than racial groupings. It is customary to lump all modern forms of man under the one zoological species, *Homo sapiens,* although the validity of applying to man in general an adjective which means "wise" or "knowing" is somewhat questionable. A sapient man must use the term *Homo sapiens* with considerable mental reservation. These great primary divisions of man might be called subspecies, but it is better not to give them any definite place in zoological hierarchies of classification, because zoologists do not agree among themselves as to the definitions of their taxonomic terms.

WHITE DIVISION

The first of these great divisions may be called White, or Caucasoid. Both terms are misnomers—the former because the range of skin pigmentation in this division is from dark brown through fish-belly white to raw beef color; the latter because this division has not diffused from the Caucasus as a center of development, but almost certainly from an area somewhat farther east.

This diversified White division of mankind is united by the common possession of a few physical characters which are mostly generalized rather than specialized. The first of these are hair form and hair distribution. Hair form in the White stock is never woolly and never attains the coarse straightness of Mongoloid hair. It is usually wavy, although it ranges from a fine straight variety to loosely curled types which are not wiry or frizzly. Beard and body hair are rarely sparse, and ordinarily strongly developed. Baldness in males is common from middle years onward. The profile of the face is usually straight; there is little or no protrusion of the jaws, or prognathism (except in the most primitive White races). This lack of prognathism may be regarded as an advanced character. The external nose rarely shows excessive breadth and is usually medium to high in

the bridge. Very narrow noses and convex or aquiline noses
(which are specialized) attain their maximum frequency in this
division. Ears are somewhat larger than in Mongoloids and
much larger than in Negroids. The lobe of the ear probably
attains its maximum development in Whites. Lateral compression of the cheekbones and lack of anterior jut of these bones
which form the side walls of the face are at a maximum among
certain White races. The maximum is also reached in forward
thrust of the bony eminence of the chin. The bony ridges which
surmount the orbits of the eye are usually larger than in Negroids and Mongoloids and at times very large indeed. The
bony palate and the teeth are usually reduced in size as compared with the other main divisions of mankind. The pattern of
the cranial sutures (the lines of articulation of the vault bones
of the skull) is usually more intricate and tortuous than in
Negroids or Mongoloids. The tarsal bones, which form the
arches of the foot, are somewhat larger and articulated into
stronger vaults; the great toe is more nearly in the long axis of
the foot, the lesser toes are more vestigial, and all of the toes
have retained less grasping or prehensile power than in the
other main stocks.

Of course all of these general characteristics of the White
division are subject not only to wide individual variation, but
also to marked racial variation; and some of them show individual overlappings with the Negroid and Mongoloid divisions which are not ascribable to mixture with those stocks.

Australoid

Within this White group by far the most primitive race is
the archaic Australoid, which probably reached the antipodal
continent before the end of the Pleistocene or glacial period
over an islanded route which presented fewer wide gaps than it
now does. These aboriginal Australians are reminiscent of fossil types of man in their huge brow ridges, low and receding
foreheads, protrusive jaws, feeble chins, large palates, and big

teeth. They have exaggeratedly broad and fleshy-tipped noses adorning extremely short broad faces, and their skins vary from a medium red-brown to a dark chocolate color (in exposed parts). However, their hair is not woolly or frizzly, but usually wavy; and, although of a generally dark brown to black shade, in some groups it is frequently tawny or gingerish in children and adolescents. The adult males have abundant beards and heavy body hair. The brain cases are small and very narrow relative to their length (dolichocephalic). This race is usually of medium stature, but the trunk is often relatively short and the legs long, with meager, Negroidal shanks. The Australian race is probably not, as some think, an unmixed remnant of the men of the Old Stone Age, but is rather an archaic White type which has been modified in a slightly Negroid direction by mixture with its predecessors in the Australian continent—the now extinct Tasmanians. These latter appear to have been a very primitive stock with even darker skins and with woolly or frizzly hair. They probably represented early pygmy Negritos —first migrants into the Antipodes—who subsequently received some accretions of Australoid blood. Apparently the pure Australian strains, found in the west and south of Australia, include more heavily set and hairy men than the central and northern Australians, who lack the Negroid shanks and the deeper shades of skin color of the latter groups, and more frequently display blondness. In the far north of Australia, neighboring New Guinea, definitely Negroid traits are seen as a result of mixture with the Papuans and Melanesians (Oceanic Negroids). The Harvard-Adelaide Expedition, now engaged in studies of physical anthropology in Australia, has recently discovered in a refuge area back of Cairns, Queensland, a very short-statured or pygmoid group probably derived from the earliest of all Australian inhabitants—people with bulbous foreheads, yellow skins, broad noses, convex upper lips, and prognathous jaws; in fact, very close to the Negritos of inner New Guinea, and surely related to the Tasmanians.

Ainu

Much less primitive than the Australians, but still representative of the more archaic elements in the White division of
mankind, is the Ainu race, domiciled in the islands to the north
of Japan, the outlying remnant of an ancient population stratum
which probably extended at one time across Siberia into Europe.
They are usually called the "Hairy Ainu" because the men
can boast of the most luxuriant beards and the furriest bodies
to be found in the human species. The head hair is dark brown
to black and wavy in form. The eyes are dark brown, and the
skin, where visible through the hair, a dirty white. The Ainu
are short, sturdily built people. Their heads are long and relatively, but not absolutely, narrow. They have far more capacious
brain cases than the Australians, almost equally short faces,
but foreheads which are not inordinately sloping and brow
ridges which, though well developed, are not enormous. The
jaws of the Ainu show comparatively little projection, although
the palates are large and the teeth strong and well formed. The
root of the nose is deeply depressed, and this organ is broad
and fleshy, but not notably low-bridged. The lips are of moderate thickness, the ears of the long European type with well-
developed lobes. These Ainu, who possess a very primitive
culture, seem to me to be closer in physical type to the men
who inhabited the caves of Europe during the last of the glacial
period and who are associated with naturalistic cave art, than
is any other contemporaneous group. The Ainu are definitely
related to the Australians, but they represent a more highly
evolved and relatively unpigmented type, without suspicion of
Negrito admixture. Strains of Ainu race blood are to be found
in eastern Europe, especially in Russia, where the novelist
Tolstoy was a notorious double for a typical Ainu. However,
in Russia the head form commonly associated with this type is
round, or brachycephalic, and the features of the face are somewhat more refined than in the true Ainu.

Australian

Ainu

Classic Mediterranean

Arabo - Mediterranean

Nordic

Iranian Plateau

Mediterranean

Apart from these two archaic and vestigial stocks, the most ancient and far-flung White race is that which is usually called Mediterranean. It occupies most of the basin of that inland sea and sends outliers northwestward in Europe to the British Isles, down through the Sahara Desert, and eastward as far as India and farther. This race is fundamentally very dark brunet white or light brown in skin color, has black or dark brown hair and dark eyes, and is dolichocephalic, or long-headed (head breadth in the living less than 77 per cent of head length). The form of the hair varies from slight wave to loose curl, and the growth on the face and on the body is scanty. The face is usually oval, sometimes rather long and narrow, more rarely shortish and square. There is little or no jaw protrusion, and the teeth and palate are small. The nose is usually narrow and high-bridged with a thin tip; it may be straight, convex, or aquiline with a delicate depressed tip; it is occasionally rather infantile, somewhat blobby, and slightly concave. Stature in this group is prevailingly medium to short, but in some subraces tall. Slender body builds are almost invariable.

This basic Eur-African, brunet, long-headed race must be divided into several subraces. The first of these is the Classic Mediterranean type, as exemplified in ancient and modern Egyptians, many Arabs, Berbers, Italians, Spaniards, and some Britons. This subrace is characterized by short to medium stature, slender build, smoothness and gracility of the contours of bones of head, face, and postcranial skeleton; forehead of medium height, somewhat rounded and with submedium to moderate slope; eyebrow ridges feebly developed; cheekbones flat; nose straight, narrow, and of medium height; chin pointed and not very prominent; light brown to brunet white complexion; hair often deeply waved and sometimes curly; face elongated oval in shape.

A somewhat more primitive variety, or subrace, may be distinguished as the Crude Mediterranean type. The bony contours are more rugged and angular, the brow ridges larger, the face shorter and squarer with more protruding cheekbones and jaw angles, the nose broader and lower with slight tendency toward concavity of the bridge, the chin less prominent but squarer and often cleft, beard and body hair somewhat less sparse.

Another Mediterranean subrace may be designated as the Arabo-Mediterranean. It shows most of the gracility of the Classic type, but tends to be slightly taller, with longer face and very high-bridged, narrow nose, usually beaked or aquiline, with thin and depressed tip. The chin is pointed but juts strongly forward. Pigmentation is very dark.

Finally we have the Atlanto-Mediterranean subrace of this great stock, which is much taller and rather more heavily built. The skeleton is more rugged and the face is especially long, with a heavy bilateral chin. The nose is straight or convex; the cheekbones and jaw angles moderately pronounced. This type is usually very white in skin color and sometimes shows a ruddy tinge. The hair and eyes are dark.

Iranian Plateau

Closely allied with these last two varieties of the Mediterranean race, the Arabo-Mediterranean and Atlanto-Mediterranean subraces, is another physical type which perhaps should receive separate racial classification, on a parity with the great Mediterranean race. This type, recently distinguished by Dr. Henry Field's researches in Iran and Iraq, may be called provisionally the Iranian Plateau race.

In pigmentation, stature, and body build it is not distinguishable from the medium varieties of the Mediterranean race. It is outstanding, however, in its very large, extremely dolichocephalic head with markedly protuberant occiput, high sloping forehead, and strong brow ridges. Its most characteristic feature is its great nasality. The nasal bones jut out strongly from beneath the overhanging glabella. They are high, moderately broad, and hooked. The nasal tip is depressed and of thin to medium thickness. The cheekbones, or malars, are prominent and the face, which is elongated, has a strong chin and noticeable jaw angles. The beard and body hair in this type are very strongly developed. This Iranian Plateau race, with its specialized and hereditarily dominant features of the nasal skeleton and the external nose, is particularly strongly represented in Persia and Mesopotamia, but extends into northwestern India. It now seems probable that most of the convex and hooked noses, which are so common in the Near East and have diffused from that area, are due to this Iranian Plateau stock, which has passed on these features in many mixtures with other racial groups.

Nordic

The Nordic race is certainly a depigmented offshoot from the basic long-headed Mediterranean stock. It deserves separate racial classification only because its blond hair (ash or golden), its pure blue or gray eyes, and its pink or ruddy skin indicate that it is the result of a radical mutation toward suppression of pigment, fixed by a long process of inbreeding and selection in an isolated area. This area of differentiation is almost certainly the great steppe region approximately north of the Aral Sea. The only other alternative is the Scandinavian region, which seems rather to be a refuge area and only a secondary center of fixation and distribution of the Nordic race. Of course, the Baltic region is the present focus of Nordic habitat and diffusion, but it seems probable that the Nordic race developed in Late Paleolithic times before the Scandinavian peninsula was free of the ice sheet.

Moderate to fairly tall stature and robust framework are characteristic of this race. The head is sometimes frankly dolichocephalic, but more often mesocephalic (of medium breadth in relation to its length) because its breadth has increased, as contrasted with most Mediterranean races, and its length is sometimes slightly diminished. The face is longish, the cheekbones usually flat but sometimes fairly prominent, the nose prevailingly straight, high-bridged, and thin, but occasionally arched. The chin is often heavy and prominent. Subvarieties include a gracile type which is much like the Mediterranean except in pigmentation, but larger, with slightly more elongated face and longer, thinner nose. This is the ash-blond, pale blue or gray-eyed, flat-cheeked type with a rather weak and usually pointed chin. A taller, stronger, more ruggedly built variety is the golden-blond, blue-eyed type with heavier brow ridges; more sloping forehead; outstanding cheekbones; square jaws; long, deep, bilateral chin; and prominent, often convex, nose. Apart from pigmentation, its morphological similarities to parallel Mediterranean types lie particularly with the Atlanto-Mediterranean subrace, but it also has affinities with the brunet Iranian Plateau race.

Alpine

The basic differentiation of the White division toward round-headedness, or brachycephaly (relation of breadth of head to length in the living 82 per cent or over), is the Alpine race. This type almost certainly developed on the western slopes of the central Asiatic Plateau, probably in the neighborhood of the Hindu Kush and the Pamirs. Its diffusion westward occurred somewhat later than that of the blond, long-headed Nordics. The Alpine race is nearly as brunet in pigmentation as the Mediterranean race, but dark brown hair and light or medium brown eyes are probably commoner. The body build is medium to short, but broad and rotund, with stumpy extremities and long trunk. Hair form is only slightly wavy and often straight, the hair somewhat coarser than in Mediterraneans. Body and beard hair are much more heavily developed than in Mediterranean or Nordic races and comparable with, or superior to, that found in the Iranian Plateau race. The head is globular with a steep occiput; the neck is short and thick. The

Alpine

East Baltic

Armenoid

Dinaric

Mongoloid

Mongoloid

forehead is broad, high, and often steep; the temples bulging. Brow ridges are moderately to heavily developed. The nose is rather short, broad, and fleshy in the tip and bridge, but of medium height and usually straight. Although the face is wide and the cheeks full, the malars, or cheekbones, do not appear unduly prominent because of the great breadth of the head and an actual lack of size development and jut in the cheekbones themselves. The jaws are square at the hinder angles in the thinner-faced types, but may appear rounded in fat-faced individuals. The chin is well developed, but may be either pointed or bilateral. Lips are moderate in thickness—fuller than those of the Nordic and perhaps a little thinner than those observed in most Mediterraneans. The palate is broad and short. This Alpine race has obviously Ainu affinities, but differs from that race in its round head, in its lesser hirsuteness, and in a greater refinement of facial features associated with a broader, squatter body build.

There are other round-headed types which belong to the White division, and especially we may note the brunet, sugar-loaf-headed, beaky Armenoids, the tall, long-faced, hook-nosed Dinarics, and the square-headed, ash-blond, saddle-nosed East Baltics. As I consider that all these belong in the category of secondary, or composite, races, or indeed are merely hybrid types, I shall discuss them under the subject of mixtures between allied races.

Within this great White division of mankind I have recognized the following principal races: Australoid, Ainu, Mediterranean, Iranian Plateau, Nordic, and Alpine. These I regard as primary races in the sense that it seems probable that they have differentiated from a common stock, each through inbreeding, the selection of germinal variations, mutations, and environmental adaptations, rather than through intermixture. Secondary races are, on the contrary, composite groups which have arisen through the crossing of two or more primary races, followed by a period of inbreeding in isolation during which a stabilized physical type emerges from the blending of the racial features of the parent strains. The order in which these primary races of the White division have been enumerated is quite probably that of their development and diffusion. The Australoid race represents the retention of the most primitive and archaic features and is almost certainly the oldest and first in order of diffusion of this division. It must have been evolved well before the end of the Pleistocene or glacial period, and it seems probable that its continued evolution has been retarded or stopped in the present-day Australians, either through their isolation in an island continent, which seems to have had a repressive or inhibiting effect upon mammalian evolution, or for other reasons which we do not understand. It is probably a fact familiar to all of you that Australia contains no indigenous mammals above the level of the pouched marsupials, with the exception of man and the dingo dog, which presumably accompanied him in his migration thither. Traces of Australoid-like fossil types occur in South Africa and in the Upper Paleolithic or late glacial deposits of Europe, as well as in Palestine and in Java. They will be found, no doubt, in many other areas of the Old World as excavations proceed. It is impossible at present to fix the area of differentiation of this ancient race— it may have been anywhere from the Indian peninsula westward to the Syrian and Palestinian coasts of the Mediterranean. The Ainu race seems to represent the further evolution of this same type in northeastern Asia and is even closer to the Late Paleolithic types of man found in Europe than are the Australians. The Mediterranean race is surely a further evolution and refinement of this same basic stock, of which the center of characterization appears to have been Mesopotamia, whence it spread in all directions. The Iranian Plateau race may have arisen in that area by mutations of Ainu-like proto-race, particularly effecting nasalization. The depigmentation which characterizes the Nordic stock must have taken place, again, as a result of mutations in the steppe region northeast of the Caspian. Probably the latest racial mutant in this division was toward round-headedness, or brachycephaly, a phenomenon which seemingly occurred on the western slopes of the Tibetan Plateau, resulting in the formation of the Alpine race.

However, these racial developments in the White stock inter-digitated with evolutionary trends which gave origin to two other great divisions of mankind, each with its own quota of racial differentiae.

NEGROID DIVISION

The Negroid division of mankind is characterized by some strongly specialized features which suggest advanced and late evolutionary trends. On the other hand, it also retains some primitive and generalized physical characters. Skin color ranging from a reddish-brown through darker shades to a sooty black indicates a heavy deposition of a granular melanotic pigment in the lower layers of the epidermis. This pigmentation must be related to the need of protection of the underlying tissues from the destructive effects of ultra-violet light, which is especially powerful in the tropics. It is a fair assumption that human stocks have differentiated toward black and white, or toward heavily pigmented and pigmentless conditions, from a generalized intermediate status in which skin color was light brown or yellow-brown. It is very difficult to get away from the notion that extremely heavy pigment in the skin is a tropical adaptation of comparatively recent origin.

The head hair of the Negrito or Negro arises from a curved follicle imbedded in the skin, is markedly flattened in cross section, and grows into tiny tight spirals of a form which is rather ineptly called woolly. This short, tightly curved hair is certainly a specialized development from a primitive wavy type of only slightly flattened or oval cross section. Dixon has suggested that woolly head hair forms "a natural mat which by its included air-spaces must serve as a most excellent insulator for the brain against the intense heat of the sun." * This theory is ingenious, if not convincing. It has been frequently alleged also that the very broad noses of the Negroids, with their wide-open nostrils, are tropical adaptations which enable their possessors to snuff up great draughts of moist warm air, in contradistinction to the narrow, pinched noses developed in northern climes for the purpose of admitting only as much cold air as may be warmed in passage through the high, arched nose with its more extensive heat-radiating surfaces. I am somewhat skeptical of these interpretations, although there can be little doubt that the selection of fit variations in these two directions must have taken place in the tropic and northern frigid zones, respectively. In any event, the flaring wings of the Negroid nose, together with its bulbous tip, wide bridge and root, are specialized developments from the primitive or infantile condition. The thickened, puffy, and everted lips of the Negro are also very advanced features. Apes, like elder statesmen, have very thin lips. The simian lips are stretched over a muzzle bulging with big teeth; the senile lips have caved into the mouth because of lost teeth and artificial dentures. Thin lips do not denote determination in either case. Another evidence of evolutionary specialization in the Negroid division is the practical denudation of the body of its covering coat of hair—a variable feature in different Negroid races and not so extreme as that characteristic of the Mongoloids. The Negroid ear also is extraordinarily small and reduced, with nothing of the primitive about it except an absence or slight development of the degenerative fatty lobule found in Whites and Mongoloids.

There are also some Negroid features which are primitive and almost anthropoidal. Particularly notable in this category are prognathism, or jaw protrusion (more pronounced in this division than in any other modern race save the Australoids), the very feeble chin eminence of the mandible, the elongation of the bones of the forearm, the primitive conformation of the

* Dixon, Roland B., *The Racial History of Man*, p. 480. N. Y., 1923.

foot arches and of the toes, the *plica semilunaris* (a crescentic cartilaginous plate in the inner corner of the eye—alleged remnant of the third, or nictating, eyelid of reptiles). On the other hand, the elongation of the lower leg or shank in the Negro, together with the attentuation of the calf muscles and a special mechanical advantage afforded to these muscles by the low-set and out-thrust heel bones, may be specializations. Altogether, the assemblage of divisional characters suggests a mélange of primitive features blended with those of high specialization, and a protracted evolutionary history.

The Pygmy Negritos

The tiny pygmy Negritos contest with the Australoids the honor of being the most archaic of existing human races. On the basis of distribution they seem to take priority over the latter in the tropical parts of the Old World. For they are found exclusively in so-called marginal areas—refuge places in the most remote interiors of jungles or in isolated islands. More specifically, in Africa they dwell in scattered groups in the thick Congo forests; on the mainland of Asia they may be discovered as mixed remnants in some of the jungle tribes of the southern Indian peninsula and in the Malay Peninsula, in the adjacent Andaman Islands, in the remote interior of New Guinea, in a similar position in the Philippines, and possibly, again as a mixed remnant, in the hinterland of Queensland, Australia, at the base of the York Peninsula. Undoubtedly they preceded the Australian race in Australia and were the first inhabitants of New Guinea.

The characteristics of the Negrito race as a whole are: extremely small stature and general body size, red-brown to medium brown skin color with black hair and dark brown eyes, very tightly curled or woolly hair. It seems necessary to recognize two strongly demarcated subraces of Negritos which probably exist in the African and Oceanic areas alike, although their respective distributions have not been accurately ascertained.

The first of these I may call the adult type of long-headed pygmy, the second the infantile type of round-headed pygmy. The adult type has the general body build of a well-formed adult male, although diminutive in size. The shoulders are broad, the chest deep, the hips narrow, the arms and legs of normal size and well developed. The infantile type has narrow shoulders, small chest, relatively broader hips, pot belly, and smoother, childlike extremities. The adult type tends toward dolichocephaly, has a long and relatively narrow face, a big nose which widens out like a funnel from a narrow root, or of the so-called button type, which is very low and concave in the bridge and blossoms out into a thick tip with round nostrils directed forward and spreading wings. This adult type usually has a peculiar bulbous forehead with a central eminence which is shaped something like a shield whose point is directed downward. The jaws are markedly protuberant; the upper integumental lip (part on which the mustache grows) is very long and strongly convex; the membranous lips are thin, and the mouth is wide; the chin is long, but fugitive. This type of pygmy usually has a moderately developed beard and fairly abundant body hair, sometimes of a slightly reddish color.

The infantile type is very different. In the first place, the head is globular and the face is very broad and short. The head hair is probably woollier than in the adult type, and there is little development of beard or body hair. The nose is always very wide and bulbous, with a low bridge which is prevailingly saddle-shaped. The tip of the nose is never long and depressed, as it sometimes is in the adult type. The jaws in the infantile type are not so markedly projecting, the integumental lips less long and convex, and the membranous lips are thicker and sometimes present a good deal of the puffiness and eversion found in the true, full-sized Negro. The skin color of the infantile type is perhaps more variable than in the adult type, and is sometimes considerably darker.

Tentatively it may be suggested that the adult long-headed

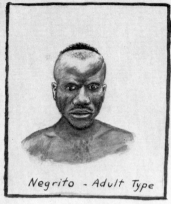

Negrito - Adult Type

Negrito - Infantile Type

Negro - Forest Type

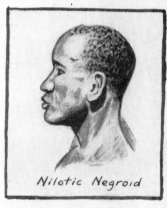

Nilotic Negroid

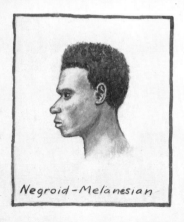

Negroid - Melanesian

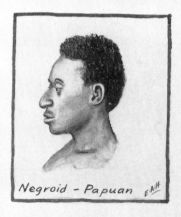

Negroid - Papuan

E.A.H.

pygmy type in Africa seems to be commonest in the western Congo region, as contrasted with the more eastern and southern distribution of the infantile type. In the Malay Peninsula it appears that both types are present among the Semang, whereas the Andaman Islanders and the Aetas of the Philippines (both Negrito groups) seem to be prevailingly or exclusively of the infantile, brachycephalic type. In the interior of New Guinea the adult, long-headed, bearded type with big nose seems to have been remarked oftenest, although the infantile type is probably also present.

Theories as to the origin of these two distinct pygmy Negrito types are necessarily speculative. My present view is that the long-headed, adult type was first differentiated, and that the infantile, round-headed type represents a somewhat later mutation, either from the adult type or from some protopygmy stock of presumably mesocephalic, or medium-headed, form, and perhaps lacking some of the extreme features of the adult type. The infantile type must have undergone the process which is ordinarily called "foetalization"—the retention of characters usually displayed in prenatal or infantile life. The juxtaposition of the two races in the Congo, with the long-headed type farther west, suggests the priority of the latter, which seems ordinarily to occupy a more marginal position than the infantile type. The extinct Tasmanians probably represented one or other of these pygmy Negrito types with slight Australoid admixture.

The Negro Races

The full differentiation of the normal-sized Negro races is best observed in the African continent. Among the pygmies of the Congo forests are larger groups of agricultural Negroes of medium stature (165 to 167 cm.) with heavy shoulders and torsos, long arms, short and moderately well-muscled legs. Body hair is more sparsely developed than in the adult type of pygmy; thin beards are not uncommon. The hair is woolly and the skin color is dark brown or often nearly black. This is the most primitive type of full-grown Negro—called by Sir Harry Johnston the "Forest Negro." The head is narrower and longer than that of the dolichocephalic pygmy, the brow ridges heavier, the forehead less bulbous, more retreating, and lower. The face of this type of Negro is very protrusive, with strongly marked cheekbones, long, fleeting chin, broad-bridged nose with thick tip and flaring wings, puffy and everted lips. The face is proportionately short and broad. Variations of this standardized West African or Forest Negro type are found all over tropical Africa, but especially in the thickest rain forest. There can be little doubt that the Forest Negro was differentiated from the pygmy, probably the long-headed type of Negrito. I see no reason for supposing that this differentiation took place anywhere else than within and on the periphery of the Congo forest belt itself. While these Forest Negroes are indeed in the thickest jungle areas, they have also spread out into the opener forests and park lands. Their culture is always much higher than that of the very primitive hunters and food-gatherers represented by the pygmies.

There are also in Africa several Negroid subraces which probably owe their origin to slight accretions of White blood in the Forest Negro stock. The first of these is the Nilotic Negro, inhabiting the Sudd area and the headwaters of that region.

These Nilotics are enormously tall, elongated of leg, short of body, and narrow of shoulder and chest. They have very black, almost hairless skins, and their shanks are of the exaggeratedly calfless variety. Hair is very woolly, heads usually long, faces broad and short. However, the jaws are not excessively protruding, and the nose is not unduly coarse. Finally, the lips are not rolled outward and blubbery to the extent found in the most pronounced Forest Negro type, nor is the chin so retreating and the forehead so low. Although these modifications away from the burly, thickset Negro type may be due to series of mutations, it is more probable that they are caused by admixture with the tall, slender, brunet White stocks of East Africa which are called Hamites. As one goes further east in the Lake region toward the Horn of Africa, effects of White admixture may be seen in more and more pronounced form, until they tend to submerge most of the Negroid features in the pastoral Bahima aristocrats; and, finally, the Negro blood fades out almost completely in the Galla. The result of White increments has generally been to elongate the body, straighten the facial profile, and refine the nose and lips. The effect on skin color and on hair form is usually not so apparent.

The Oceanic Negroids inhabit New Guinea and the neighboring islands. The terms Melanesian and Papuan are principally linguistic rather than racial. There are, however, at least two physical types of Oceanic Negroids, neither of which appears to be racially pure. Hair form does not usually present the extremely small spirals characteristic of the Negrito and the African Negro, but tends to be frizzled out into a mop. It seems probable, however, that truly woolly hair does occur. Skin color is quite variable—through various shades of brown to almost black. In general, most of these Oceanic Negroids are long-headed, but round-headedness is found, particularly in some of the short pygmoid stocks. Apart from the less specialized hair curvature, the principal deviations from the fully developed African Forest Negro stock are in the face. Negroid meagerness of the legs, relative shortness of the trunk, and elongated forearms are apparently as consistently present as in the Africans. The forehead of the Oceanic Negroid is commonly somewhat more sloping than that of the African, and the brow ridges are much larger. The face is less prognathous and the lips less thick and everted. Two contrasted Oceanic types are particularly distinguished by their noses. The one has a rather ordinary Negroid nose, low and somewhat broad, with perhaps less thickness of the tip and more circular nostrils than are characteristic of African Negroes. This type, which is often identified with the Melanesian linguistic stock, seems not to have much of a growth of body hair. The other type has less rounded and more sloping forehead, with bigger brow ridges. The nose is very anomalous indeed, since it is broad and high-rooted, but convex with a thick and depressed tip. This nose is often called pseudo-Semitic. In this so-called Papuan type the beard is well developed, the membranous lips thin, with the upper integumental lip very long and convex. Body hair is by no means sparse, and tawny or reddish shades occur in some immature individuals. The head hair is not usually very tightly curled, although it must be classified as frizzly or curly.

A recent examination of the physical evidence in this part of the world leads me to believe that the truly Negro racial type in the African sense can hardly be said to exist in the Mela-nesian-Papuan area. I am inclined to believe that the full-grown Negroid types are largely the result of mixtures of two sepa-rate pygmy Negrito races with the Australoid race. Such a hy-pothesis would account for the heavy brow ridges, depressed nasal root, and modified curve of the hair found in most New Guinea Negroids. However, it would not explain the pseudo-Semitic nose with its remarkably depressed tip. There are but two reasonable explanations for the latter. The first is that the long, funnel-shaped Negrito nose seen in inland New Guinea may have been specialized into the hooked Papuan type. On the whole, this seems improbable. The other and preferable alter-native involves the supposition that New Guinea must have been invaded by some convex-nosed stock which has left its dominant feature as a legacy to some of the Negroid-Austra-loid combinations. It is difficult to find any origin for this hooked nose outside of the Iranian Plateau race, and the no-tion of a migration of stocks from this area into New Guinea and the merging of their nasal form with that of the Negroids is a little hard to swallow. The noses are also incredible, but real.

THE FOETALIZED MONGOLOIDS

Nearly all close students of racial history agree that the great Mongoloid division of mankind has been the latest in its diffusion over the habitable world and was probably the last to differentiate. The evidence for this opinion is based largely upon historical and stratigraphic evidence as to the sequence of racial types all over the world. In Polynesia, Melanesia, Micronesia, and the Indo-Malayan Archipelago the mixed Mongoloids seem to be the latest arrivals. They were preceded by mixtures of Negroids and some sort of Whites, or by one or the other separately. In the New World the earliest populations seem to have been long-heads who display little or nothing of the Mongoloid specializations of the bones of the face. Some of them are vaguely Australoid, some almost Negroid, some like crude variations upon the Mediterranean White pattern. While it would be definitely rash to postulate, as some have, a sequence of migrations to the New World in the order of Australoid, Negroid, White, and finally Mongoloid, it would appear wholly possible that the earliest and most primitive inhabitants, now found largely in marginal and refuge areas, may have been blends of more anciently distributed stocks. In eastern Asia the archaeological evidence of sequence of physical types is very incomplete; but here, too, long-headed non-Mongoloid stocks seem to have preceded the brachycephalic, straight-haired, yellow-skinned races. The outstanding non-Mongoloid remnant is, of course, the Ainu race in the north of Japan. Finally, in Europe Mongoloid types do not appear until virtually historic times. The Lapps seem to have been a proto-Mongoloid stock with Mongoloid features imperfectly developed, and there are suggestions of a Mongoloid strain in the East Baltic stocks—especially the Finns. There are vague hints of Mongoloid characteristics in some of the Upper Palaeolithic and Mesolithic skeletons; but, on the whole, it seems probable that fully Mongoloid types did not appear in Europe until the Hunnic invasions, if then.

Mongoloid physical characters are more strongly expressed in the soft parts of the body than in the skeleton. On the whole, they are concentrated in the skull, as is the case with most racial features. Modern Mongoloids of apparently unmixed stock are prevailingly round-headed, but long-headed Mongoloids do exist. Among these may be enumerated the Tungus, the Chuckchi, and the Eastern Eskimo, although the last two are not innocent of some slight suspicion of admixture of an earlier non-Mongoloid stock. The round-head has a relatively great breadth and a relatively diminished length. This proportion is generally to be observed in the foetus during the last two or three months of intra-uterine life, and seems to be the stock embryonic head shape. Races which in adult years are long-headed tend usually at birth and during infancy to be somewhat more brachycephalic. Brachycephalization may then be considered provisionally as the retention of a foetal condition. The sutures between the bones of the skull vault in Mongoloids tend to be, on the whole, very simple, and not tortuous as in some other divisions of mankind. This condition is also paralleled in the foetus and the infant. The dovetailing of the sutures does not develop before the second or third year of life and becomes increasingly intricate during the earlier stages of the growth period. The Mongoloid skull also retains the smoothly rounded frontal bone of infancy and childhood and usually lacks any strong development of the brow ridges, which are adult features. The nasal skeleton is infantile in its low root and bridge, although the narrowing of the nasal bones at the superior end, frequently seen in Mongoloids, is the reverse of infantile. The comparative absence of facial protrusion and the relatively great transverse breadth of the jaws, together with the small development of the mastoid processes and the frequent gaps in the bony tympanic plate which forms the anterior portion of the auditory entrance, the low, short, broad bony palate, and the shallowness of the glenoid fossa (the socket into which the jawbone is jointed) are also infantile features. There are, however, some features of the Mongoloid skull which are not babyish. The most notable of these is the strong anterior and lateral jutting of the malars, or cheekbones. Others are the commonly elongated face and the flaring hinder angles of the jaws. The incisor teeth which are hollowed behind like scoop shovels are found occasionally in primitive man (e.g. Sinanthropus) and can hardly be considered foetalized, or infantile. In the postcranial skeleton the Mongoloid may show certain modifications caused by a barefoot, bent-knee gait, but there is nothing very distinctive from a racial viewpoint in the bones of the appendages, the girdles, or the vertebral column.

The pigmentation of the skin of the Mongoloid is usually yellowish brown, sometimes with reddish shades, and occasionally with an almost clear yellow tone. This latter is exceptional. Yet I think that it must be admitted that yellow is more to the fore in Mongoloids than in Negroes or brunet Whites. It seems probable that this yellow color is due to the presence of carotin diffused from the subcutaneous fat. Whether or not it may be due to diet is an open question. Over-indulgence in carrots will make the skin yellow, but there is no particular reason for supposing that Mongoloids are excessively addicted to that vegetable. On the whole, it seems improbable that diet has anything to do with their yellowish skin pigmentation.

Hair form, hair texture, hair pigmentation and distribution are undoubtedly specialized in the Mongoloids. The hair sheaths are so deeply pigmented as to give a blue tinge to the black hair color, but there is not so much melanotic pigment in Mongoloid hair as in that of Negroids. The form of the Mongoloid head hair is straight; the hairs have an almost circular cross section and are, in general, of large diameter. This divergence from the presumably primitive wavy form is as marked as that of the tiny spiral coils found in Negritos. The denudation of body surfaces has apparently gone farther in Mongoloids than in most Negroids. This is again a specialized condition, although it might be considered a retention of the infantile (not the foetal) condition.

Certain heavy deposits of subcutaneous fat are characteristic of the Mongoloid—especially over the cheekbones and at the angles of the jaws, also in the eyelids. The fold of skin which often extends across the upper eyelid, obscuring its eyelash implantations and cutting across the inner corner of the eye (thus covering the caruncula) is generally known as the Mongoloid fold. It is a frequent manifestation in foetuses and infants of European racial stocks and sometimes occurs in Negroes. However, it is far the most common, although variable in the degree of its development, among the Mongoloid stocks. This epicanthic, or Mongoloid, fold seems to be related, in some fashion, to skin slackness as a result of the flat, infantile nasal root. The Mongoloid nose is merely a babyish nose, showing little or no evidence of specialization. The lips also are unremarkable. The external ear shows less size reduction than is generally observable in Negroids.

The present area of concentration of the pure Mongoloid race is in northeastern Asia, where a full development of Mongoloid characters is found in such peoples as the Goldi, Giliak, Buriat, and Tungus. The Mongols proper show signs of admixture with a hook-nosed stock. Again, most of the Chinese and the peoples in southeastern Asia, as well as the Tibetans, are obviously Mongolized on the top of other racial elements. The area of differentiation of the pure Mongoloid type may be somewhat to the west of the present focus, and north of the Tibetan Plateau. Environment may have had something to do with the obviously late mutations which resulted in this well-delimited physical division of mankind, but there is no clear evidence that this form of man is particularly adapted to Arctic environment, nor to the desert and steppe region. A favorite theory is that recently advanced and elaborated by J. R. de la H. Marett, who is of the opinion that the Mongoloid is a hypothyroid type, particularly adapted for liquid economy. Our present knowledge of endocrinology and of the relation of diet to the functions of the ductless glands permits us neither to refute nor to confirm this theory. On the whole, it may be said to be suspiciously plausible.

Apart from brachycephaly, or round-headedness, the Mongoloid and brunet White Alpine types have little in common, and it is almost certainly wrong to identify them with each other. Nevertheless, it seems probable that their areas of differentiation were not far apart, the Alpines possibly on the western slopes of the central Asiatic Plateau, the Mongoloids to the north. The Mongoloid hair form seems to be dominant and possibly also the cheekbones and the epicanthic fold of the eye (although the evidence with regard to the latter is somewhat contradictory). On the other hand, the infantile Mongoloid nose is probably recessive. Professor Franz Weidenreich's attempt to relate Sinanthropus, the fossil Pleistocene man of China, to Mongoloids, on the basis mainly of the occasional occurrence of shovel-shaped incisors in both stocks, seems to me quite unconvincing. The evidence as it now stands suggests that the Mongoloid division of mankind did not become evolutionarily differentiated until after the close of the glacial period —not more than 20,000 years ago. All of the other main divisions of mankind seem to have been developed at least as far back as the Upper Pleistocene. However, further excavations in Asia may yield evidence of a greater antiquity of the Mongoloid type. Certainly, on the incomplete showing of the yet-unpublished Upper Palaeolithic skulls from Chou Kou Tien, the Late Pleistocene men of northern China were not Mongoloid, but more closely akin to the so-called Aurignacian and Cro-Magnon types of Europe.

Professor Griffith Taylor's theory of zones and strata of racial differentiation and migration, independently advocated by my late colleague Roland Dixon, is based primarily upon the ideas of the diffusion of mammals from the central Asiatic area advanced originally by the palaeontologist Matthew. According to this theory the focus of mammalian evolution (including the higher primates and man) has always been in central Asia. Different races, evolving in this zoological Garden of Eden, have spread in successive waves over the world, so that the most primitive racial types are now found upon the margins of the land areas of which the Asiatic Plateau is the center. There is, in general, a great deal to be said for this theory on the basis of the distribution of fossil types and present races. Assuming, however, that the first primitive human types were evolved at least as early as the Upper Pliocene period, this zones and strata theory ought to reveal protohuman anthropoid apes in the New World and archaic fossil types of man down in the tip of South America. There is absolutely no evidence that morphologically archaic men ever reached the American continent, and there are no fossil anthropoid apes in the New World. The theory seems to work fairly well if one leaves out the Americas.

It seems to me that we may postulate no single *umbilicus hominum,* no one center of human evolution. The generalized and fossil manlike apes spread themselves over a wide zone from northern India westward to the extremity of central Europe and all through the African continent. The various anthropoid stocks which gave rise to man were also probably widely diffused. It is difficult, however, to explain the distribution of the pygmy Negritos except on the hypothesis that they originally developed in, and spread from, some area between the present African and Oceanic foci. If the presence of a Negrito substratum can actually be demonstrated in the Indian peninsula, that is the probable area of the early development of this very archaic type. Suggestions of Negrito remnants in the hill and jungle tribes of southern India are by no means absent. On the other hand, there seems to be no good reason for denying the African full-grown Negro type an evolution *in situ* from the earlier Negrito stocks in Africa. Again, as I have stated, the Melanesian and Papuan Negroids of New Guinea and other islands may well have sprung from admixture of the Negroids with Australians and other stocks.

In Pleistocene times archaic types of men with protruding jaws, low foreheads, and big brow ridges seem to have ranged as far south as Northern Rhodesia, as far west as the Channel Islands, and in the Oriental region at least down to Java and probably to Australia. At present it is not possible to determine the places of origin of these apelike low-brows. It does, however, seem unlikely that they migrated to other parts of the Old World either from South Africa or from western Europe. My quarrel with the Matthew-Griffith Taylor theory of single repeated evolutions from a central Asiatic focus is that its adherents rather disingenuously employ a circular type of argument. If they find a nearly human fossil ape in South Africa or a very primitive man like the Rhodesian type, they insist that the presence of these archaic forms on the extreme marginal areas is evidence that they must have developed at the most remote possible point from the actual locus of the finds. This is *lucus a non lucendo*. But if the most archaic types of man are also found (as they are) in China and Java, very near to the postulated center of evolution, they get round the difficulty by arguing that these approximate points were at some remote period the periphery of human distribution, and that these were once marginal types. Thus every find is grist for their mill. In order to be logical they should admit the presence of the most apelike forms in or near central Asia as equally conclusive evidence that man originated in southern Australia, at Cape Horn, or in Ireland.

Personally, I have always found it advisable to distrust these simple and orderly theories, because their logic is usually specious. No fossil Negritos have been found superimposed upon Neanderthal-like forms either in central Asia or in any other place. Nevertheless, however strongly one reacts against this facile hypothesis, it is hard to get away from the evidence that the Australoids seem to have wandered southeastward and prob-

ably westward from some point to the south of the central
Asiatic Plateau, that the Negritos apparently came from the
same general region, that most of the White stocks seem to have
poured westward and southward from the Iranian Plateau, the
Mesopotamian area, and the steppes to the north, and that the
Mongoloid drift has emanated from the region to the north of
this same plateau. Of course, evolution has continued in many
parts of the world, but the supposition that man actually evolved
from apelike ancestors at different times in several continents
has little to support it. Much can be said for a separate evolution of the true Negro from the Negrito in Africa, but it is
hardly probable that the Negrito differentiated from some ape
in Africa and then wandered as far as the Philippines, or that
the Oceanic Negroids could have trekked to New Guinea from
the Dark Continent. I have changed my mind to some extent
since I last wrote about this subject (1931), and it is perfectly
possible that I may change it again. With the advance of knowledge consistency ceases to be a jewel and is nothing more than
an obdurate chunk of useless rock.

IV

THE MAKING AND MIXING OF HUMAN RACES:

2. THE FORMATION OF SECONDARY OR COMPOSITE RACES

SECONDARY, OR composite, races arise from the blending of primary stocks which have already undergone long differentiation and selection in isolated regions. The secondary races are formed when, for various reasons, a more recently evolved racial stock moves into a territory already fully occupied by some more ancient race. It follows that the substratum in the blend is usually represented by the more primitive race, and the outcome of the mixture is likely to depend upon the relative numbers of the newcomers as contrasted with the old settlers and also upon the number of dominant physical variations possessed by each race. Since it seems probable that the later evolved races have, on the whole, more dominant physical features, we should expect most of their racial characters to survive at the expense of those of the older stocks. However, when the invaders come in relatively small numbers they may be absorbed into the mass of the earlier races without making any very great impression upon the physical features of the latter. Or they may segregate themselves as an alien aristocracy which gradually receives increments of the blood of the primitive stock. These phenomena have taken place in Negro Africa where the Bantu-speaking peoples, especially in East and South

Africa, have undergone minor infusions of White blood, and, in the Lake Region, have settled among them a pastoral warrior caste called the Bahima, which obviously carries a great deal of White blood. The Bantu, however, are so predominantly Negro that they cannot be recognized as a secondary race. They are merely Negroes with some White admixture.

It seems necessary to conclude that secondary races are not formed unless very large numbers of two races intermingle. Too great a preponderance of one or the other stock merely results in the slight adulteration of that stock. The secondary race is not formed until a long-continued period of interbreeding and subsequent inbreeding of the hybrids has resulted in the stabilization of the blend so that a certain uniformity of physical type is attained. By the time this standardized combination has been fixed, memory of the different elements which have gone into the blend has usually been lost or is preserved only in vague historical legends and in folklore.

Generally speaking, secondary races are of much more recent origin than the primary races. Some of them, indeed, seem to have been formed in the last two or three thousand years. This is certainly true in the case of the Polynesians. The process is continuing, but only in the few areas where primary races are in contact.

Secondary races which have been formed from the crossing of primary races drawn from different main divisions of mankind—such as Negroid, Mongoloid, and White—are much more obvious and more easily distinguishable than those which have grown up within one single division by the subsequent interbreeding of races differentiated from the one prototypical stock. In fact, it might be advisable to limit the term "secondary race" to such as have been formed by the intermixture of primary races drawn from different basic divisions of our species.

THE ENIGMATIC BUSHMAN-HOTTENTOT RACE

Certainly the oldest secondary race with which we are acquainted, and by far the most enigmatic in its origins, is the Bushman-Hottentot group, which until recently occupied South Africa. This race shows a very perplexing combination of Negritoid and Mongoloid features, and is ranked by many anthropologists as an early and primary race. Before we discuss the question we may describe the physical characteristics, distribution, and probable migrations of this stock. The Bushmen in South Africa were primitive hunters and food-gatherers, while the Hottentots were later arrivals who possessed a cattle culture. Since the Bushmen are the earlier and purer representatives of the race, we may begin with them.

The Bushmen are so short in stature that they may be called pygmoid, if not pygmy. Their skin color is yellow-brown, with yellowish tints much more prominent than in Negroid stocks. The anatomy of the foot is more primitive than in any other type of man in which this organ has been carefully studied. The females have a localized deposit of fat on the buttocks and the upper outside areas of the thighs which forms an enormous bustle, or cushion. A very slight development of this fatty deposit also occurs in the males. This feature is known as steatopygia—fat buttocks. It has given rise to very many interesting speculations, the favorite of which is that it serves the same purpose as the hump of the camel—a reserve larder to be drawn upon in time of food shortage. Steatopygia has also been compared with possibly analogous deposits of fat on the rumps of certain sheep, and with a similar accumulation around the base of the tail of the mouse lemur—a tiny and primitive primate which aestivates (sleeps through the dry season). In my unregenerate youth I was once rash enough to hint that steatopygia in man might be the relic of hibernation or aestivation in some of our protohuman ancestors. The evidence of human statuettes found in the caves of western Europe during the later phases of the glacial period clearly shows that these localized deposits of fat were characteristic of the females of some of the Upper Palaeolithic races. If the Aurignacian ladies subsisted upon their gluteal fat during the long winters of the glacial period, it is hard to understand how their husbands survived the winter, squatting on their unpadded ischial tuberosities, wide awake and shivering. This steatopygia is evidently in part a secondary sexual character, because its development in the males is at most meager. The sex limitation appears to militate against the theory of steatopygia being in any broad sense a useful or functional adaptation. Some degree of development of this feature is said to occur occasionally among the Congo pygmies, or Negritos, and sporadically in some of the other Negroid stocks of Africa. However, it is racially characteristic of no present-day people except the Bushmen and the Hottentots. It must be regarded as a specialization, rather than a primitive character.

The Bushmen-Hottentot stock also possesses certain peculiarities of the conformation of the external genitalia. In the male Bushmen, apparently because of shortness of the suspensory ligament, the flaccid penis assumes a horizontal or semierect position. In the female Hottentots (and probably in the Bushwomen) the labia minora of the vulva are peculiarly elongated to form the so-called "Hottentot apron." It seems very doubtful that this feature is due to artificial deformation. So far as I am aware these peculiarities are limited to the Bushman-Hottentot stock.

The body of the Bushman or Hottentot is almost devoid of hair. The head hair grows in tiny spirals not more than one millimeter in diameter and is further grouped in twisted clumps separated by bare spaces on the scalp. This type of hair is called "peppercorn." It seems to be the most highly specialized variety of Negroid hair. Peppercorn hair may occur sporadically among the Negritos and Negroes. I do not think that it is a standard adult feature of any racial group except the Bushman-Hotten-

Winter's Night in the Glacial Period

tot. Its frequent occurrence in Negro babies suggests that it may be the retention of an infantile character.

The skull of the Bushman tends to be relatively long and narrow and that of the Hottentot even more so. The foreheads are rounded, as in many Negroids, and the brow ridges are small. The root and bridge of the nose are extraordinarily broad and flat—much more so than in most Negroids and Negritos. In fact, the conformation of this part of the nose is somewhat Mongoloid. The cheekbones jut forward very strongly and are also laterally prominent. Further, they have laid upon them a pad of fat which is similar to that found in Mongoloids. The orbits of the eyes are low, the eye opening is slitlike and frequently slanted upward and outward from the nose, and the Mongoloid fold is commonly present. The tip of the Bushman or Hottentot nose is short and moderately thick, but in no wise so bulbous as the nose of the Negrito or that of many Negroes. The nostrils look forward and the wings, or alae, are flaring. The face of the Bushman and the Hottentot shows comparatively little prognathism. The lips are thick and everted, but not so blubbery as in the fully developed African Negro. The short face is terminated by a rather feeble pointed chin. Since the cheekbones project, the entire face takes on a triangular form.

The Bushman also has, frequently if not consistently, a peculiar form of ear. Like the ear of the Negro, it is absolutely small and relatively short and broad. In the typical Bushman ear the helix, or rim, is very deeply rolled, and its upper surface is horizontal and (it is alleged) frequently soldered to the head. There is little or no lobe to the ear. The slit between the cartilaginous flap called the tragus, which extends over the auditory opening, and the opposite cartilaginous ridge, or antitragus, is very narrow and directed diagonally downward and forward. The typical ear thus described is very peculiar indeed. It is apparently by no means always present in the Bushman—at least in all of its various peculiarities. It also occurs sporadically among the Hottentots.

Available data make it difficult to distinguish between the physical characteristics of the Bushman and the Hottentot. In general, it appears that the Hottentot has a longer, narrower, and relatively higher head, more prognathism, relatively wider nose, and more variable stature. It is commonly believed that the Hottentot is only a Bushman with a minor admixture of true Negro blood and possibly some Hamitic, brunet White blood. The physical divergences of the Hottentot from the Bushman, as heretofore tentatively indicated, support this suggestion.

Now, the remarkably and truly enigmatic fact about the Bushman-Hottentot stock is that it combines ultra-Negroid hair form and moderately Negroid lip form with skin color which is at least quasi-Mongoloid, malar development that is fully Mongoloid, eye folds that have their maximum distribution among Mongoloids, and a somewhat Mongoloid nose. Pygmy stature, steatopygia, together with the curious ear and the characteristic variations of the genitalia, are neither distinctively Negroid nor Mongoloid, but apparently *sui generis*. How can we account for this extraordinary combination of extreme physical variations?

The simplest theory would derive the Bushman-Hottentot stock from a blend of Mongoloid with pygmy Negrito. Then, presumably, the features surviving in the distinctive Bushman-Hottentot blend would be the dominants. Incidentally, it may be stated that most of the racial features of the Bushman-Hottentot do seem to be dominant variations. This theory would postulate the dominance of the tightly curled Negrito hair over the straight Mongoloid, the highly evolved cheekbones over the less developed, the persistence of the Mongoloid eyes, the root and bridge of the Mongoloid nose, and the Negroid thickness and lip eversion. Of these postulates the one least supported by observation of recent Negroid-Mongoloid crosses is that of nose form. However, there are very few data relating to Negro-Mongoloid crosses.

A greater difficulty in the way of accepting this Mongoloid-Negrito theory as the explanation of the Bushman-Hottentot racial blend is the absence of a fully Mongoloid stock in Africa. So far as present anthropological evidence is concerned, there is no Mongoloid stock in Africa and there never has been such an African Mongoloid stock. Again, the archaeological evidence of the presence of Bushmen in South Africa quite clearly suggests that the Bushmen had reached the southern tip of the continent at a very remote time—at least as early as the end of the last glacial period—perhaps 20,000 years back. Considering the apparently very late distribution of the Mongoloid stock in Asia and Europe, it is hard to believe that a fully developed Mongoloid stock could have penetrated as far as central Africa and there could have mixed with the pygmy Negritos before the end of the glacial period.

Finally, one almost insurmountable obstacle to this theory lies in the fact that no Bushman- or Hottentot-like stock is found in southeastern Asia or in Oceania, where we know that areas inhabited by pygmy Negritos have been overrun by later peoples who are to some extent Mongoloid. If a cross between a Negrito and a Mongoloid produces a Bushman, surely something of the kind should occur in the Malay Peninsula and the Philippines. But there is no such animal in that part of the world.

An interpretation of the Bushman-Hottentot enigma much favored by some anthropologists is that this stock represents a sort of a racial prototype in which there are generalized precursors of Negroid and Mongoloid features. I take strong exception to this view because practically none of the features found in the Bushmen and Hottentots can be regarded as in any sense primitive or generalized. The head hair, for example, is perhaps the most highly specialized type of hirsute covering which can be found among the races of man. The ear is also very far removed from the primitive and the anthropoidal. I do not know the answer to this Bushman-Hottentot riddle, but the nearest I can come to a satisfactory solution is something of this sort. The ancestors of the Bushman-Hottentots may have been more or less fully developed pygmy Negrito types which evolved somewhere in Asia in a district contiguous to, or not far away from, the region which later gave rise to the Mongoloid mutations. These Negritos received some infusion of proto-Mongoloid stock, carrying with it potentialities for the development of Mongoloid features, before the migration to Africa began. In the African environment there occurred in this somewhat mixed stock a further development of some of the ancestral Negrito features together with a partial expression of Mongoloid tendencies. Whatever is Mongoloid in the Bushman-Hottentot must have been carried with the original migrants in solution when they arrived in Africa. The absence of Bushman-like types in Asia I should attribute to the fact that the Negritos have been completely swamped by recurring Mongoloid invasions, and that the fully developed and culturally more advanced Mongoloids may not have mixed with the Oceanic Negritos in sufficient numbers to produce a Bushman-like hybrid. My postulate is that the Bushman is physically and by blood much more Negrito than Mongoloid, and that a similar type in the Oceanic area would be expected only if a predominantly Negrito population should receive a minor infusion of Mongoloid blood. This may or may not be the correct explanation of the phenomena under discussion. Nature seems to have been unable to make up her mind whether to produce a Negrito or a Mongoloid, just as earlier she manifested a similar indecision as to whether the duck-bill should be a reptile or a mammal. Evolution occasionally vacillates.

TRI-HYBRID RACES

The East Indian Race

The great Indian peninsula teems with peoples (and other animals) today and was probably one of the earliest homes of man. Men of the Old Stone Age lived here in presumably large numbers, but unfortunately none of their remains has yet been discovered, because there has been very little exploration of the Pleistocene deposits of India. The Siwalik foothills of the Himalayas have, however, yielded the greatest abundance of anthropoid ape fossils belonging to the Upper Tertiary period. (This "abundance" consists of a few teeth and bits of jaws.) It may be predicted that the remains of fossil man himself will be found in India as soon as the proper areas are exploited by properly trained archaeologists.

Although the various primary races which have inhabited India have fused into a number of quite easily distinguishable secondary racial types, there is no generally recognized name which may be applied to the dominating composite race of modern India. This lack is partly ascribable to the unfortunate mistake made by Columbus whereby the American race was given the name "Indian," thus relegating the real Indians to the position of unsuccessful contestants for the racial application of their own geographical designation. The term Hindu, commonly used, applies, of course, to a religion which is by no means universal in India. The name Dravidian, which I have sometimes employed, is a little better, since it denotes a great linguistic family whose speakers are aborigines of India. Nevertheless, it is always unwise to use a linguistic family name for the designation of a physical race. However, either East Indian or Dravidian must serve. The invention of new names is likely to add to an existing confusion.

The stature of the East Indian is commonly short to medium and the build slender. It is possible, however, that insufficient food and malnutrition may be in some measure responsible for small body size in this race. The skin color is medium brown to dark brown, varying considerably in the different regions and in the numerous castes. The head hair is invariably black in color, prevailingly wavy, and oftener curly than straight. Beard and body hair are usually moderately to strongly developed. The head form is nearly always long and narrow, with a somewhat rounded forehead and a moderate development of the brow ridges. The face is oval and neither very short nor noticeably long. The cheekbones are of medium prominence, and the chin is likely to be pointed and somewhat weak. There is little jaw protrusion. The profile of the nose is prevailingly straight, the root either medium in height or low and depressed, the bridge rather wide and not remarkable in elevation, the tip and wings moderately broad. The lips are thicker than those of most Europeans, but lack the Negroidal fullness and eversion.

This description indicates a somewhat neutral physical combination without high or low points of featural development. Actually, there is great individual and group variability among the inhabitants of India, and the composite type sketched above is clearly the result of the blending of more extreme types. These latter may be observed to retain sharper racial features in out-of-the-way regions where race mixture has been less intensive. We can reconstruct the processes of amalgamation by which the East Indian race has been built up by studying the contributing elements in the order of their probable antiquity in India.

In various remote jungle spots in the south of the peninsula there survive tribes which are either Negritoid or really Negrito. They have the short stature, very dark skin, woolly hair, prognathism, wide, flat noses, and protuberant lips which characterize certain types of the Oceanic Negrito. In other refuge areas there is to be found a type which is often called pre-Dravidian or Veddoid. Stature is again short and skin color dark, but the head is longer and narrower than in the Negrito type; head hair is wavy and body hair is more fully developed; the brow ridges are rather heavy, the root of the nose low and sunken. The jaws are protrusive, the lips somewhat thick, and the chin peculiarly weak and fleeting. This type has affinities with the Australoid and seems to have been superimposed upon an early and sparse Negrito population. The next strain which came into India, and apparently in large numbers, seems to have been a primitive, brunet White, Mediterranean element—dark-haired, long-headed, oval-faced, and lacking prognathism, with a straight and narrow nose. This White element has, to a considerable extent, swamped the preceding stocks, straightened the facial profile, narrowed the nose, thinned the lips, and made the chin more prominent. It has also had some slight effect, in all probability, of diminishing skin pigment. Thus the East Indian, or Dravidian, race seems to have been composed by adding a major Veddoid or Australoid component to a minor substratum of Negrito, then swamping the blend with brunet, Mediterranean White. It seems probable that this White element was responsible for the introduction of the Aryan languages, which may have come into India about 1500 B.C. In the northwest of the country there have also been admixtures of the hook-nosed, dolichocephalic Iranian Plateau race, which is more notably hairy than the other Indian stocks. This admixture seems to have resulted in tall stature. Finally, in Kashmir there is evidence of some infusion of a blond stock, doubtless Nordic. Here and there Mongoloids have trickled into India through the Tibetan passes, but, on the whole, the Mongoloid accretions seem to have been so slight as to leave very little impression upon the composite racial type. It is interesting to note that the higher Indian castes usually display fewer of the primitive racial elements than do the low castes, in whatever part of the country. But as one goes south the earlier strata in the populations appear more strongly represented in the blends, so that the southern Indian Brahmin, although carrying more Mediterranean race features than his caste inferiors, is yet more aboriginal in appearance than the lower-caste person farther to the north.

The Polynesian Race

Polynesia is a word derived from the Greek, meaning "many islands." It refers to the numerous archipelagos and to the scattered single islands which dot the middle Pacific. Some of these islands are high and mountainous; others are low coral atolls. These were probably the last parts of the earth to be occupied by man, since to reach them a considerable skill in navigation is required. A nearly equilateral triangle, roughly 5,000 miles on a side, with the apices at Hawaii, New Zealand, and Easter Islands, includes almost the whole of Polynesia. On the west side are the Samoan, Tongan, Cook, Society, Tuamotu, and Marquesas groups, whereas the isolated corners are occupied by those islands previously mentioned. All of the Polynesians speak related languages, affiliated to Melanesian and Malayan, and through these to the Mon-Khmer of southeastern Asia.

It seems improbable that the earliest peopling of Polynesia could have taken place much before 500 B.C., and its occupation by primitive peoples was apparently completed about the middle of the fourteenth century A.D. Although the physical types of Polynesians vary individually and, to some extent, in the different island groups, there has been evolved a smooth and recognizable racial blend which, with local modifications, prevails all over the vast area.

The stature of Polynesians is consistently tall, and their bodies are heavy and muscular. They lack the Mongoloid blockiness, the Negroid linearity and poorly developed legs. They approximate European ideals of body build. Both males and females tend to become fat from middle age onwards. Skin color varies from a pleasing light brown to deeper, richer brown shades. In the Marquesas and in New Zealand tattooing designs of a very elaborate character are incised on many parts of the body. Of course, tattooing is a practicable means of bodily adornment only for people who have comparatively light skin color. Otherwise the designs will not show. Hair color is usually black or very dark brown. In the Marquesas, and probably elsewhere, reddish hair occurs associated with bluish or greenish eyes. Ordinarily, eyes are dark brown. The head hair is moderately wavy with occasional tendencies toward curliness and straightness. Frizzly hair is not characteristic of any Polynesian

Bushman

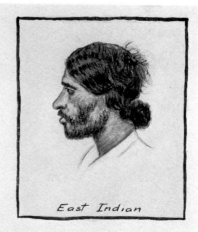

East Indian

Polynesian

Indonesian-Malay

American Indian
- Lacandone

North American Indian

group but occurs in individuals. Body hair is sparse as in Negroids and Mongoloids.

Most present-day Polynesians are round-headed, or brachycephalic, although skeletal remains of the older populations usually show a former prevalence of dolichocephaly, or longheadedness. The back of the head is characteristically flat and steep; the vault is high, the forehead lofty but sloping, with a tendency toward narrowness. Brow ridges are moderately to strongly developed. The eminence over the root of the nose—glabella—is prominent, and the root of the nose is somewhat depressed, broad, and of medium height. A moderate breadth and elevation of the nasal bridge is characteristic. The profile of the nose is prevailingly straight, but both convex and concave forms occur, the former more commonly in adult males, the latter in females and children. The tip and wings of the nose are somewhat heavier than in most northern Europeans, but in no wise bulbous or flaring. The cheekbones are more strongly developed than in Whites, and tend to be heavily padded with flesh. However, this portion of the face is not exaggerated in projection so as to give a Mongoloid appearance to the countenance. The lips are fuller than in Europeans but not blubbery; the chin is deep and strong and the hinder angles of the jaws are prominent. On the whole, the face tends to be both broad and long. Usually the eyes are prominent, full, and heavy-lidded, with wide palpebral openings and absence of the internal Mongoloid fold. The latter does indeed occur in individual instances, but it can hardly be said to be a standard Polynesian feature.

The Polynesians are a very comely race with beautifully made bodies and handsome faces. They exhibit none of the featural disharmony which many theorists have associated with race crossing. Clearly enough, they are of tri-hybrid origin—a Negroid or Negritoid element, plus a very strong infusion of brunet White stock, with a slight Mongoloid dash to top off. Arguments about their racial origin center upon the question whether the different elements were blended as the consequence of separate migrations into the Pacific area of Negroids, Whites, and Mongoloids, in that order; or whether, on the contrary, all of the racial strains were carried in solution by each of the successive waves of migrants. Probably the best explanation of the sequence of types and the routes of the migrations is that given by my late colleague, Roland B. Dixon, on the basis of a detailed survey of cranial material, classified, however, by a somewhat arbitrary and not altogether satisfactory scheme.* He found that in Easter Island and in the whole southeastern portion of the area the dominant type is, or was, a long-headed variety which gives evidence of being mixed Negroid. These Negroids, he thinks, were the first comers, who had developed in the so-called Melanesian area (New Guinea and the neighboring islands). These dark-skinned, curly-, wavy-, or frizzly-haired peoples gradually worked their way eastward as their skill in navigation increased. Apparently, however, they left the northern and southwestern corners of the triangle (Hawaii and New Zealand) empty.

The second group of migrants, according to Dixon, came down from the north by the way of the Ellice and Gilbert groups, rather than from the west via Melanesia. These were long-heads with narrow noses, belonging presumably to White stocks. I should think that they were mainly of Mediterranean race, although possibly with some Nordic admixture. These newcomers first reached Samoa and Tonga and ultimately got to Easter Island, although they also failed to reach either Hawaii or New Zealand. They were possessed of much higher cultures than their predecessors. Finally, the last wave, which may have come as late as the early part of the Christian period, was composed largely of peoples whom Dixon calls "Alpines" (brachycephals with relatively high heads and relatively narrow noses). It seems to me probable that these were the invaders who actually introduced the Mongoloid strains, although they were probably not pure Mongoloids but mixed with White

* Dixon, R. B., *The Racial History of Man*, pp. 377-387. N. Y., 1923.

stock. Dixon thinks that they came by way of Micronesia. They poured into western Polynesia and moved northward and east-ward as well as southward. Dixon suggests that New Zealand received its first population from this round-headed wave, which had taken on no little of Negroid and White long-headed ad-mixture as a result of its previous contact with the older west-ern Polynesian population. This round-headed group also colo-nized Hawaii. Dixon is much puzzled by the presence in Hawaii of a round-headed, broad-nosed type which he calls "Palae-Alpine," otherwise almost unrepresented in the area. The in-flexibility of his scheme of skull classification makes it neces-sary for him to regard this as a separate racial strain. However, a knowledge of the genetic effects of race mixture makes it per-fectly clear that the broad noses of the Hawaiian round-heads may be either Mongoloid or Negroid features carried in solu-tion to northern Polynesia and segregated out there as a result of inbreeding. That a Negroid substratum is also found in the Hawaiians seems to me undeniable.

Now, I do not pretend to assert that Dixon's account of the racial history of Polynesia is correct in all of its details. Dixon was a student who specialized upon the Polynesian area and had a vast store of erudition concerning its history and cultures. However, as I have intimated, his particular method of skull analysis involved the postulate that various divisions of the length-breadth and length-height indices of the skull and of the nasal index occur exclusively in certain specific racial types. He made little or no allowance for individual variation and sex dif-ference. Every shift in one of these three component indices (each divided into three arbitrary categories) necessitated the assumption of the presence of a different race. Dixon used to refer jocularly to his *Racial History of Man* as "my crime." Actually, it was not even a misdemeanor, but rather a brilliant analysis of all available cranial material in the world in which certain theoretical and dubious postulates were followed out to their logical conclusion. This much-criticized work is one of the most stimulating forays into the field of physical anthropology ever made by an ethnologist or ethnographer. If we dismiss as incapable of present verification the detail of Dixon's scheme as applied to Polynesia, it is nevertheless fairly certain that its main outlines are correct. A basic Negroidal element has been swamped by a strong infusion of White blood, to which has been added a dash of the Mongoloid. The absence of very coarse straight hair, fully developed Mongoloid cheekbones, and Mongoloid eye folds suggests that the Mongoloid strains are of minor strength, since these are usually dominant characters. Again, since Negroid hair is dominant over the straight fine or wavy fine White hair forms, it is certain that the absence of frizzly and very curly hair in Polynesia indicates that Negroid strains must have been far weaker in the population than those of the Whites. Since round-headedness seems to dominate or to persist at the expense of the long-headed variation, it seems probable that the Polynesian areas in which long-headedness still survives were colonized first by long-heads and received very little infusion of later brachycephals. Conversely, the absence of contemporary dolichocephals in such groups as the Hawaiian Islands does not prove that they never existed there, since, in any event, they would have been submerged by the round-heads. Archaeological sequences of skull types alone can furnish the solution of these problems.

COMPOSITE RACES WITH MONGOLOID OVERLAY

The Indonesian-Malay Race

Indo-China, Japan, and the Malay Archipelago are peopled, in large part, by a composite, or secondary, race which has been formed by the Mongolization of one or more submerged earlier racial elements. Throughout the most of this area there are evidences of the presence of dark-skinned, curly- or frizzly-haired peoples with long heads. Occasionally there survive, as in the

Malay Peninsula and the Andaman Islands, isolated enclaves of Negritos who are brachycephalic. Probably there are also submerged Australoid strains present in minor proportions. However, all of these primitive strata have been overlaid first with a thick stratum of long-headed, brunet, White stock, and then thoroughly swamped with Mongoloid populations stemming from the mainland of Asia. The generalized Indonesian-Malay racial type may be described as follows: Stature is nearly always short or below medium, while the body build tends to be lateral, or squat. The shoulders and chest are broad, the trunk relatively long, the limbs short and sturdy. Skin color is yellow-brown, eyes dark brown, and hair blue-black. Head hair is nearly as straight and coarse as in the full Mongoloid types, but varies toward waviness and curl among groups or individuals in whom the submerged racial strata are strongly represented. There is very little hair upon the face and the body. The head form is nearly always brachycephalic, the face very broad and short with flaring hinder angles of the jaws. Foreheads are wide and sloping, with small to medium development of the brow ridges. The cheekbones reach a Mongoloid stage of anterior and lateral jut; there is usually some degree of development of the internal or Mongoloid eye fold, but it rarely sweeps across the whole upper lid from the outer to the inner corner as in the full Mongoloid type, exemplified in northeastern Siberia by such peoples as the Goldi, the Giliak, and the Buriats. The nose is very short, broad, and flat, with a root which is commonly saddle-shaped, a tip which is turned up but not unduly thick, nostrils directed forward and with somewhat flaring wings. This Indonesian-Malay type is likely to show a fair amount of prognathism and lips which are much thicker and more strongly outrolled than are characteristic of a pure Mongoloid type. These rather thick membranous lips are edged by a definitely raised line or lip seam.

In certain areas, such as parts of the interior of Borneo, it appears that the Mongoloid overlay of the population is very thin or even lacking. Here one encounters long-headed, brown-skinned individuals with wavy hair and slender body build. These seem to represent an earlier population of an apparently brunet White stock identical with, or akin to, the fundamental Mediterranean race. Below that and occasionally apparent in individuals and groups are the definitely Negroid and pre-Dravidian or Australoid elements. Dixon and Griffith Taylor have traced incontrovertibly the succession of racial types in these areas and have found the darker-skinned, long-headed, and curly-haired peoples invariably to be marginal in distribution, or to inhabit refuge areas. The influx of Mongoloid brachy-cephals from the mainland of Asia was certainly late. These Mongoloid invaders, coming in great numbers and bringing more advanced cultures, have mixed with the earlier races and imposed upon the blend their dominant features—brachycephaly, Mongoloid cheekbones, and hair form. Their squat body builds also seem to survive at the expense of the more slender and linear types usually represented in earlier stocks, with the exception of the Negritos. However, in prognathism, lip thickness and eversion, in the form of the nose, and in the occasional cropping out of curved head hair, we must recognize the influence of the more primitive stocks.

The American Indian

The racial unity of the American Indian has long been an article of faith among the majority of American anthropologists under the influence of Boas and Hrdlička. Neither of these veteran and eminent anthropologists is willing to attribute a dominating role to heredity in the formation of physical types. Professor Boas has been for upwards of half a century the most thoroughgoing protagonist of theories of environmental adaptation in the formation of bodily characteristics, and has been responsible for some very fruitful researches upon bodily changes which have taken place in the children of immigrants to the United States. Certainly his work indicating the lack of fixity or permanence of certain allegedly racial features is of great value. I think, however, that Professor Boas' attitude toward racial questions has been formed in part as a result of his honest abhorrence of racial discrimination and prejudice. He has reacted so violently against the injustice and nonsense of theories of racial inferiority or superiority that he has bent the larger part of his very remarkable scientific talent to the refutation of theories of racial difference and to the attempt to demonstrate that race is really very little more than environmental variation plus imagination and psychological "conditioning." In my opinion he has gone too far and has allowed his scientific judgment to be influenced by his emotional bias.

It is rather more difficult to interpret the views and attitude of Dr. Aleš Hrdlička. This great physical anthropologist has perhaps done more solid and worth-while scientific work upon the American Indian than any other two or three persons combined. On that subject he has several firm convictions which approach the status of obsessions. The first of these is that America was peopled from Asia in comparatively recent times— certainly some millennia after the final retreat of the last ice sheet. The second is that all of the American aborigines were fundamentally Mongoloid in racial origin and that a stratigraphic sequence of various skull types and the present distribution of brachycephaly and dolichocephaly are of no particular racial significance. On the whole, Dr. Hrdlička's attitude toward the question of race is not dissimilar to that of Professor Boas, although Hrdlička does not crusade against race. Rather he occupies himself with the physical anthropological description of various groups of Indians or of other peoples without bothering to come to grips with the troublesome question of race.

It is somewhat difficult to give a generalized description of the physical characteristics of the American Indian race, if it is a unified race, because among Indians these features are nearly all subject to wide variation not only in individuals but also in large groups. Body build, for example, ranges from very short, squat types to those which are comparatively tall and slender. Head form runs the gamut from the most globular to the most elongate and narrow. Almost any kind of a nose may and does occur, from the most infantile concave types with upturned tips to the most nobly beaked and convex. However, this reservation should be made: exaggeratedly broad noses with thick bulbous tips and coarse flaring alae are practically nonexistent in the American Indian. The more or less homogeneous racial features which characterize the American Indians are as follows: straight, coarse, black hair and dark eyes, sparse development of body hair, yellow-brown skin color, Mongoloid lateral and anterior prominence of the cheekbones. Some qualification has to be made concerning even these few generally distributed Indian features. In the first place, there is a good deal more wavy hair among the American Indians than is commonly credited to them, and not infrequently the hair can be described with accuracy as very dark brown rather than black. Again, the skin tones range from an almost yellow shade through indubitably reddish or coppery brown tones to something which is not far from a brunet and rather sallow white.

Perhaps the best way to demonstrate the variability of the American Indian in physical characteristics is to describe a few of the most strongly contrasting of contemporary types, and then to proceed with an account of the sequences of cranial types found in archaeological deposits of prehistoric and historic age. First let us sketch the physical features of the ideal, or conventionalized North American Indian as represented upon the Buffalo Nickel. He has, naturally, the coarse, lank black hair, the leathery, yellow-brown skin, and the great malars, or cheekbones, of the Mongoloid. But instead of an infantile upturned Mongoloid nose, he possesses a sharply cut convex beak, high in the bridge, depressed and somewhat fleshy in the tip, but in no wise coarse. His lips are not full, and his mouth is set in a wide thin line. His chin is very strongly developed, his forehead sloping and marked by heavy brow ridges. The skin of the face from middle age onwards tends to wrinkle deeply, and the bold modeling of the underlying bony structures stands out in high relief. This countenance is really markedly different from the babyish flat moonface of the full Mongoloid type. The eye too is, on the whole, wide open, and is not likely to have a Mongoloid fold across the inner corner. This sort of Indian can be either round-headed or long-headed and may occur almost anywhere in North America. Perhaps he is most typical of the plains tribes—especially the Sioux.

In marked contrast with the Buffalo Nickel Indian is a little-known type which exists in the remote forests of Yucatan and probably elsewhere in Middle and South America. This type has been described among the Maya-speaking Lacandones by my colleague, Alfred M. Tozzer. Stature is short and body build medium to stocky. The skin color is golden brown—somewhat lighter than that of most of the inhabitants of the Yucatan peninsula. The long black head hair is wavy and not infrequently curly. In the children it is often bleached by the sun to a reddish hue. The beard of the adult male is considerable, especially on the chin, where it is allowed to grow as a tuft. Presumably the body hair is not so sparse as in ordinary Maya Indians. The head is very brachycephalic (average length-breadth index 86.5). The face is broad with well-developed cheekbones, which do not show, however, the extreme Mongoloid projection. The nose may be straight, convex, or concave, but tends to be somewhat bulbous at the tip and to have considerably more flaring wings than are ordinarily found in Whites. The jaws project somewhat, and the lips are on the thick side—especially the lower lip. The chin is rather retreating. The features which impress one as un-Indian, or non-Mongoloid, are notably the hair form and distribution and the coarse modeling of the face. We know so little about the physical anthropology of the forest tribes of South America that it is impossible to trace the distribution of these rather primitive, non-Mongoloid types. However, it is apparent from occasional photographs that wavy black hair, blunt wide noses, thick lips, and heavy eyebrow ridges are often combined in somewhat brutal types of countenances which recall the pre-Dravidian, slightly Australoid features of some of the southern tribes of India.

Possibly the most fully developed Mongoloid types among the American aborigines occur in the Eskimo. Here, apparently, hair is straightest, skin most yellow, and eyes most frequently Mongoloid in the shape of their palpebral openings and in the folds of the upper lids. The cheekbones reach the maximum flare and the most marked anterior jut; the face is long with very prominent jaw angles. The fatty padding of the cheekbones is pronounced and the brow ridges are poorly developed. The root and bridge of the nose are very low. Yet the nose is very narrow, as is also the head. There is almost no development of beard, and hair on the short, squat bodies is very sparse. The face in the Eskimo is not, however, so flat as that of the extremely developed Mongoloid types found in northeastern Asia.

The varieties of physical types of American Indians suggest that the earlier inhabitants of the continent were not really Mongoloid, but showed blends of features more or less resembling attenuated Negroid or Negritoid and Australoid variations. So far as I am aware, there are no natives of the American continent who can be described accurately as predominantly Negroid or Australoid, apart from the imported African Negroes and the hybrids which have arisen from their recent mixtures with other races. Nevertheless, non-Mongoloid types crop out here and there, and the evidence of cranial material from archaeological deposits is fairly unequivocal. In most areas where archaeological excavations have been carried out long-headed, or dolichocephalic, types underlie the later-coming brachycephals. Some of these earlier long-heads have heavy brow ridges and rather short faces with broad nasal apertures and low nasal bridges. In some, protrusion of the tooth-bearing parts of the jaws is associated with rather Negroid conformation of the nose and poorly developed chins. The cheekbones in these types are quite variable in development, but usually bigger and more prominent than are to be observed in modern White races. Whatever the lowest stratum of the American aboriginal population may have been, it was certainly non-Mongoloid, and probably dark-skinned with wavy to curly hair. There is also some indirect evidence that an early White stock reached the New World long before the coming of Columbus. Long-heads with sloping foreheads, large brow ridges, robust cheekbones, great curving beaks of noses, and heavy prominent chins are especially strong among the remains of the eastern Woodlands Indians of the United States. Portraits of these eastern Indians, now mostly extinct, depict them with ruddy skins, long, oval faces, and not infrequently with wavy hair. They do not look particularly Mongoloid. They recall in some respects the Iranian Plateau race, but I have never seen them represented with the heavy beards which characterize that Near Eastern race. The brachycephalic types which overlie the long-heads in the archaeological deposits of many regions of North America usually carry the Mongoloid cheekbones, but normally in association with the prominent, convex nasal bones and the heavy, outthrust lower jaws which occur in the modern Plains Indians. The infantile nose and the flat, fatty face of the fully developed Mongoloid is usually conspicuous by its absence.

I am inclined to believe that the earliest migrants to the New World were small, long-headed persons with heavy brow ridges, prognathous faces, broad noses, dark skins, and wavy or curly hair. They would represent such a racial combination as occurs when a primitive brunet Mediterranean White has taken on some Australoid and Negroid or Negritoid features—much like the Todas of Nilgiri Hills in southern India. Perhaps the next waves brought big-nosed dolichocephals of the Iranian Plateau race, but already slightly Mongolized, straighter in head hair, and with more sparse body hair and incipient Mongolization of the cheekbones. There followed the later and more dominant round-heads, with possibly a full development of

Mongoloid specializations. In the ensuing mixtures of strains in the New World, Mongoloid skin color, Mongoloid hair form, and Mongoloid cheekbones were ordinarily dominant, but the beaky nose of the western Asiatic highlands nearly always survives at the expense of the low-bridged Mongolian blob. The most interesting feature of physical type distribution in the Americas is that the farther south one goes along the backbone of the continents and the farther east into the Plains and forest areas, away from the cordillera, the less Mongoloid in general are the characteristics of the Indians and the more likely they are to be long-headed. Such a distribution again confirms the Dixon-Taylor theory of migrations of successively less primitive racial types, presumably from the central Asiatic land mass, with the pushing out into marginal and refuge areas of the primitive pioneers and the submerging of these elements in the more desirable areas and those nearer to the centers of distribution and of higher evolution. Thus the peripheral zones tend to show the survivors of the earliest and physically the most primitive migrants, whereas they are represented archaeologically in the deeper layers of deposits in the more central area, and in contemporary populations by the partial survival of their physical characteristics in mixtures with the more highly evolved newcomers.

COMPOSITE WHITE RACES

The Armenoid Race

The term "Armenoid race," popularized by the German anthropologist, von Luschan, has been widely employed to designate an easily recognizable physical type which is at home in Anatolia and is represented by many immigrants in eastern Europe, central Europe, and elsewhere. There has also grown up the anthropological habit of referring to eastern and central European Jews who have hooked noses and round heads as "Armenoid Jews," on the assumption that they are, for the most part, descendants of persons belonging to the Armenoid race who had been converted to Judaism. The conventional description of the Armenoid race is as follows: body build is medium to broad, and stature medium or below medium; skin is olive colored or yellowish white, hair black or very dark brown; eyes dark brown to light brown. Head hair is slightly wavy, but often straight; body hair is abundant, and eyebrows and beards are especially thick. The eyebrows often meet over the root of the nose. The head is of a peculiar shape—very flat at the back and rising to a peak from a long sloping forehead; it is pronouncedly brachycephalic, by virtue of very abbreviated length and considerable width. The face has rather prominent cheekbones, but is, on the whole, of medium width and length. Brow ridges are moderately developed. The nose is remarkable for its convexity and the length and fleshiness of its drooping tip. This tip is frequently rather oblong in shape and dips below its attachment to the humped bony nasal bridge, thus creating an undulating profile. The lips are of moderate to full development, the chin usually of medium size and pointed, but considerably overshadowed by the projection of the nose. The jaw angles are sharp, but the hinder width of the jaw is not excessive. Studies of Armenians and Syrians by some of the younger Harvard anthropologists—Carl Seltzer, Walter Cline, and Byron Hughes—have recently proved that the so-called Armenoid race is really a rather unstable blend of several different racial elements which have interbred in the Near East. It is doubtful whether it deserves classification as a secondary, or composite, race; it is more in the nature of a subrace. Unpublished researches of Dr. Byron Hughes on some 1500 adult male Armenians residing in the United States and upon a considerable number of first-generation Americans of Armenian parentage have cleared up the Armenian racial problem quite conclusively. The type varies markedly in different regions of Armenia, apparently according to the varying proportions of the racial constituents which are in the blend. These are ordinary brunet long-headed Mediterraneans with dark skins and curly hair, round-headed brunet Alpines with square faces and blobby noses and thickset build; the brunet dolichocephalic Iranian Plateau race, recently isolated by Dr. Henry Field, with a final dash of blond, long-headed, horse-faced, fair-skinned and blue-eyed Nordics. The least important and least constant element in the blend is this Nordic strain. When present, it has the effect of elevating stature, modifying the dark eyes to mixed and often greenish tints, and possibly of elongating the face.

The Armenoid head form seems to be the result of the survival of Alpine brachycephaly, perhaps modified to some extent by artificial flattening of the back of the head due to their method of cradling infants. The baby is tightly swathed and laid upon its back so that the occiput rests upon a fairly soft cushion. Whether this practice actually deforms and flattens the back of the head is still a matter of argument. It probably has that effect, at any rate, upon malnourished or rickety individuals in whom the cranial bones are soft and lack resilience. This flattening is apparently diminished in the American-born children of Armenian parents. It is possible, of course, that the Armenoid sugar-loaf skull may have been derived by a disharmonic combination of the short head of the brachycephalic Alpine with the high and moderately wide heads found in the Iranian Plateau stock and in the rugged Atlanto-Mediterranean subrace which seems to be a variant of the smaller Mediterranean long-headed brunet race. The Armenoid nose, which comes in a good many forms, seems to have been inherited mainly from that of the Iranian Plateau race, but the tip has been thickened and the alae spread by the influence of the Alpine strain, which has a short, fleshy nose. The heavy beard and body hair are present in both the Alpine and Iranian Plateau races, and it is expected that they should survive in the blend.

The Dinaric Race

Another subrace which has been frequently discussed is that which Deniker has called the Dinaric race. Its center of distribution is in Jugoslavia, but it has ramifications into Switzerland, the Austrian Tyrol, and neighboring regions. This race is remarkable for very tall stature, brachycephaly, long convex noses, and deep faces with heavy chins. Pigmentation is usually brunet—white as to skin color, and brown or black as to hair color—but there is considerable variation toward mixed and light eyes and medium to light hair tints. In the Dinaric the head is very high and relatively short, but perhaps it is not so strongly peaked as in the Armenoid. The face is much longer and more massive, the nose rather more finely cut and perhaps thinner in the tip; the chin is heavier and projects farther forward. Body and beard hair in these Dinarics are ordinarily heavily developed. The dominant strains in this mixed type are Iranian Plateau, Alpine, and Nordic; but the Nordic seems much more heavily represented than it is in the Armenoid subrace. The great stature, facial elongation, and comparatively light pigmentation often observed in skin, hair, and eyes, seem to be due to a strong Nordic component, or perhaps to hybrid vigor. The extreme brachycephaly is presumably derived from the Alpine strain, although it is rather puzzling to find the cephalic index in this type even higher than in the Alpine race itself. Combinations quite indistinguishable from this Dinaric race are found as group or individual variations wherever these same White strains occur in mixtures.

East Baltic Race

In Finland, Poland, and the Baltic states there dwells a well-differentiated and stabilized physical type which is usually called the "East Baltic Race." The most outstanding feature of this type is its feeble pigmentation of skin, hair, and eyes. The hair is tow-color, or almost white, more rarely a pale yellow; the eyes gray or light blue; the skin tawny white or rosy white, but more usually the former. The head hair is straight, and the body hair usually somewhat sparse. Stature is medium to tall, and the body build is ordinarily thickset. The head is very brachycephalic and somewhat flat at the back, whence the nickname "square-heads." Foreheads are high and rather vertical, always of considerable breadth. Brow ridges are not large. The face seems very square because the cheekbones are prominent and the jaw angles flaring. The chin is usually well developed. The nose tends to be rather broad and low; often it has a concave profile and the tip is short, so that the nostrils are roundish and directed forward. A long upper lip and some alveolar prognathism, thin membranous lips, and a flattish face frequently characterize this type.

Anthropologists are considerably perplexed about the origin of the East Baltic race. A common opinion attributes it to a cross of the blond, long-headed Nordic race with the brunet, round-headed Alpine race. The assumption is that the blondness comes from the Nordics and the brachycephaly and blocky body build from the Alpines. I am afraid this theory has been influenced by the presupposition that blondness is exclusively the property of the Nordic race, and when found elsewhere must be the result of intermixture with that race. The difficulty is that the East Baltics are actually blonder than the original Nordics, whereas blondness in inheritance seems recessive and ought to survive in East Baltic crosses, as elsewhere, only in an attenuated, mixed pigmental form. Of course, it may be argued that the Baltic environment tends to select blondness for survival, so that once it crops out as a mutation the sunless climate tends to preserve it and to cause rapid increase of persons exhibiting this condition. However, if this argument is advanced, it is hard to refute the contention that Baltic blondness could have originated in any stock domiciled for a considerable portion in that habitat, whether it happened to be long-headed or round-headed. Although there is actually plenty of evidence of the admixture of the blond, long-headed Nordic Swedes with the round-heads of Finland, it seems highly improbable that all of the East Baltic brachycephals could have derived their blondness from this source.

The suggestion that Lapp blood is heavily represented in the Finns and Scandinavians is usually violently repudiated by the anthropologists of those nations. The Lapps are a people who have remained at a somewhat primitive stage of culture, partially, no doubt, because of the limited natural resources of their far northern habitat. They speak an Asiatic language belonging to the Ural-Altaic family. However, Finnish is also a non-Indo-European or non-Aryan language which stems from the same great linguistic family. The Lapps are very short and brachycephalic, with straight dark hair, dark eyes, and yellowish skins. Cheekbones have an almost Mongoloid prominence; eyes are often slitlike and oblique; and the nose is concave and low in the bridge. However, the Lapps by no means represent a fully developed Mongoloid type. One can say that they are either proto-Mongoloid or mixed Mongoloid; but, on the whole, Mongoloid features are usually attenuated and frequently absent. If it were not for the blondness of the Finns, they could be explained by the hypothesis of a mixture between the brachycephalic Lapps and the brachycephalic Alpines, resulting in longer faces, increased stature, and the adulteration of the Mongoloid featural tendencies which the Lapps present. However, the fact remains that they are indubitably blond—in fact, blond almost to the verge of albinism. If we add a Nordic element to the cross, we still have a good deal more of blondness and considerably less of other Nordic traits than might be expected to survive—such as the thin, high-bridged nose, and possibly the tall, slender body build. I do not feel at all certain of the answer to this problem, but I am sure that all three of these racial elements have gone into the production of the East Baltic type and that the Alpine and Lapp strains are probably considerably stronger than the Nordic. An ordinary Nordic-Alpine cross, such as is common enough in western and central Europe, does not produce a type which is identical with the East Baltic. It is likely to result in mixed or near-blond pigmentation and a round head, but in pseudo-Mongoloid cheekbones and nose. My own suggestion is that East Baltic blondness is due to physiological disturbance set up primarily by mixture between Alpines and Lapps, and selected for multiplication and survival by the Baltic climate. Of course such blondness has been reinforced by some infusion of Nordic blood, but the origin of Nordic blondness is, in itself, somewhat of a mystery. It is certain that the Nordic is a derivative from a dolichocephalic brunet type, which stems back to Upper Paleolithic times and is fundamentally a variant of the basic European long-heads.

The Keltic Subrace

In Scotland, Ireland, and to a lesser extent in England, Wales, and Cornwall, there occurs a very tall, long-headed type with a long, compressed face, high, narrow nose, deep jaws, and a curiously disharmonic pigment combination. The hair is usually very dark brown, sometimes black, and wavy or even curly. Beard and body hair are moderately developed. The skin color is light and occasionally very florid; the eyes are usually deep blue. Very frequently in this type the hair is red and the eyes are greenish. It is easy enough to get at the derivation of these Keltic types, because the parent strains are abundantly present in the same area. They are, on the one hand, the conventional Nordic type—dolichocephalic, blond as to hair and blue or gray as to eye color—on the other, an even taller, longer-headed, brunet stock with curly or wavy hair, the Atlanto-Mediterranean subrace. Into this mixture also go some of the smaller brunet, long-headed strains as exemplified in the Cockney Englishman and in the Classic Mediterranean types of Spain, Italy, and North Africa. Why the pigmentation linkage should have broken down in the British Isles so that the blue eyes are combined with dark hair is difficult to explain. A similar combination occurs in Brittany, where, however, the head form and body build seem to have been derived from an Alpine strain. In this case body build is blocky and heads are round.

I am accustomed to designate these tall dolichocephalic brunets with blue eyes, and the corresponding redheads, as Keltics, because these types are most characteristically found in the areas where Keltic languages still survive—especially Irish and Scotch or Gaelic, the older Keltic dialects. Red hair seems to be the result of the crossing of a feebly pigmented blond stock, with hair containing only melanotic pigment and a little red-gold pigment, and of a black-haired or dark brown-haired stock in which the melanotic pigment masks the presence of red-gold pigment in considerable quantity. Then, occasionally, as a result of some process of Mendelian segregation, the red-gold pigment appears in individuals in a double dose, with the ordinarily black or melanotic pigment either absent or but feebly represented.

THE PSYCHOLOGICAL AND CULTURAL IMPLICATIONS OF RACE

The groups which we call races are distinguished by morphological and metric variations presumed to be due to heredity. It is a reasonable supposition that anatomical racial variations are correlated with physiological variations, also due in part to heredity. Pigmentation, hair form, and most of the other morphological features used for racial discrimination are really nothing more than anatomical expressions of physiological differences. The mechanism which controls growth and sex differentiation is the endocrine system, commonly known as the ductless glands. The functioning of this little-known endocrine system is presumably influenced in part by one's individual, familial, and racial heredity, in part by environment (nutrition, light, air, et cetera). Little is known of the racial variations of the ductless glands, but we do know that malfunctioning of the pituitary, the thyroid, and perhaps others of the endocrine system, brings physical modifications in the affected individual which distort the anatomical and metric features usually supposed to be controlled by race. Thus, one imperfectly understood type of endocrine pathology produces round-headed individuals with concave noses, internal eye folds, and other pseudo-Mongoloid characteristics. Such phenomena have led Sir Arthur Keith and others to conclude that differences in endocrine balance must in the long run be responsible for racial variations. However, as yet very little is known of these matters. Yet I suppose that no endocrinologist or student of human physiology would doubt that racial physiological differences are probably more numerous and important than racial anatomical variations. The few attempts which have been made to investigate racial physiological differences have usually been frustrated in part by the fact that different races are likely to exist under different environmental conditions. Thus, when differences are established in some physiological function, there is still doubt whether they are hereditary and racial, or merely environmental. The fact that Maya Indians have basal metabolisms distinctly above the standard predicted for northern Whites may be due to one or more of several factors: occupation, diet, climate, or race. We suspect that environment determines or selects certain physiological variations which manifest themselves in anatomical racial characteristics and become fixed in inheritance. At any rate, no one questions the association of physiological and anatomical variation and their interdependence.

I doubt that psychologists with a sound background of physiological training would deny the possibility of some generalized differences of temperament and mentality in hereditarily and anatomically distinguishable groups of mankind, but the mention of such a possibility flicks on the raw the practitioners of "Social Science." They like to believe that all psychological variations are conditioned by differences in human cultures, because they know nothing about the human organism but a great deal about its cultural manifestations. Psychology has not yet

advanced to a point where it can measure and appraise accurately the temperament and the mentality of different individuals living under similar environmental and cultural conditions and apparently of the same race. Such tests of individual
mentality and ability as exist depend, for the most part, upon
the subject's facility in the manipulation of his environment and
extent of his participation in the group culture. The tests are
fitted to single specific cultural environments and cannot be
transferred from one to another. Since different races usually
have distinct cultural environments, it is almost impossible to
pursue studies of racial psychological differences which have
any scientific validity. This difficulty obtains even in the case of
psychological comparisons of Negroes and Whites in the United
States. Thus, we really know nothing at all about racial psychological differences and cannot assert that they exist and
back up our statement with any solid body of evidence. We are
justified in postulating their reality on *a priori* grounds, but at
the same time it is hardly conceivable that they can be of any
great importance in comparison with individual psychological
differences which may be observed within any one race.

All reputable anthropologists condemn the malignant nonsense about racial psychology which is preached and published
by those who try to justify the oppression of ethnic minorities.
Political theories about race are nothing more than instruments
of propaganda, devised for the child minds of totalitarian
populations. Unfortunately this pseudo-scientific stuff appeals
to morons everywhere. For this reason anthropologists and
others who oppose racial injustice have tended to go beyond the
legitimate statement that racial psychological differences have
not been demonstrated and have alleged that they do not in fact
exist. I doubt that the exigencies of democratic principles and
of humanitarian conduct justify such statements. In the absence
of valid scientific knowledge we must neither deny nor assert.
We can only say that German "racial psychology" is tripe.

The task of the physical anthropologist is to devise means of classifying man into physical racial groups. If he succeeds in this, he may then turn his groups over to the psychologist. The latter must have a sound physical basis of racial classification before he can get on with his job of studying racial psychology. If you cannot tell a rat from a mouse, you would better refrain from embarking upon an investigation of their psychological differences.

I have found it perfectly feasible to divide large samples of populations into physical groups and then to study their differences in certain crude sociological categories. This process has been carried out in the case of criminals of several racial and parentage groups in the United States and in other noncriminal material collected here and in Ireland. The method used is simple enough. Various racial groups are sorted out on the basis of individual combinations of head form, hair color, eye color, et cetera. I merely use the stock combinations recognized by anthropologists as characteristic of the various White races. Of course, my critics object that the physical groups thus selected are not "races"; but, since I can show that each group is physically homogeneous and differs from every other group, I am quite indifferent about nomenclature. You may call them "races," "breeds," or "types." If you do not like my findings, you may take the easy way out, which is to call me names. The data are impregnable.

Even if it is contended that these selected groups are merely assortments of individuals who fortuitously possess identical arbitrary combinations of physical characters, the sociological differences between them are incontestable. They diverge from each other markedly in occupation, education, marital status, and in nature of criminal offense (if any). The differences are not entirely due to nationality and ethnic tradition, because none of the physical groups is homogeneous in this respect.

These behavioral differences between physically divergent groups suggest that the latter are also psychologically diverse. Of course, all of the sociological variations are complicated by questions of the influence of urban or rural habitat, climate, nutrition, and so on. They do not indicate that race is the paramount cause of behavioral difference, but merely that race is not an entirely negligible factor. When we consider the vast range of individual variation in physique, psychology, and behavior within a single race, it is remarkable that we should find any sociological difference at all between racial groups. If the physical groupings possess neither biological nor statistical validity, the social differentiations found are nothing short of miracles. This is the view taken by my sociological friends, who do not believe in miracles unless they are performed by sociologists. I do not believe in sociological miracles, even when they are promised under the New Deal.

V

THE MAKING AND MIXING OF HUMAN RACES:

3. THE RESULTS OF RADICAL RACE MIXTURES BETWEEN PRIMARY RACES

THE ENTIRE subject of race has been so obscured by low-lying clouds of ignorance, prejudice, and superstition that few serious students have attempted to penetrate its miasmic confines. This is a generally insalubrious field for the timid and the cautious investigator, but the gases are thickest and most poisonous in the depressed areas which are the sites of hybridization. Up to the last decade of the previous century practically nothing had been written on the subject of race mixture which could not be dismissed as *a priori* speculations of scientists, idle and unreliable tales of travelers and of other old wives, or sheer balderdash. When in 1916 I decided to offer some lectures in Harvard College on applied physical anthropology, I was forced to combine Criminal Anthropology and Race Mixture into a single half-year course, not because race mixture is a phenomenon of criminal anthropology or *vice versa,* but because there was not enough halfway reliable knowledge of either subject to justify more than a dozen or fifteen lectures. Now, however, there is such a large mass of comparatively valid data that these two subjects have long been divorced in the Harvard curriculum, and it is hard enough to summarize either one in a concentrated half-year's lecture course.

I must expend a little time in dealing with the ancient errors in regard to race mixture, since most of them are still alive and kicking. Many of these hoary lies and venerable superstitions have achieved a specious appearance of validity through centuries of repetition. They are like centenarians who receive publicity and homage merely because they have so incredibly survived their usefulness and their legitimate span of life.

The system of zoological classification devised by Linnaeus divided animals into large groups and smaller groups on the basis of extent of physical resemblance. Thus animals were in one kingdom, plants in another; within the animal kingdom were the subkingdoms of invertebrates and vertebrates, and within the vertebrates five classes—fish, amphibians, reptiles, birds, and mammals. The mutual resemblances of animals within any category indicated community of descent, and the finer the classification, the more closely related to each other were its included members. The conceptual scheme is logically valid; but it is in fact nothing more than a pigeonholing of animals so that like are crammed into the same cubbyhole, and the less unlike are stuffed into adjacent compartments. The higher vertebrates which we call mammals are divided into subclasses (monotremes, marsupials, and placentals); the subclasses into orders, the orders into genera, the genera into species, and the species into varieties. Now, man by structure belongs to the class of mammals and to the order of primates, which latter includes also the apes, monkeys, lemurs, and tarsiers. Within the order of primates, man is generally given a family to himself—the Hominidae—although some democratic classificationists wish to put him in the family of the great anthropoid apes. Assuming that all varieties of man—extant and extinct—belong to one family, it is fairly certain that the differences which distinguish such fossil forms as *Sinanthropus* or *Pithecanthropus erectus* from all modern types ought to be reckoned as generic differences. If this is the case, all of the existing races of man may then be lumped into one genus—the well-known *Genus homo*. Another view maintains that the present-day races all belong to a smaller zoological category—the species *Homo sapiens*—consisting of several varieties which are synonymous with races.

The difficulty with all of this classificatory business is that it assumes that the names given to the various categories correspond to some sort of eternal biological verities—definite and immutable. As a matter of fact, the various divisions and subdivisions of zoological classification are largely arbitrary. It is a rather shocking fact that zoologists have never really agreed upon the number and nature of the criteria which determine the grades of their classifications, so that each one uses his own judgment and the hoary traditions of taxonomy without really stopping to examine the validity and logical consistency of either. Thus a part of the taxonomic lore is that a species is an inbreeding group which does not normally cross with members of other species. If such crosses occur they are supposed to be relatively, if not absolutely, sterile. Of course this idea is purely theoretical. It does not rest upon any substantial knowledge of the breeding habits of animals in a state of nature. Zuckerman has reported 9 cases of intergeneric crosses among the primates which are lodged in the London zoo, 9 cases of interspecific crosses in monkeys, and 8 in lemurs. Thus the bland assumption that species as established by the Linnaean classification are inbreeding groups is a fiction.

Zoologists establish species and subspecies in wild animals on the basis of variations in coat color and many other anatomical trivialities. A similar application of the principles of taxonomy to the classification of human groups would doubtless necessitate the recognition of several different species of modern man. Yet all existing types of modern man interbreed.

Back in the days when human hybridization was purely a matter of speculation and prejudice, a good deal of emphasis was laid upon the specific diversity of man. Particularly it was widely held that the Negro is a different species from the White.

A sociological extension of this Linnaean concept enabled the White man to regard the Negro as an inferior species of animal which could be domesticated for the use of the superior White, like the horse, the ox, and the fowl. As a corollary of this convenient idea of specific distinction there arose the notion that crosses between Negroes and Whites or between Whites and Mongoloids were contrary to nature. No one with his eyes open could assert that sterility resulted from such crosses, but relative infertility and general biological inferiority of the hydrids were generally claimed. The familiar case of the mule—a hybrid between the ass and the horse—was brought forward by way of analogy. Mules are usually sterile and frequently perverse in behavior, although notoriously tough and strong. Hence the term "mulatto." As a result of social prejudice and pseudo-scientific lore of this kind, the public, and even persons who considered themselves scientists, came to believe that race mixture between radically divergent races—primary races— resulted in diminution of fertility in the offspring, decreased vitality, and general biological inferiority.

These beliefs were backed up by observations of travelers upon crosses between Whites and natives of different races in various out-of-the-way places. The general consensus of such casual judgments was that the half-breed receives all of the inferior qualities of both parent stocks and is heir to none of their virtues or abilities. Of course, very few made allowances for the fact that mixture between dominant and subjugated races takes place under a social ban and commonly between the inferiors of both races so that the results of such matings can hardly be expected to march upon the heights of humanity.

Experimentation with animals and plants now enables the geneticist to describe and explain the effects of inbreeding and outbreeding upon living organisms. The qualities and physical characteristics which are developed in the individual result from the combinations of the genes or inheritance units of the parental germ plasms which are present in the fertilized human egg.

There are 48 human chromosomes, each of which includes a vast number of genes, apparently strung like beads on a wire. Half of these chromosomes, or 24, come from each parent, and each one pairs with a corresponding mate. Out of these pairings come the combinations of the parental genes which are found in each chromosome. In the genes the factors for the development of certain bodily variations are either dominant or recessive. A dominant gene from one parent may be paired with a recessive gene (which would develop a different variation) from the other parent. In this case the variation which springs from the dominant gene expresses itself in the individual, while the recessive gene is carried in suppression—it does not show. If both of the genes from the respective parents are the same, the double dose of dominants or of recessives causes the individual to develop the one or other featural variation as the case may be. He is genetically pure, or homozygous, for that character. In chance pairings, where only two contrasted genes are represented in the development of a character, the combinations in the offspring occur in the ratio of one double dominant and one double recessive, to two mixed or impure dominants. As the impure, or heterozygous, dominants show the dominant character, the actual appearance in the offspring is that of three dominants to one recessive. However, in the formation of most physical characteristics many inheritance units are concerned—not a single pair. The resulting combinations can still be calculated, but it comes to be a very elaborate process. When many pairs of factors or genes are involved in the production of a single physical feature, the apparent result of this complicated process of Mendelian dominance and segregation is blending. Thus, the nose of the mulatto (a person half-Negro and half-White) appears to be a mosaic of details, some derived from each parent stock, and it is exactly that. However, the composite or hybrid nose nevertheless receives its morphological minutiae, in all probability, from Mendelian inheritance involving multiple factors.

Since inheritance factors are so numerous and so minute and controlled experimentation in human genetics is impracticable, about all that we can do in studies of race mixture is to observe the variations which seem to persist in the hybrids and to guess that these are dominant characters. The process of Mendelian segregation and dominance occurs in every mating, whether it is racially mixed or supposedly pure. Scattered and rough observations suggest that more highly evolved characters tend to dominate over the more primitive ones and that the normal usually dominates over the abnormal, the healthy over the pathological. It is to be hoped that these cheerful genetic indications will be substantiated by future research.

Now, this is what happens when a single stock is inbred. In the original matings the various pairs of parents are probably heterozygous for many characters—that is, they show many dominant features, although their germ plasms carry for these traits suppressed recessive genes. When the offspring of these first matings are again interbred and the process is continued generation after generation, segregation and recombination take place so that the pure dominants and pure recessives are brought out into the open. The segregation of the pure recessives uncovers the underlying weaknesses in the stock, and the inferiors are revealed in all of their degradation. On the other hand, the dominants are gradually brought to a homozygous, or genetically pure, condition, so that their apparent strength does not mask any genetic frailties which are likely to crop out by recombination in the recessives of the next generation. Evidently much good may be accomplished by this process of inbreeding, but only if selection is practiced upon the segregated offspring. The unfit recessives must be eliminated. Probably such elimination actually does take place under stringent primitive conditions in human stocks, when only the strong survive. Certainly it is inoperative in societies which coddle the feeble-minded, foster the insane, and encourage the criminalistic. All of these are biological inferiors. There are, however, one or two "outs" about inbreeding. In the first place, since weaknesses seem, on the whole, to be more numerous in human stocks than points of strength, the number of inferiors resulting from inbreeding and segregation is rather appalling. In the second place, for some reason as yet unexplained, continued inbreeding in a numerically small group seems often to bring about considerable size diminution, some deterioration in bodily health, and a diminished fertility. Probably none of these undesirable effects is produced if the inbreeding group is sufficiently large to preclude too closely consanguinous marriages. On the whole, however, inbreeding cannot be recommended as a measure of race improvement unless, beginning with a vigorous and numerous stock, it is accompanied by extirpation of the inferior recessives. It is a matter of course that in inbred groups new characters arise only through variation or mutation. The original range of disabilities and abilities is not enlarged. The qualities of the original pure races are merely perpetuated and accentuated in the process of segregation.

In the case of outbreeding, on the contrary, the ranges of variations of the stocks involved are merged and doubtless extended. Recessive characters are covered up by dominants in the first-generation hybrids; there is a general glossing over of imperfections. At first blush things look better; a general improvement seems to have been effected. Of course, the weaknesses are still there, but the sepulchers have been whitened. If this process of outbreeding is extended with more and more new stocks thrown into the pool, the ultimate result is a multiplicity of types which consist of mosaics of the dominant features derived from the several contributing stocks, with a varying number of recessive traits cropping out in most of them, according to the chance doubling-up of this or that recessive factor which permits its appearance in the individual. Of course, the majority of the apparently dominant features will be heterozygous—that is, carrying the recessive factor concealed.

However, in man initial outbreeding is usually followed by

inbreeding of the resulting hybrids. Primary crossing may go on, but secondary inbreeding and backcrossing are more frequent. Thus, in the United States at the present time race mixture between Negroes and Whites probably consists principally of backcrosses of Negroids (a term preferable to mulatto) either with Whites or with those of predominantly Negro blood. There are, apparently, very few crosses of pure Whites with pure Negroes.

Inbreeding after primary crosses brings about segregation in the second generation and thereafter. Then, if interbreeding goes on in all directions among the hybrids, we may expect about one-quarter of recessive traits to manifest themselves and three-quarters of dominant traits, whenever these recessive and dominant traits are determined through the combinations of single pairs of genes. Of course, most human features are probably controlled by more than one pair of genes, so that the actual effect of interbreeding seems to be blending of characters in the hybrids. Again, owing to the multiplicity of characters and inheritance factors involved, no single person receives all of the dominants nor all of the recessives. As inbreeding proceeds, generation after generation, new types set up by combinations of dominant features become more and more widely spread, and recessive features crop out less and less often.

If we assume that the human abilities and disabilities which appertain to psychological endowment are similarly inherited according to Mendelian laws, and that the superior qualities are dominant, it is evident that the hybrid race will tend to be one in which mosaics of dominant physical features inherited from both parent stocks will be accompanied by the manifestation of the dominant mental and temperamental characteristics of both races as they combine in individuals. A certain proportion of luckless individuals will doubtless receive the double doses of recessive genes which bring out the less desirable qualities of both parental races. A very few of those particularly unfortunate will doubtless get a majority of these unfavorable variations and will be thoroughly undesirable. In the great bulk of the population, points of weakness will be balanced and glossed over by points of strength. In the end you come out with what you put in, except in so far as the recessives or undesirables are eliminated by natural selection or by some purposeful social selection. Otherwise the recessive factors are merely covered over and concealed by the dominants. However, it is, in fact, a little better than that. In the first place, the range of abilities of the hybrid stock is considerably enlarged; there is greater versatility. Again, there are produced in this fortuitous process of the combinations within enlarged ranges of hereditary features, a few who get the pick of the abilities of both races. If you believe that, on the whole, civilization progresses, not by the inching forward of the masses of the population, but rather under the leadership of supermen who advance by leaps and bounds, the production of the few persons of extraordinary ability made possible by race mixture enormously facilitates social and cultural progress. I subscribe to that belief, partially if not wholly, and I am willing to have the imbeciles if we can get the geniuses.

Nevertheless, the modern trends in human evolution—whether physical or social—suggest that this "great man" theory of progress does not work any too well unless the general level of the population—biological and psychological—is kept up. Even if there is a handful of men of genius in a population of morons, the supermen can do little with the inferiors because the latter are stupid and ineducable. They destroy the gifted individuals out of resentment of their superiority or inability to understand their principles and cultural products, and are dominated rather by predatory and crude opportunists who are not supermen at all, but only cunning brutes who know how to batten upon the unintelligence of the masses.

But to get back to outbreeding—it has one other advantage which is difficult to explain biologically, but has been observed frequently in the lower animals and sometimes in man. In the first generations of hybrids there may occur an increase in bodily size and an addition to bodily strength which is called heterosis, or hybrid vigor. With continued inbreeding of the hybrids this increment of size is gradually diminished in some cases, but in others it is rather persistent. This phenomenon is thought to be connected in some way with heterozygosity in the new combination of dominants from one stock with recessives from the other.

Taking it all in all, it is undeniable that a stock can be improved by inbreeding and selection which eliminates the inferior recessives. This process, however, may be accompanied by some diminution in size and fertility on the part of the dominants. Outbreeding, on the contrary, is likely to carry with it increase in size and vigor and certainly a wider range of physical and mental potentialities. It should be noted that hybrid vigor seems to include increased fertility, and often improved vitality and longevity. But outbreeding also produces its crops of persons in whom the inferior, recessive genes are doubled and come to outward expression. The variety of inferiors, as of average individuals and of superiors, is also increased. There is no way to beat the genetic game simply by breeding. You can breed for better types and get them, but there are also thrown off in the process runts and inferiors which must not be allowed to perpetuate their infirmities and deficiencies.

RECENT NEGRO-WHITE MIXTURES

Old World

Among the radical race mixtures, those which have attracted the most lay attention are the crosses between Whites and Negroes, especially when these involve the partially depigmented Whites whom we call blonds. Here we have the extremes of variation of skin color, hair color, eye color, facial projection, nose form, lip form, et cetera. In Africa race mixture between

Whites and Negroes is of such long standing that several sub-races have grown up from the infusion of minor amounts of White blood into the Negroes. Most of the contributing White stocks have been members of the brunet, long-headed Mediterranean race. In North America, and especially in our own country, a good deal of Nordic blond stock has combined with Negro blood.

In Africa, from glancing at the characteristics of predominantly Negro groups, such as the Nilotic Negroes and East African tribes (e.g. the Masai), we can discern the effect of adding a very little White blood to the Negro. If the Negro blood is still vastly in excess, there is little if any change in skin color. Indeed, skin color seems in some cases to get even darker, since White blood often adds a tanning potentiality. Nor is the woolly hair of the Negro much affected by small infusions of White blood. The most prominent effect is in body build. The legs tend to get very long indeed, while the trunk remains comparatively short and is relatively narrow. Stature increases enormously. By far the tallest peoples in the world are Africans with a minor proportion of White blood. Probably a little White blood does not greatly increase the amount of beard and body hair, which is sparse in the Negro.

In the head the effect of the White cross seems to manifest itself by a straightening out of the facial profile. Jaw protrusion decreases. Often the head gets somewhat wider; the dolichocephaly of the original Negro is modified toward mesocephaly or even brachycephaly. It seems probable that the height of the nose is slightly increased and the lips are a little thinned. Almost certainly the face elongates, and the chin becomes heavier and projects further forward. However, we are referring here to the generalized picture which is presented by a few Whites mixing with a great many Negroes. And, for the most part, in Africa the crosses are of such long standing that the results can only be inferred. It is not possible to trace them genetically by generations and by proportions of blood.

¾ Australian ¼ White F3

Hottentot - Boer

½ English ½ Polynesian

½ Chinese ½ Polynesian

½ Negro ¼ Indian ¼ White

¼ Negro ¾ White

E.A.H.

The best body of family data pertaining to crosses of Negroes and Whites in the United States is that collected by Caroline Bond Day, a graduate of Radcliffe College, and analyzed and published by her under my direction.* Mrs. Day is an approximate mulatto, and has been able to secure unique genealogical data and photographs on more than 350 mixed-blood families. All of these families were visited and studied by Mrs. Day, personally, in various towns and cities. In each case she secured sociological and genealogical data, often photographs of families covering two to six generations, usually hair samples of the individuals studied, and sometimes anthropometric measurements and observations. The most of this data is stored in a a locked file in the Peabody Museum at Harvard University. About 50 families were published with the consent of the members involved. The series is not as valuable anthropometrically as it is from the morphological and genealogical viewpoint. Many of the living members of the families studied were inaccessible, or unwilling to be measured. The fractions of blood represented in the measured series of persons are so numerous that they make small and insufficient samples when divided up into age and sex groups.

Mrs. Day took the most elaborate pains to determine as far as possible the exact amounts of White and Negro blood involved in the crosses, but the absolute proportions are always a matter of some doubt, largely because it is necessary to take the word of informants as to whether this or that ancestor was, according to family tradition, a full Negro. Unfortunately no one can be 100 per cent certain that a person with any particular set of Negroid features has no drop of White blood, even when that person is present in the flesh. It is hardly possible to ascertain the precise racial composition of one's defunct progenitors.

I am going to describe in nontechnical terms the physical re-

* Day, Caroline Bond, *Harvard African Studies*, Vol. X, 1932. *Varia Africana* V.

sults of Negro-White crosses, as determined by Mrs. Day. First I shall indicate the apparent inheritance of separate morphological features and then the usual combinations into types according to blood fractions.

Woolly Negro hair, when crossed with wavy or straight White hair, is dominant or partially dominant. However, when White blood amounts to three-eighths, the hair usually becomes frizzly rather than woolly and considerably longer. The shift from predominantly woolly to predominantly frizzly actually takes place in some individuals with as little as one-eighth of White blood, but some putatively pure Negroes are also recorded to have frizzly hair. When the White blood is increased to more than one-half, the hair becomes first of all merely curly, with large spirals, then deeply wavy, and finally, when the Negro blood amounts to less than one-quarter, there remains a moderate but permanent wave, or the hair may be straight. With the increase of White blood the hair tends to become longer in the women. If the contributing White stock is one which has golden or ash-blond hair, the dead black hair of the Negro is transformed first of all to a probably less intense black, then to the very dark brown which is often called black in Europeans, but which shows its true brown color in transmitted light. Further increments of White blood bring out the regular shades of red-brown, golden brown, and flat brown tints, with occasional pure golden and red shades. Red hair sometimes appears in persons with the percentage of White blood as little as three-eighths. Light brown hair and reddish-brown hair are common whenever the strain of White blood amounts to one-half or more. Pure ash-blonds in Mrs. Day's series are found only in quadroons (one-fourth Negro).

In the first hybrid generation the dark brown or black skin color of the Negro is reduced on the average to a light brown, either reddish or yellowish, probably according to the nature of the contributing White stock, whether florid or sallow. But variations also occur in first-generation hybrids and in mulattoes (half-Negro and half-White) of whatever hybrid generation. Further, within any class of a given blood composition there are the approximately pure dominants and the corresponding recessives, who tend to show physical characters approaching more nearly to one or the other parent stock than would be suspected from their equality of blood composition. Three-quarters White persons usually present a skin color no darker than that of the Mediterranean Whites, such as southern Italians. Often it is much lighter. Here again, it depends largely upon the blondness or brunetness of the White race involved. Pink-white skin color is recorded in a fair number of supposedly half-Negroes. A rather common phenomenon in these slightly Negroid peoples is large and very dark freckles which run together in masses. There are also parts of the body which tend to remain unduly dark in color. These are especially the eyelids and the region below the eyes, the sacral area of the back, and probably the external genital organs. In these hybrids there is a very pronounced tendency for the skin to get darker with advancing age. Often parts exposed to the sun tan more heavily than is common among the brunet Whites. Differences between exposed and unexposed areas of the body are usually very great.

Eye color in some of the blackest Negroes is so dark that the pupil can scarcely be distinguished from the iris. The white of the eye is yellowish and often stained with brown patches. With as much as three-eighths of White blood the iris becomes lighter, but is usually still a homogeneous dark brown or light brown. Flecks and patches of yellow tend to persist in the sclera ("white" of the eye), even in persons who are nearly White. When the blond White stock is strongly in the ascendancy, various shades of mixed eyes, with greenish or grayish backgrounds and brown, yellow, or orange pigmented areas around the pupil, appear. Very frequently the eye is sharply zoned. Quite indescribable and very peculiar forms of mixed eyes are often seen. It may be doubted that pure gray or blue eyes are ever found in Negroid blonds, although eyes which are predominantly gray or blue occur in half-Whites and in persons with less than half of Negro blood. Absolutely pure blue or gray eyes are comparatively rare even in the purest White stock of the lightest skin pigmentation.

A strong infusion of White blood in a Negro stock generally raises the root and bridge of the nose. Often the bony bridge remains somewhat broad, the tip thick and short, the wings of the nostrils flaring. With further increase of White blood the nose gets much longer and thinner at the tip, and the flare of the wings is diminished. A convex septum is a very persistent feature. Usually some Negroid features are retained in the nose up to the quadroon, or one-quarter Negro. However, the average quadroon or octoroon has a nose generally indistinguishable from that of most Whites.

Lip thickness and eversion tend also to diminish with increments of White blood. The lip seam is a very persistent feature. Beard and body hair also get thicker as White blood increases. The small, finely shaped Negro ear seems to yield readily to the larger, more crudely modeled White types which are commonly outstanding and have longer lobules.

The most remarkable phenomenon observed in Negro-White crosses is the apparent segregation and dominance within each group of a stated blood composition, three-quarters Negro, half-Negro, one-quarter Negro, and so on. In each class a certain proportion will appear more Negroid than would be expected from their blood proportions, another small proportion will lean more strongly to the White features, whereas the rest will show a certain homogeneity of blend. Thus, a mulatto who is strongly dominant in White features will sometimes be light enough in skin color and European enough in other features to pass for a Mediterranean White; while, on the other hand, the mulatto with Negroid dominant features may be as dark in skin color and as generally Negroid as a person who has three-quarters or even more of Negro blood. So the dominants and recessives of any blood class tend to be indistinguishable from intermediates of the next classes of increased or diminished proportions of Negro blood. Hence it is impossible to determine blood composition by experience in observation, except on a basis of favoring odds which are about two to one. One's guess is that dominants, recessives, and intermediates within any blood class occur in about the proportions of 1-1-2.

The other interesting phenomenon is a tendency for linkages of certain physical features to occur irrespective of blood proportions. Mrs. Day has frequently demonstrated to me that finely cut, straight noses, straight, nonprognathous faces, and thin lips in Negro-White hybrids are likely to go with the darker shades of skin color and with woolly or frizzly hair. On the other hand, light yellowish skin color, lighter, finer, and curlier hair, are more frequently associated with prognathism, flat, broad noses, and thick lips. The former seems to be a combination of Mendelian dominants, the latter, possibly, of Mendelian recessives.

Age changes in almost every type tend to bring out the more Negroidal characters of pigmentation and hair form.

Our knowledge of the fertility, vitality, and pathology of the Negro-White mixed blood as compared with the Negro or with the pure White is very deficient. The reason for this is that the Negroid or mixed-blood has usually been lumped with the Negro in comparative studies. The result is that little is known of the pathology of either which can be attributed confidently to racial composition. Certainly I am acquainted with no evidence which indicates that the Negro-White hybrid is inferior in biological status to the pure Negro. Dr. George D. Williams,* in a study of tuberculosis in the Negro population of Macon, Georgia, has been unable to distinguish between the mixed-bloods and the full-bloods in the incidence of this disease. He finds the significant correlations are rather with economic status

* Williams, George D. and Applewhite, Joseph D., "Tuberculosis in the Negroes of Georgia," *American Journal of Hygiene*, Vol. 29, No. 2, Sec. A, 1939, pp. 61-110.

and living conditions. *A priori* one would expect that the hybrid would inherit some of the immunities and some of the susceptibilities of each parent race. The prominence of Negro athletes in certain types of modern sports has awakened universal interest. It may be noted that the majority of these athletes appear to be mixed-bloods, ranging in proportions from predominantly Negro to near-White.

There is no real evidence that fertility in the Negroid is impaired. However, there can be little doubt that birth control is widely practiced among the mixed-bloods of higher economic status, as it is in the Whites. Since these hybrids are keenly aware of the anomalous social situation in which they find themselves, and since they resent it bitterly, they are frequently unwilling to bring into the world children who will have to suffer the social injustice which is the lot of the Negro and the Negroid. Consequently, there are indications that the birth rate in the educated and comparatively prosperous mulatto class is low.

The social and psychological status of the Negroid has frequently been made the subject of investigation. There can be no doubt that, on the whole, the mixed-bloods are somewhat more highly placed in the economic scale and often enjoy educational advantages superior to those of the full Negro. However, it is very difficult indeed to decide to what extent this apparent social and economic superiority of the Negroid is attributable to his inherently greater ability. It is undeniable that from the earlier days of slavery some discrimination has been practiced in favor of the lighter-skinned Negroids, as contrasted with the full Negroes. Higher intelligence quotients which have been found in some investigations to characterize the mixed-bloods may be attributable in some measure to the better educational and social opportunities which those with perceptible amounts of White blood often enjoy. Certainly there is no whit of evidence suggesting that the Negroid is less intelligent and efficient in mundane affairs than the pure Negro. The bulk of data seems to indicate the contrary, but no evaluation of the racial significance of these putative differences can be made.

Frequently it has been suggested that mulattoes are more neurotic and less stable mentally than the pure Negroes. I know of no substantial body of data which validates this claim. It is conceivable that the mental conflicts which arise in the mixed-blood are more frequent and more severe than in the case of the pure Negro, for the reason that the mixed-blood knows himself to be of a bi-racial descent and yet is usually forced to cast his lot with the side of his ancestry which has always been treated as an inferior race and has been consistently oppressed.

There is, in summary, no adequate basis for the claim that the person in whose veins flows the blood of both Negroes and Whites is inferior psychologically, physiologically, or in any other way to the parent races. Individual ability depends upon family and individual inheritance rather than upon race. From a genetic viewpoint it could be predicted that the occasional Negroids who have received the most favorable inheritance combinations should exhibit qualities superior to those manifested by any pure Whites or pure Negroes. That many mulattoes are brilliantly intellectual is a matter of fact confirmed by my personal observations. However, there is as yet no objective way of taking a census of high intellectual ability; and the rating of genius, like kissing, goes by choosing.

With equality of opportunity there is no doubt that the contributions of the Negroid to North American civilization would be as substantial as they are in Brazil, where race prejudice is, reputedly, at a minimum.

WHITE-MONGOLOID CROSSES

Until recently there have been no anthropological studies of the crosses of Mongoloids with Whites, except such as have been accomplished in the case of the American Indian, who, as we have seen, is by no means a pure Mongoloid, but a definitely composite race with a strong Mongoloid overlay. Even now the only data available pertain to crosses between Europeans and Chinese, and these are scanty. Actually the Chinese are not full Mongoloids, but, like the American Indian, carry various submerged or apparent strains of non-Mongoloid origin. Frequently, therefore, Mongoloid physical characters in the Chinese do not reach their full development. They are partially suppressed. I am in possession of no information concerning crosses of Whites with such apparently Simon-pure Mongoloids as the Buriats, Goldi, Giliak, and Tungus.

Mr. Yun-Juei Tao has recently contributed a valuable and unique monograph upon the results of Chinese-European crosses in France and in Germany.* These studies merit a brief summary. Mr. Tao examined the matings of 13 German women and 32 French women who had married Chinese. He also studied one marriage in which the mother was a Chinese woman. In the German crosses nearly 62 per cent of the fathers were tradesmen, and the rest were students or workers in the skilled trades. In the French-Chinese crosses 72 per cent of the Chinese fathers were laborers, 17 per cent were students, and the rest miscellaneously employed. In Germany the mixed families enjoyed the happy and moderately prosperous life of the small burgher. In France most of them were quite poor, and often the women were daily workers. In both countries the children were, as a rule, strongly attached to their fathers and were brought up to speak French or German, but not Chinese. This of course would be due to the influence of the mothers. The average age of fathers of 45 families was 38.7 years, and of mothers 32.5 years. From these matings were born 71 children: 40 boys and 31 girls, an average of 1.5 children per family. These, of course, were not completed marriages, and more children could be expected. The suggestion is, however, that

* Chinese-European Crosses, Yun-Juei Tao, *Zeitschrift f. Morphologie u. Anthropologie,* 1935, pp. 349-408.

these matings were not especially prolific. No record of still-births was secured.

In crosses between Whites and Mongoloids we expect the principal results of interest to pertain to the inheritance of skin color, of hair color and hair form, of the shape of the face and of the malars, and finally of the eye folds and eye openings. Of all the children studied by Tao, only three were recorded to have pink-white skins, and these were infants less than one year old. All the rest had skin shades ranging from yellowish white to brown. Of course, only 14 of the European mothers are known to have had pink skins; the rest (27) were dark in skin color or unobserved. It is suggested that the yellowish skin tints are dominant over pale white and pink-white. Tao noticed that the pink shades seen occasionally in the younger hybrids disappeared as they grew older and their pigmentation deepened. In 11 families in which the mother was freckled and the father free from freckles, the children were unfreckled. Freckles or dark spots were visible on the faces of two adults of mixed blood and in two children who were the results of an F_1 (first filial generation) backcross with a European. The material indicates that freckles are not dominant, but are likely to develop as a phenomenon of advancing age in persons of mixed pigmentation. The same is true of pigmented moles in Whites.

The pigmented patch in the sacral region which is called the Mongoloid spot is stated by Chemin to occur in 89 per cent of Chinese children during the first year of life, but to diminish in frequency with advancing age until only 19 per cent show it between the ages of 3 and 8 years. It is recorded in nearly 32 per cent of 60 F_1 European-Chinese hybrids under the age of 12 years, but is said to be fainter and to disappear more rapidly than in the pure Chinese. It has been suggested that the appearance of the sacral spot is controlled by two pairs of genetic factors, one for pigmentation present or absent, the other pair for suppression or manifestation of the pigmentation if present. Under these circumstances we should expect 50 per cent of the

Chinese-Europeans to show the spot in early life, but only 32 per cent actually do.

All of the fathers of these children had black hair, but in the mothers hair color ranged from "dark blond" to dark brown. All of the children under 12 years of age showed hair color of intermediate shades, and in 9 individuals from 7 families very young children had lighter hair color than the mother. Of 6 adult F_1 hybrids 5 had dark brown hair and one had black hair. The backcrossings show very diverse hair shades—a fact taken to be evidence of segregation. Evidently here, as in other cases of race mixture, a confusing factor is the tendency of the recessive blondness to express itself in infancy and to be obliterated by progressive pigmentation through the later years of growth. No simple Mendelian formula appears to explain the phenomena of the inheritance of hair color.

It is interesting to note that Tao recorded 6 of 31 Chinese fathers with wavy hair. The European mothers had, for the most part, wavy hair, but a few had straight hair. The straight European hair is finer than the straight Chinese hair. Of 17 F_1 hybrids, 14 had coarse, straight hair; and the others with different hair form were very young. It is thus indicated that a full dominance of straightness and coarseness manifests itself in adult years. The Chinese hair is of greater diameter than that of the Europeans, and it seems probable that the fine, straight hair or wavy hair of the young hybrids is eventually replaced by coarser as well as straighter hair.

All of the fathers had dark brown eyes, whereas the mothers exhibited a range from blue to dark brown. All of the F_1 hybrids have eyes of various shades of brown, 4 of them darker than those of the father. It is thus evident, as demonstrated in many other cases, that dark eyes are dominant. Segregation is shown by the fact that one individual born from a backcross with a European has blue eyes. The whites of the eyes in the Chinese fathers are flecked with yellow and in the F_1 hybrids are bluish in infancy, but apparently acquire the pigment spots in later life. Slanting eye openings appear to persist at the expense of the straight forms, but the presence of nearly one-fourth of straight eyes in the F_1 hybrids suggests that dominance of the slant eye is not complete and that more than one inheritance factor is involved.

The opening of the Chinese eye is narrow, or low, as contrasted with that of the European. Tao observed that all children appeared to have wide palpebral openings. It is doubtful whether this condition would persist to maturity. The internal epicanthic, or Mongoloid, fold of the upper eyelid was found in 25 of 31 Chinese fathers and in 50 of 60 F_1 hybrid children. This observation suggests that the epicanthic fold is dominant. Three of six adult F_1 hybrids also exhibit this fold, whereas three individuals sprung from European backcrosses lack it.

The metric data in this study of Chinese-European crosses are unsatisfactory because of the tender age of the subjects involved. However, there is some evidence of the dominance of brachycephaly. Tao also observed that all of the F_1 Chinese-European hybrids over 5 years of age had higher nasal roots and bridges than the Chinese, but wider alae and larger nostrils than the Europeans. Lips are apparently thicker than in Europeans, chins longer and more projecting than those of the Chinese.

None of the results of this study is contrary to the expectation of the anthropologist who has studied race mixture. The dominance of straight hair, dark hair, dark eyes, and epicanthic folds has been observed in other crosses.

The general results of studies of primary racial crosses between Negroes and Whites and between Mongoloids and Whites offer interesting evidence as to the types of featural mosaics which are stabilized in the hybrids and afford also many indications of the dominance of this or that morphological variation. On the whole, they support the contention that inheritance is Mendelian with segregation and dominance. However, it is clear enough that dominance is often incomplete and that most bodily features are not controlled by the interaction of a single pair of genetic factors. It is for this reason that it is commonly stated that racial mixtures result in blends. They are not really blends, but mosaics.

Hybrid vigor in size and strength has not as yet been demonstrated for hybrids of the types we have been discussing. It is suggested in the stature of Negroids in Africa, but I do not think that this indication is supported substantially by the American data. In my own series of Negro and Negroid criminals, both numerically large, the Negroids, or mixed-bloods, are taller than the putatively pure Negroes, but shorter than the Old American White criminals. But the mixed-bloods are the heaviest and the Whites the lightest. There is, then, the possibility of hybrid vigor in weight, but it is only a possibility.

VI

THE MAKING AND MIXING OF HUMAN RACES:

4. MIXTURES BETWEEN PRIMARY AND SECONDARY RACES AND BETWEEN ALLIED RACES

SECONDARY, OR composite, races are stabilized blends derived from the intermixture of primary races. Presumably, most of the members of such races are heterozygous dominants in the majority of their features and homozygous, or double, dominants in others. Since the heterozygous individuals are genetically less stable than those which are homozygous, we should expect crossings between two secondary races to bring about the breakdown of type combinations found in each and the formation of new ones. New arrays of dominants and recessives would be derived from the segregation of factors in the combined stocks.

If a secondary race crosses with a primary race which has previously contributed to that secondary blend, the reinforcement of characters derived from that primary race may skew the hybrids over toward the original features of the primary race. For example, if Polynesians are a tri-hybrid race derived from White, Negroid, and Mongoloid elements, crossings of Whites with Polynesians may produce more European-looking hybrids than would be anticipated in such a race mixture, because the White strain is present, although often recessive, in the Polynesian stock. If a Polynesian crosses with a Mongoloid or a Negroid, the hybrid is correspondingly overweighted by the latent proportions of those races already present in the Polynesian.

The breaking up and recombination of characters resulting from secondary racial admixture sometimes provides a clue to the origins of the composite races, since the elements fused in the secondary races are resolved in the mixture. Again, individual cases of unusual crossings between races which are not at present in contact, except perhaps in certain cosmopolitan regions, often clarify the origins of secondary races which have sprung up elsewhere in the world.

HOTTENTOT-WHITE MIXTURE IN SOUTH AFRICA

Any physical anthropologist will tell you that the classic study of race mixture is *Die Rehobother Bastards,* published in 1913 by Professor Eugen Fischer, of Berlin University. This investigation was the first serious attempt to apply Mendel's Law of Heredity to all of the metric and morphological characters observed in an inbred hybrid group. Rehoboth is a town in the southwest portion of the Union of South Africa. It was formerly included in German Southwest Africa. It is inhabited by the descendants of crosses between Boers and Hottentots, together with Negro and Hottentot servants and dependents. The Boers and other European settlers in the early days of South Africa not infrequently took Hottentot wives. They probably preferred them to Negro women, since the Negroes were slaves and the Hottentots were a free people with considerable wealth in cattle. Perhaps these Dutchmen also admired steatopygia. German women, of course, were scarce. Since the Hottentot-Boer marriages were frowned upon by the pure Boers and those who contracted them were disowned, the hybrids were driven back upon themselves. A group of these mixed folk eventually reached the town of Rehoboth about 1870. By this time they had become a well-integrated social unit. Pride in their origin had been inculcated, and the names of their European ancestors had been preserved. Only marriages between hybrids or "Bastards" were countenanced, and the pedigrees of most families were known for several generations. Probably about 31 families and 300 souls reached Rehoboth in the original migration. The Rehoboth Bastards were welded into a people by a succession of struggles with the surrounding natives.

Fischer examined the records of ancestry and concluded that of 37 male progenitors 17 were Dutch, 11 German, and 19 of dubious origin. Apart from these original 37 ancestors, he found 61 other names of European origin. It is evident that the Europeans must have been a mixed lot ethnically—Dutch, German, French Huguenot, and other scattered strains.

The Hottentots, as we have seen, are a secondary, or composite, race—derived from a major Bushman element with probably minor infusions of Hamitic, brunet White, and Bantu Negro. But the Bushmen themselves are a problematic race with mixed Negroid and Mongoloid characteristics. I have suggested that they sprung originally from a very archaic blend of proto-Mongoloids and pygmy Negritos. The Hottentots are extremely variable in size. Some of them are almost pygmoid and others of nearly medium stature. It is difficult to say how much of this statural variation has been brought about by recent intermixture with the tall Negroes of South Africa. Hottentots are indistinguishable from Bushmen in their yellow-brown skin color, their peppercorn hair, Mongoloid eyes and cheekbones, flat noses, peculiarities of the external genital organs, and steatopygia. Recent studies suggest that the Hottentots are more dolichocephalic than the Bushmen, more prognathous, and in a few other features slightly more Negroid. Whatever the exact composition of the Hottentot blend, it can have had little in common with the strains represented in the undeniably mixed Europeans who were the fathers of the Bastard stock. *A priori* we should expect a good deal of blondness in the European fathers, together with even more individuals of intermediate pigmentation and some few brunets. We should also expect finer hair—wavy or straight—taller stature, and more round-headedness. Certainly, all forms of the length-breadth head index must have been represented among these Boers and Germans, with a probable predominance of brachycephaly.

Fischer measured and observed only 310 of the Rehoboth hybrids, presumably because he found them rather unwilling subjects. He first of all attempted to classify them according to the number of generations they were removed from the primary cross, but this method turned out to be unsatisfactory. Ultimately he was forced to divide his material into three groups: those in which Hottentot and European blood occurred in about equal parts, and those with predominance of European and Hottentot strains, respectively. We may first summarize Fischer's findings in regard to the metric and morphological characteristics of these exotic hybrids.

The mean stature of all Bastard men is 168.4 cm. (66.30 in.), as contrasted with 167.5 cm., given as the average of the modern Dutch by Fischer. Since the Hottentots are much shorter than the Dutch, there is the possibility of heterosis—that manifestation of hybrid vigor whereby the mixed stock exceeds the size of both parental races. Similar figures suggest that the Bastard women are taller than Dutch or South German women and a great deal taller than Hottentot women. At any rate, it is certain that the Bastards approach or equal the medium to tall stature of the European side of their ancestry. Among the men of the subgroup in which European blood predominates mean stature is 174 cm. (68.5 in.), a very tall average for any race. They are somewhat taller than the half-breed group (167 cm.) and the predominatingly Hottentot group (168 cm.). Fischer says the men are more slender than Europeans of the same stature. The women are slight until the age of about thirty years, and grow fat thereafter.

Steatopygia, the peculiar accumulation of fat on the buttocks observed particularly in Hottentot and Bushmen women, but present to a slight degree in the men of these stocks, was not discernible in the Bastard men. Fischer observed it in the women, as far as it could be seen under the heavy European clothing which they wore. He thinks that it begins to develop in about the fifteenth year and reaches its full status at the age of thirty. He notes that the older women are fat and move with a clumsy, waddling gait like Dutch women. Hottentot women get thin in old age and are more agile. No peculiarities of the proportions of body segments were observed, with the possible exception of rather long legs.

The heads of Bastards are long, as are those of the Hottentots; and their breadth seems to fall between the narrow averages of the Hottentots and the wide mean values found in southern Germans. Actually the Bastard population is on the verge of dolichocephaly (length-breadth index: men 75.8, women 76.7). These values are nearer the Hottentot than the Boer or Dutch averages and suggest a rather unusual swing toward long-headedness. Of course, we do not know the cranial indices of the European male ancestors of these hybrids.

The most striking change in the proportions of the Hottentot-Boer hybrids is the elongation of the face. Fischer states that face length exceeds that of both parent stocks. The Hottentots have short, triangular faces; the Boers are probably quite variable in facial proportions. The forehead width of Bastards also shows heterosis, according to Fischer. The nose is usually a composite organ in this mixed people. The root tends to be rather broad, flat, and low; but the bridge is variable in height. The eyes are rather far apart as in the Hottentots. A certain amount of alveolar prognathism, or protrusion of the tooth-bearing borders of the jaws, is discernible.

Only about one-quarter of the Bastards have the narrow slitlike eye openings which are characteristic of the Hottentots. Eye folds covering the inner corner of the eye seem to be present in nearly one-half of the children and one-quarter of the adults.

Fischer's classification of folds is not altogether clear. As far as I am aware, however, he was the first to recognize the median fold which overhangs the middle portion of the upper eyelid. This feature, found extensively in adult Europeans, occurs in many of the middle-aged and elderly male Bastards.

Lip thickness apparently varies with the blood proportions. The lips in the predominantly European group are thin or moderately thick. Thickness and eversion seem to increase with increments of Hottentot blood. A very bright lip seam at the boundary of the membranous and integumental lips is found in half the the near-Hottentot and half-blood groups, and in one-quarter of the near-European group.

The chin in the hybrid is usually better developed, less pointed, and heavier than in the Hottentot. Notable is the occasional appearance of the small, heavily rolled type of ear which is called the Bushman ear. All of the features of this ear do not appear, as a rule, in any single individual, but nearly one-fifth show some trace of it.

In general, the group with the highest proportion of European blood looks most like the European. Occasionally a very flat-faced, Mongoloid-appearing person may be noticed, and here and there an extremely Negroid type crops out.

Fischer says that skin color in the Rehoboth Bastards is as light as that of the southern European, although a grayish brown tint is sometimes observed. Yellow and brown skin colors are rare. The group with the most European blood has the least pigmentation. The Bastard tans very deeply, so that the difference between exposed and unexposed areas is very great.

All varieties of hair form except straight occur in the Rehoboth hybrids. Hair form seems to follow the blood proportions and the most nearly straight hair occurs in the near-European group. Young children sometimes have the peppercorn hair found in the Bushmen and Hottentots. Some of the very young children have blond hair, but the hair darkens markedly with increasing age. Although many medium shades occur, there are no pure blonds among the adults. The darkest hair is found in the group with the most Hottentot blood. Blue eyes may be observed in some of the near-Europeans. Yellow specks generally occur in the whites of the eyes.

Generally speaking, the Rehoboth hybrids appear to look like Europeans in infancy and during childhood, but as they grow older most of the European resemblances disappear. Fischer says that the same growth rhythm is manifest in the hybrids as is noted in other races (an initial phase of very rapid growth in the first two years, a somewhat slower growth up to puberty, an adolescent spurt, and a final period of very slight increase). It is probable that menstruation is later in the Rehoboth girls than in the Hottentots. Marriage among this people is very late, whether because of economic discretion or late maturation I cannot say. It usually takes place at the ages of 25 to 27 years in men and at 20 to 23 years in women.

The marriages of the Rehoboth hybrids are extraordinarily fertile. The average number of offspring per marriage is 7.4. It is very improbable that this figure falls below the averages of either parent stock.

Fischer noted that in general this people seems to enjoy excellent health, and many of them live to be very old. He noticed nothing extraordinary in their pathology.

Professor Fischer deserves great credit for his attempt in this study to trace Mendelian inheritance of physical features in families according to known proportions of blood. This effort resulted in the establishment of a number of probabilities in regard to Mendelian segregation and dominance. Thus, evidence is offered to demonstrate that dark hair and dark eyes are dominant over light hair and light eyes, woolly and curly hair form over slightly curly, wavy, and straight hair. Fischer also suggests the probability of low nasal indices dominating over high indices, convex nasal bridges over concave, straight eyes over oblique eyes, and other features. Unfortunately the data are usually inadequate for definite proof.

The sociology of these hybrids between Boers and Hottentots is of great interest. European culture predominates; partly, however, because of the influence of missionaries. The form of government used by the Bastards before they came under the German protectorate was highly reminiscent of Hottentot tribal rule. A captain led the people by hereditary right. With him were associated an under-captain, a magistrate, and seven councilors. All of these offices were elective, but tended to become hereditary in certain families. The Bastards were stratified socially. The upper crust consisted of the "good old families," well-to-do, and with the most European blood and the most influence and energy. This group married within itself and monopolized offices and political influence. Hangers-on were poorer families of predominantly European blood, but possibly of less ancient hybrid lineage and less distinguished history. The lower class had more Hottentot blood and often backcrossed with Hottentots. This lower class was despised by the aristocracy and complained of oppression.

The Rehoboth hybrids are a pastoral people living on very good grazing land. The tenure of land was first in common, but ultimately individual ownership grew up—first of houses and adjacent land, with the rest of the land in common. Finally the common lands were apportioned by the council, considerably to the dissatisfaction of the lower classes. The well-to-do Bastard has a town house, a country house, many cattle, and hordes of Hottentot and Negro servants. These hybrids have developed very little material culture of their own and are averse to agriculture. Their social customs are an interesting mixture of Boer and Hottentot. They are bi-lingual, but Hottentot speech is primary. Dwellings grade down from the Boer type of house to the Hottentot hut and kraal. In fact, their culture is hybridized to about the same extent as their physiques.

This pioneer study of Fischer indicated that hybrid vigor does occur in this cross of widely separated races, that fertility and vitality are by no means impaired, and that Mendelian inheritance seems to be operative in race mixture. No subsequent study of equal scope has been undertaken in South Africa. Observations of recent writers tend to confirm Fischer's results. However, Fischer has been criticized on the ground that his assumption of pure Hottentot ancestry on the distaff side of the Rehoboth Bastards is dubious. Hottentot mixtures with Negroes and with Whites are of such long standing in South Africa that it is unsafe to postulate pure Hottentot lineage for these hybrids. Again, Fischer doubts that a new and relatively homogeneous race could arise out of such mixtures as have taken place in this area. He considers the hybrids to be unstable, individual mosaics of racial features inherited from one or other parental stock, according to Mendelian rules. The more generally approved opinion is that stabilized secondary races can and do originate from such crosses, if inbreeding and selection follow upon widespread primary intermixture.

EAST INDIAN-WHITE MIXTURES

According to the census of 1931, the official number of "Anglo-Indians," or hybrids between Europeans and Indians, in India and Burma was 138,395, of which 19,200 were in Burma.* This figure represents an increase of 122.9 per cent from the census of 1881. Probably the total of persons of mixed Indian and European blood is considerably larger than the number mentioned. The origin of this group in India dates back to the Portuguese occupation in the early sixteenth century, and especially to intermarriage between British and natives in the days of the East India Company. Race mixture has continued ever since. The European strains include more Portuguese, Dutch, and French than is commonly supposed. Armenians, Jews, West Indians, and other Negroids have also added ingredients. Studies of this large mixed population have been almost negligible. Cedric Dover, himself an Anglo-Indian, has

* Dover, Cedric, *Half-Caste*, p. 117. London, 1937.

contributed some valuable historical notes and comments in a polemical book on race mixture which discusses the question from a mainly sociological point of view. Actual physical anthropological data on the subject are apparently restricted to a short paper written by Edgar Thurston* in 1898, and to the incomplete publication of some measurements made by Annandale and analyzed by P. C. Mahalanobis.†

The East Indians represent blends in various proportions of a minor and very ancient Negroid or Negritoid strain with a heavier Australoid or proto-Australoid element, both of which are overlaid and swamped by an ancient admixture of one or more varieties of brunet Whites, probably mostly of Mediterranean race. It is quite possible that the Iranian Plateau race and even the blond Nordic race have contributed sizable elements to the blend in various parts of the country. These highly composite and rather variable Indians have then crossed in recent times with all sorts of Europeans. The result is rather discouraging from the point of view of genetic analysis. As far as I am aware, no modern studies of race mixture in family groups have been carried out. We must then depend upon the very meager and unsatisfactory data offered by Thurston and Mahalanobis.

Thurston studied 130 adult male Eurasians in the Madras presidency. His subjects were drawn from the poorest class of Eurasians, mostly clerks and petty urban employees. He says that they marry very young—often in childhood—and bring up a plethora of children in poverty, hunger, and dirt. Fifty marriages of men with a mean age of 34 years had produced 207 children (average 4.1), of whom 91 had died in infancy. We

* Thurston, Edgar, "Eurasians of Madras and Malabar," *Madras Government Museum Bulletins,* Vol. II., No. 2, 1898.

† Mahalanobis, P. C., "Anthropological Observations on the Anglo-Indians of Calcutta," *Records of the Indian Museum,* 1922, pp. 1-96. "Analysis of Race Mixture in Bengal," *Journal and Proceedings of the Asiatic Society of Bengal,* 1927, N. S. Vol. 23, Article 24, pp. 301-333.

may consider briefly the metric and morphological features of this small Eurasian group.

Their stature (166.6 cm., or 5 feet 5½ inches), is considerably above that of any of the Indian caste groups with whom they are compared and below that of the English of Madras. Their average weight (in clothing) is only 107½ lbs. Their absolute chest circumferences are substantially the same as those of several pure Indian groups and castes, but chest circumference relative to stature is inferior to all of these Indians and vastly below that of the Madras English. Their head lengths and head breadths are essentially those of the Madras Brahmins, who have wider heads than low-caste Indians. The cephalic index of the Eurasians (76) is slightly higher than that of other groups, with the exception of the Brahmins. The Eurasians have lower nasal indices than any of the pure Indian groups. Thurston states that the lowering of the index is not due to diminution of nasal breadth, but to greater nasal length. He adds that long, narrow noses go with the taller, fairer-skinned Eurasian individuals.

Skin color in these Eurasians ranges from sooty black through yellow-brown to sallow white. In exceptional cases the skin color is rosy. Nearly all of his 130 males had been extensively tattooed, although in some cases the marks were obscured by dark pigmentation of the skin. Thurston mentions the progressive pigmentation of the skin with advancing age and also irregularities of pigmentation, such as extremely dark genitalia and dark patches on the knees, elbows, and neck. Hair color is uniformly black and hair form straight or curly, but never woolly. Eyebrows are thick and frequently concurrent. Baldness and premature graying are common. Eye color is variable, with a predominance of dark tints. Thurston found but one blue-eyed individual.

It is quite clear that the Eurasians examined by Thurston were disproportionately selected both from the lowest social and economic classes and from the groups in which European blood was distinctly in the minority. Yet his data show stature intermediate between the Indians and the English, head breadth exceeding that of the lower-caste Indians, tendency toward leptorrhiny, or a narrow-nosed condition, and variable pigmentation. Feeble chest circumference in relation to stature is possibly due in part to malnutrition.

Cedric Dover in *Half-Caste* discusses the social and economic position of the Anglo-Indian. The majority are found in the large towns and are in the service of the government. The census of 1931 shows that 336 per thousand are engaged in transportation, 103 in public administration, 107 in industry, 94 in trade, 84 in the professions, 56 in the public forces (chiefly police), 32 in agriculture, and 31 in domestic service. In short, this literate and urban class constitutes a most important section of the rank and file of the Indian government. Dover also cites many cases of intermarriage of Eurasians with Indians of noble birth and with Europeans in high official positions. He describes the important part played by the Eurasians during the Mutiny, in which they were loyal to the English. He gives them a large measure of the credit for saving India for the English. He also cites many individual instances of distinction gained by the Eurasians in politics, medicine, law, and literature.

It is clear enough that the Anglo-Indians are among the chief instruments for the preservation of British rule in India. Their position amply indicates their intelligence and their ability to acquire European educations. Their rapid increase is sufficient evidence of their fertility. Data pertaining to their biological status are admittedly inadequate. The sedentary nature of their occupations probably is associated with slightness of physique, but we have no means of knowing to what extent their inferior physical endowment, if it is inferior, is the result of environment as contrasted with inheritance. Dover speaks of the athletic prowess of many Eurasians who have had the advantage of the upper class education. Thurston also found that poor

Eurasian boys who were brought up in an English school were physically well developed.

KISARESE-DUTCH CROSSES

The only modern scientific study of race mixture which has been carried on in the Far East is that of Rodenwaldt, who investigated crosses of Dutch and other Europeans with the natives of the island of Kisar in the Timor Archipelago.* On this small island lives a colony of hybrids which originated from intermixture of the soldiers of the Dutch East India Company with the Kisarese, beginning about 1750. The latter consist of three social classes—nobility, farmers, and common people. The nobility are of mixed Mongoloid stock and belong to the Indonesian-Malay composite race. The farmers and common people evidently have a strong strain of Oceanic Negroid, blended to some extent with Malay. The racial situation is so complicated and Rodenwaldt studied so few subjects, either hybrid or of the pure native stock, that his extremely elaborate and careful work yields very few conclusive and dependable results. It is not worth while in this brief summary to enter into a detailed discussion of the physical anthropology of the numerous tiny groups into which it was necessary to subdivide his scanty material.

The Kisarese, or Mestizos, form an inbreeding group with a material and social culture slightly superior to that of the natives. Those with the most European blood hold administrative positions and are engaged in commerce and in professions. With decrease of European blood the occupational level sinks, and agriculture is the principal pursuit. Rodenwaldt says the hybrids are far superior to the natives in ability and intelligence. They are comparatively healthy and highly fertile. Sixteen marriages in the last two generations produced an

* Rodenwaldt, Ernst, *Die Mestizen auf Kisar*, Batavia, 1927.

average of 7.3 children per marriage. The investigator could find no evidence of degeneracy through inbreeding.

In most characteristics the Kisarese hybrids apparently are intermediate between the natives and the Dutch. There is no evidence of heterosis, or hybrid vigor. Rodenwaldt made a conscientious effort to trace the inheritance of physical features by the application of Mendelian rules, but his data are altogether inadequate. However, he was able to establish the probability of segregation and dominance in some few metric and morphological features. Hybrid noses with a dominance of high bridges, dominance of great head breadth, intermediate and progressive pigmentation of hair, skin, and eyes, with juvenile blondness, are a few of the phenomena encountered.

AUSTRALIAN-WHITE MIXTURES

In Australia the physical and cultural characteristics of the aborigines are so strongly in contrast with those of the British White population that a study of hybridization between the races involved should yield results of the greatest interest. Unfortunately, little or no effort has been made to investigate this subject up to the last year. Griffith Taylor,[*] the geographer, with F. Jardine, published many years ago a short study of race mixture in New South Wales, and in the same year C. B. Davenport[†] published a few observations made in 1914 on the occasion of a short visit to Australia.

However, in May, 1938, a joint expedition of Harvard University and the University of Adelaide took the field for the purpose of securing ample and definitive data on race mixture in Australia. In this enterprise the genealogy, linguistics, so-

[*] Taylor, G., and Jardine, F., "Kamilaroi and White: A Study of Racial Mixture in New South Wales," *Journal of the Royal Society of New South Wales,* LVIII, pp. 268-294, 1925.

[†] Davenport, C. B., "Notes on Physical Anthropology of Australian Aborigines and Black-White Hybrids," *American Journal of Physical Anthropology,* VIII, pp. 73-94, 1925.

ciology, and material culture are being studied by Norman Tindale of the Museum of South Australia and the physical anthropology by Joseph B. Birdsell of Harvard. All areas of Australia and Tasmania are being investigated, and at latest reports more than 2,000 individuals had been completely studied. Western Australia remains to be visited. This material includes series of both parent stocks, half-breeds, quarterbreeds, and various other backcrosses. In two years it may be expected that fuller information on race mixture in this area will be available than for almost any other part of the world.

For the present little can be said of race mixture in Australia. The census figures for 1933 returned the number of half-castes as 20,609, but it is now estimated that they are in excess of 30,000. Primary crossings are still going on, and in some cases it will be possible to study the principals of the primary matings, together with their first-generation offspring.

Davenport measured 13 full-blood Australians and 7 F_1 hybrids at Brewarrina Mission, N. S. W. The data are insufficient to be used as a basis for any conclusion. However, it may be noted that all of Davenport's 7 F_1 hybrids had dark eyes and dark brown or black hair. He states that segregation is observable in the F_2 (second filial) generation in which blue and "hazel" eyes and some rather light skin colors appear.

In a personal communication to me, Mr. J. B. Birdsell, now at work in Australia, comments upon the ease with which F_1 hybrids may be distinguished. They are moderately dark in skin color, but have cleanly cut features, so that in everything except the wings of the nose and the breadth of the nasal bridge they approach the morphology of the northwestern European. The blend is harmonious, with most of the European features dominating. Birdsell says that F_1's are more readily accepted in the White communities than the F_2 and later generation hybrids of the same blood proportions in whom Australian characteristics have begun to segregate. In another letter Birdsell mentions a family in which both parents are F_1's and the four daughters F_2 (half-Australian, half-White). He notes that these four girls range in eye color from mixed gray to pure brown by even transitions. He also refers to progressive pigmentation, massed freckles, and the blotching frequently observed in the lighter-skinned hybrid children, as well as the presence of the sacral pigmented spot. On the whole, Birdsell reiterates, F_1 hybrids can scarcely be distinguished from the darker-skinned Whites, save by a few minor traits. Their faces tan heavily, but unexposed parts are extremely light. These first-generation hybrids are stated to be the best and most intelligent workers; and, until old age, when Australian characters tend to assert themselves, they live and are accepted by the community more or less as Whites. An F_1 hybrid offspring of a full-blood Australian and a Singhalese is unexpectedly Negroidal. A family of ¾ Australian and ¼ Hindu or East Indian blood shows also a good many Negroid characteristics. Finally, an F_1 between a Negro and an Australian shows the dominance of frizzly hair over wavy, but with a rather wide variability of hair form, suggesting multiple factors.

The preliminary indications of dominance of more highly evolved racial types over the Australoid are quite in accordance with expectation. These few scattering comments gathered from field reports of the Harvard-Adelaide expedition give some indication of the rich results which are to be anticipated from this exhaustive study of race mixture involving perhaps the most primitive anthropological type now in existence.

POLYNESIAN-WHITE CROSSES

The Pitcairn and Norfolk Islanders

Two of the finest studies of race mixture have been made by H. L. Shapiro upon the famous descendants of the mutineers of the English warship *Bounty* and their Tahitian women.* The story of the *Bounty* has been so popularized that it requires no repetition here. It is enough to say that in 1790 nine English mutineers reached the lonely isle of Pitcairn in mid-Pacific, accompanied by a dozen or fewer Tahitian women and 6 to 10 Tahitian men. In the course of a few years all of the men had been killed or had died with the exception of John Adams, who was left with the Tahitian women and their hybrid children. You doubtless remember that in this sorry plight Adams turned to religion and reformed the entire brood. The colony was lost until 1808. Between that time and 1856 about three Englishmen joined it. In 1856 the whole group of 187 individuals was moved to Norfolk Island, 900 miles east of Australia. In 1858 two of the families returned to Pitcairn, and five years later another group of 27 went back to the smaller island. There are thus two separate colonies of descendants of the mutineers, the Norfolk and Pitcairn Islanders. The first anthropological study of any of these hybrids was made by Sir Arthur Keith in 1917 upon the two Young brothers who came to London from Pitcairn as seamen on a yacht.†

In 1923 H. L. Shapiro set out to study the Pitcairners, but was carried on to Australia when a storm prevented his landing at Pitcairn. He then proceeded to Norfolk and spent five months in the study of that colony. The result was his splendid monograph upon these people. It was not until 1934 that Dr. Shapiro managed to visit Pitcairn and to complete his work on the smaller group in their original domicile. His technical study of this group has not yet appeared, but preliminary results are available in his fascinating *Heritage of the Bounty*.

Most of the Norfolk Islanders represent the fourth or fifth generation from the original cross and are approximately of

---

* Shapiro, Harry L., *Descendants of the Mutineers of the Bounty*, Memoirs of the Bernice P. Bishop Museum, Vol. XI. No. 1, 106 pages. Honolulu, 1929. Shapiro, Harry L., *The Heritage of the Bounty*, 329 pages. N. Y., 1936.

† Keith, A., "The Physical Characteristics of Two Pitcairn Islanders," *Man*, No. 88, pp. 121-131, 1917.

equal proportions of English and Tahitian blood. Shapiro studied 64 adult males, 49 adult females, and 37 children. The males exceed both of the parental stocks in stature, but the females only equal the standing height of the English and Tahitians. The Tahitians have short, broad heads and the English longer and much narrower heads. The hybrids have inherited the longer head length of the English and an intermediate head width. Tahitians also have wider faces than the English and the Norfolkers are again intermediate. The males have the longer faces of the Tahitians, and the females probably fall between the two parent stocks in facial length. The male hybrids have narrow foreheads such as are common in the Polynesian stock and nose measurements probably intermediate between the shorter and broader Tahitian nose and the longer and narrower English nose. The Norfolkers are much closer to the long-headed English in cephalic index than to the brachycephalic Polynesians. In both male and female hybrids the mean nasal index is between the low value of the English and the high average of the Tahitians, but approaches nearer to the English mean.

In eye color it is evident that deep pigmentation is dominant. The combined group of males and females has 50.4 per cent of mixed eyes, 36.3 per cent of dark eyes, and 13.3 per cent of blue eyes. Blue eyes are much commoner in men than in women. The inner epicanthic fold, fairly common among Polynesians, is very rare in the descendants of the mutineers of the *Bounty* (traces in 1.61 per cent of males and in 2.27 per cent of females). Unexposed skin color in the Norfolk Islanders is intermediate between the moderately dark skin of Tahitians and the relatively fair skin of the English. Skin color overlaps that of both parent groups, suggesting multiple factors. However, the hybrids tan to a color as dark as that of the Polynesians. Hair color is prevailingly black or dark brown, indicating a dominance of the heavily pigmented Polynesian hair. A small percentage have light brown, medium brown, or blond hair (medium brown 9.09 per cent of males, 12.76 per cent of females; blond 1.82 per cent of males, 4.26 per cent of females; light brown 2.13 per cent of females). The men have darker hair than the women. In early graying of the hair and frequent baldness the Norfolk Islanders resemble the English.

Hair form certainly segregates, since the Norfolk Islanders show all varieties—from straight to frizzly—with the former attaining 45 to 48 per cent. Frizzly hair is found in nearly 11 per cent of males and in more than 10 per cent of females. It is far commoner in these descendants of the mutineers than in the Society Islanders, a Polynesian group. The Norfolk men have much heavier beard and body hair than are found among Polynesians.

Tahitian males have high, sloping foreheads with glabella (the prominence over the root of the nose) very strongly developed. The Norfolk males resemble the Polynesians in this feature. Apparently, high, convex noses derived from the English ancestry dominate over the straight, lower-bridged noses characteristic of the Polynesians. This statement applies more accurately to the men than to the women.

Shapiro found no satisfactory English series with which to compare his descendants of the mutineers of the *Bounty*. A small group of English scientists appeared to resemble the Norfolk Islanders more closely than do the Polynesians of the Society Islands. However, this British scientist group is certainly not representative of the English general population. English convicts, studied by Goring, are farther away from the hybrids than are the Tahitians. British convicts, like other convicts, are a biologically inferior lot. The Norfolkers are not, and I suppose the same must be admitted in the case of the British scientists.

Both hybrid vigor in size and increased fertility resulted from the Polynesian-English cross. In the F_2 generation there were 9.1 offspring per marriage. In later generations the fertility decreased somewhat, probably because of changing social conditions, increased knowledge of contraception, and delay in marriage. Many of these hybrids are long-lived; the oldest in 1923 was 95 years of age. Health is in general very good, but all are subject to early loss of teeth—probably the heritage of the English. Five generations of inbreeding have shown the persistence of hybrid vigor and no physical deterioration.

Shapiro's later Pitcairn series includes 62 adult men and 62 adult women. The stature of the Pitcairn men is 1 cm. below that of the Norfolk Islanders, but its mean (173 cm.) still exceeds that of either parent race. Curiously, the Pitcairn Islanders have the short head lengths of the Polynesians and an intermediate head breadth. The Norfolk group has the long heads of the English. The Pitcairners also have narrower foreheads than either parental stock and preserve the very constricted faces of the English. Their nose width is intermediate between the averages of English and Tahitians. Skin color is not so dark as that of the Tahitians, but there are few with the fair skins of the English. Hair color is predominantly black, with moderate proportions of dark brown. Lighter shades are rare, although one adult had blond hair, and blondness appears as a temporary character in infants and children. Women have darker eyes and hair than men in the Pitcairn group. In females brown eyes predominate, and in males intermediate or mixed eyes. Again, as in the Norfolkers, convex nasal bridges appear to dominate. Both thick and thin lips appear in these people, so that the characteristics of each parental race are represented. The Pitcairners have the same shocking teeth as are found in the Norfolkers. Variability of this group is small, as in their relatives on Norfolk; partially, no doubt, because of close inbreeding.

After 145 years, the living progeny on Norfolk and Pitcairn Islands sprung from the six English mutineers who lived long enough to produce children is in excess of 800 persons. However, there has been a steady decline in fertility both on Norfolk and Pitcairn, from a maximum of 11.4 children per female on Pitcairn in 1815-1839 to 2.4 in 1890-1914 (the birth years of the mothers). On Norfolk the second generation averaged 9.1 children per mating, and the fourth 2.96. The decline in fertility seems to be partially the result of later age at marriage and earlier cessation of childbearing. It may be connected also with the growing use of contraceptives and a possible increase in venereal diseases.

Physically the Pitcairn Islanders are robust and healthy; their medical record is good. The only obvious degeneracy is in their dentition. Shapiro's subjective impression is that only two or three of the 200 inhabitants are mentally below par, a few dull, and the rest within the ordinary range of intelligence. He was struck by the relatively large number of individuals who possessed qualities of leadership or traits of personality which raised them above their neighbors.

The material culture and social organization of the inhabitants of Norfolk and Pitcairn, as described by Dr. Shapiro, present many features of extraordinary interest in their mélange of European and Polynesian elements. Some original and peculiar features of house construction were noted. The Pitcairners in conversation with English or Americans speak English with a peculiar dialect, but among themselves they use a patois consisting of "mispronounced English and Tahitian words with a spattering of coined words, the whole employed in a degenerate English syntax."

By and large, the descendants of the mutineers and the Tahitian women present an example of the effects of close and long-continued inbreeding which is biologically even more interesting than the nature of inheritance of features from two distinct racial stocks. The principal manifestations in the combined phenomena are hybrid vigor through several generations, initial increase of fertility and subsequent diminution, maintenance of health and longevity in spite of inbreeding, dominance of White racial characters. The last is due not alone to Mendelian segregation and dominance, but also to the fact that the Polynesian race carries a White element in its composition which makes the hybrids more than half White when this latent White fraction is added to the English blood.

Polynesian Mixtures in Hawaii

One of the most important areas in the world for the study of race mixture is the Hawaiian Islands. The original population of this group was, of course, the brown-skinned Polynesian race, black-haired, brown-eyed, big, and comely. The head of the Hawaiian is usually brachycephalic, the face broad and high, the nose mesorrhine (medium breadth in relation to its length). The features present the smooth blend which is characteristic of the Polynesian tri-hybrids. Apparently the hair is oftener curly or very deeply wavy than in some of the other islands of Polynesia. Possibly in the fusion of Negroid, Mongoloid, and White racial strains there may be somewhat more of the first element (and less of the third) than in, for example, the Maori of New Zealand and the Samoans. It is also possible that Negro blood may have been reinforced in supposedly pure Hawaiians by recent admixture with Portuguese, Puerto Ricans, and American Negroes.

The difficulty of the study of race mixture in Hawaii is its bewildering diversity. Foreign residents sifted in gradually until 1876, when the production of sugar was enlarged by free entry into the United States in a market protected by a tariff. From 1850 to 1936 the non-Hawaiian population of the islands increased from 2 per cent to 86 per cent.* The principal stocks involved in race mixture are Whites (including Europeans and Americans), Mongoloids (Chinese, Japanese, and Koreans), Indonesian-Malays (Filipinos), Negroes, and Negroids. The result is a racial hash including many exotic and complicated fractional blends and backcrosses, as well as large groups of F_1 and F_2 hybrids which are half-White and half-Polynesian, or half-Mongoloid and half-Polynesian. One suspects that the length of the hybridization period and the multiplicity of strains

* Adams, Romanzo, *Interracial Marriage in Hawaii*, p. 7. N. Y., 1937.

involved makes exact genealogical determination of blood composition usually difficult and frequently impossible. According to the census of 1930, the part-Hawaiians numbered 28,224, or 8.1 per cent of the civilian population.* Adams estimates that a classification of the population into five racial groups gives a total of 300,239 of more or less pure racial stock and 47,560, or 13.7 per cent, of various hybrids. Full-blooded Polynesians are estimated at about 13,000.

As far as I am aware, the first anthropological study of race mixture in Hawaii was based upon data collected by Professor A. M. Tozzer, of Harvard University, during the summers of 1916 and 1920. This material was analyzed and published by Dr. L. C. Dunn (Columbia University) in 1928.† After Dr. Tozzer's first efforts, Dr. Louis R. Sullivan of the American Museum of Natural History undertook very extensive studies in Hawaii and elsewhere in Polynesia under the auspices of his own institution and of the Bishop Museum of Honolulu and the University of Hawaii. Dr. Sullivan's untimely death interrupted the work, although some of his data were published by Dr. Clark Wissler.‡ Dr. H. L. Shapiro succeeded Dr. Sullivan at the American Museum and enlarged the scope of his work. However, Dr. Shapiro's numerous and admirable publications on the physical anthropology of Polynesia have not included as yet any detailed studies of hybridization in Hawaii.

Here I must content myself with a brief summary of the pioneer study by Dunn and Tozzer. Their total material consisted of data on 508 subjects, but these unfortunately must be divided into many small groups—most of which are inadequate for analysis.

* Adams, *Op. cit.*, pp. 18-19.
† Dunn, Leslie C., and Tozzer, Alfred M., *An Anthropometric Study of Hawaiians of Pure and Mixed Blood*, Papers of the Peabody Museum of Harvard University, Vol. XI, No. 3, pp. 90-211. Cambridge, 1928.
‡ Wissler, Clark, *Growth of Children in Hawaii; based on observations by Louis R. Sullivan*, Bernice P. Bishop Museum Memoirs, XI, pp. 105-257. Honolulu, 1930.

The European and Hawaiian types which have intermarried are very similar in bodily dimensions and proportions, aside from the greater corpulence of the Hawaiians. The F_1 and three-quarter Hawaiians have the superior weight of the maternal stock, whether owing to diet and habits of life or to the inheritance of corpulence as a dominant. The brachycephalic head form of the Hawaiians is dominant, and the European dolichocephaly appears as a recessive in the F_2 and subsequent generations. In the Norfolk Islanders the dolichocephaly of the English appeared to dominate; in the Pitcairners an intermediate head form was attained; in the Hawaiian material brachycephaly asserts itself. It should be noted, however, that brachycephaly may well have been more prevalent in the Europeans whose strains have entered into the Hawaiian crosses than in the mutineers of the *Bounty*. The F_1 hybrids are larger than the full-blood Hawaiians and quite possibly larger than the European stocks from which they have sprung.

In the F_1 hybrids the higher bridge and nasal root, together with the broad tip and base of the nose, appear as dominants, the last two features from the Polynesian strain. The darker hair color and eye color, heavy skin pigmentation, and pronounced wave of the hair also seem to be partially dominant, although segregation in the second and backcrossing generations bring out resessive blondness, lighter skin color and eye color, and straight hair. Dunn states that, on the whole, the F_1 hybrids resemble the Polynesian stock more than the European, although dominance is incomplete and most features are, in fact, intermediate.

In most of the physical characteristics in which Hawaiians and Europeans differ most markedly the Hawaiians and the Chinese are alike. Moreover, the F_1 Chinese-Hawaiians in the Dunn series are almost too few to permit dependable conclusions. It seems probable that stature is intermediate between that of the short Chinese and the tall Hawaiians. Apparently the hybrids are shorter-headed and more brachycephalic than either parent race. The face and nose in the first generation offspring seem to lean toward the Chinese type, since the former is smaller and the latter narrower than in the pure Hawaiians.

The greatest difference between Chinese and Hawaiians is in hair form, which is, without exception, straight and coarse in the former (so far as observed by Tozzer) and usually wavy or curly in the latter. Very significantly, the straight hair does not dominate completely in the first hybrid generation. Sixty per cent have the Mongoloid hair form, but the others have the Hawaiian wavy or curly varieties. But wavy hair does occur in some pure Chinese, and its presence in that stock may account for some of the curved varieties found in the F_1 Chinese-Hawaiians. One person even had "wiry" (frizzly?) hair. Dunn is uncertain how to interpret this individual. Perhaps unrecorded Negro blood may be present, and there also may have been defects in the pedigrees of the other wavy- or curly-haired F_1's.

The inner epicanthic fold appears in a majority of the F_1 hybrids and seems to be dominant. However, the data on this feature were deplorably scanty. The nose form also appears to follow that of the Chinese in that the root is usually depressed, the bridge straight in males and concave in females, the septum directed upward. On the whole, the first generation leans toward the Chinese type, as would be expected from the reinforcement of the Mongoloid strain in the Hawaiians.

For a very succinct analysis of the nature and extent of outmarriages in Hawaii we may draw upon an article published by Louis R. Sullivan in the *Honolulu Bulletin* for 1921. Much more elaborate and later data are available, but not in such a convenient form. In all probability conditions have not greatly changed. Sullivan analyzed 14,569 unselected marriages for the years 1913-1917. Mixed marriages constituted 17.8 per cent of all tabulated. He found that more American men marry women of foreign blood than marry their own race; that more than one in six American women marry Hawaiians or part-Hawaiians. In outmarriages the Hawaiian women rank first, the

Portuguese second, and the Americans third. Korean, Japanese, and Chinese women outmarry least often. Birth rates show the Asiatic-Hawaiian and the White-Hawaiian hybrids to be the most fertile of all ethnic groups, with the exception of a numerically insignificant group of Spanish. The pure Hawaiians have the highest death rates, with the Asiatic-Hawaiian and White-Hawaiian hybrids about halfway down the list of death rates ranked by race and nationality. On the basis of birth rates and death rates, the Asiatic-Hawaiians have the greatest rate of natural increase and the White-Hawaiians rank next. Full-blood Hawaiians are decreasing in numbers. (Here again a numerically insignificant Spanish group is disregarded.)

The sociology of the racially mixed groups in Hawaii is ably discussed by Romanzo Adams in his book *Interracial Marriage in Hawaii*. Lack of space prevents my elaborating this subject. The drift of opinion appears to favor the view that part-Hawaiians in their ability to succeed in modern industrial society are between the levels of performance of their parent races. The Whites and the Chinese are experienced in, and adapted to, commercial and professional competition. The pure Hawaiians have no such tradition, experience, and inclination. The part-Hawaiians tend to retain a good deal of the Hawaiian attitude. The extreme capability of the Chinese and Japanese in Hawaii is a matter of common knowledge. The opinion generally held is that the Asiatic-Hawaiian hybrids are more able and more successful than the White-Hawaiians. Adams points out that conditions in Hawaii have operated to prevent the raising of social restrictions against persons of racially mixed antecedents, so that there is at any rate economic opportunity and social mobility for all. He feels that the smaller success of the Hawaiian-White hybrids, as compared with the Chinese-Hawaiian, is due to the fact that the former have been more strongly influenced by Hawaiian traditions and ways of life. He very wisely refuses to commit himself to conclusions arrived at by the use of any statistical test of comparative ability.

On the whole, it appears that the general status of the part-Hawaiian is intermediate between that of the parent stocks, both biologically and sociologically. Evidences of hybrid vigor, whether physical, mental, or social, are neither numerous nor impressive. On the other hand, there is no suggestion that biological or sociological deterioration arises from any of these mixtures. It is even possible that the part-Hawaiians are the most fertile stock of the islands. At any rate, they seem to show the most rapid increase.

INDIAN-WHITE MIXTURES

In the New World mixtures of Whites and Negroes with American Indians have been much more extensive than is commonly believed. There can be little doubt that the populations of many countries of South America and Central America are basically Indian with varying degrees of South European White admixture. In some of the countries large Negro elements have been added. Indian strains in the Old American population of the United States are probably stronger than most of us suppose them to be, especially in the South and the West.

In the United States no thorough and extensive studies of race mixture between Whites and Indians have been undertaken in recent years, although some meritorious small investigations have been made. The pioneer in this field was Franz Boas, who in 1894 published a study of the half-blood Indian.* This study was not genetic, but dealt with groups of putatively pure-blood and half-blood Indians. In it Boas showed that the mixed race was more fertile than the pure Indian race, that the half-breeds are taller than the parental stocks from which they have sprung and less homogeneous in stature. Further, Boas found that during the early years of childhood the Indian is taller than the half-blood, and that this relation is reversed later on. The

* Boas, Franz, "The Half-Blood Indian: An Anthropometric Study," *Popular Science Monthly,* pp. 761-770, October, 1894.

half-breed has a face which is intermediate in average breadth between the high mean of the Indian and the lower value found in Whites, but nearer to that of the Indian. Thus, the influence of the Indian blood seems stronger, although the proportions of blood of the two races in the hybrids are approximately the same. Similarly, the dark hair and dark eyes of the Indian prevail among the half-breeds.

Sullivan in 1920 analyzed some of the data on mixed and pure-blood Siouan tribes which had been collected under the supervision of Professor Boas in 1893.* His series included 594 adult male full-bloods, 77 adult male half-bloods, and much smaller groups of females. In skin color, hair color, and eye color, the half-breeds seem to stand near to the pure Indians; and in amount of body hair they are intermediate between Indians and Whites. Most of the morphological observations were not sufficiently sensitive to bring out differences of detail in the groups. Actually, the bodily proportions of Sioux Indians are probably not much different from those of the British and French stocks with whom they have mixed. The half-bloods are taller than the full-bloods (and probably than the parent White stocks). The face is much higher and wider in the pure Indian. The average facial dimensions of the mixed-bloods fall between those of the Indian and White races, with a leaning toward the former. Nevertheless, the individual half-breed tends to resemble either the Indian or the White in facial proportions, rather than to be intermediate. This stricture holds for different proportions of admixture—half-White, three-quarters White, et cetera.

Not very much more than the above is known about the physical characteristics of the mixed-blood North American Indian. However, the census data relating to vital statistics for the decade 1900-1910 were very thoroughly analyzed by my

* Sullivan, Louis R., "Anthropometry of the Siouan Tribes," *Proceedings of the National Academy of Sciences,* Vol. 6, No. 3, March, 1920, pp. 131-134.

late colleague, R. B. Dixon.* His studies demonstrate that the full-blood Indian women are more sterile than the mixed-bloods and that sterility is least in the marriages in which both parents are mixed White and Indian, or mixed Negro, White, and Indian. Sterile marriages between full-bloods amount to 10.7 per cent, and for mixed marriages 6.7 per cent. There also seems to be an inverse ratio between the amount of White blood in the married couples and the proportion of childless unions.

The number of children produced in mixed-blood marriages exceeds that of the full-blood marriages. The proportion of White blood does not seem, however, materially to influence the number of offspring. Actually, the primary crosses between the full White and the pure Indian are more prolific than any of the other main classes of mixed marriages. Of the subclasses of mixed marriage, those involving Negro, Indian, and White are the most fecund. Such marriages (of 10-20 years' duration) include between 55.5 and 58.6 per cent with 6 or more children. The average number of children in full-blood marriages is 4.5 and of mixed-blood unions 5.1.

For all classes of marriages the proportion of surviving children is 74.7 per cent; for pure marriages it is 69.7 per cent, and for mixed marriages 79 per cent. The percentages of children surviving are highest when one of the parents is a full White. Thus, in primary crosses between pure Whites and pure Indians, the percentage of surviving children is 82.9, between mixed-bloods and Whites 83, while for marriages in which both parents are mixed it is only 77.6, and in marriages between full-bloods and mixed-bloods only 69.9. The last figure is only slightly higher than that for full-blood Indian marriages (69.7).

The marked superiority of the mixed-blood in fertility and vitality is not capable of simple interpretation. It does not imply necessarily that the hybrids are biologically superior to the pure

* Dixon, Roland B., *Indian Population in the United States and Alaska*, Bureau of the Census, 1915.

Indians. Probably many of the pure Indians are too disgruntled at American civilization to wish to produce many offspring. Further, the marriages including a White parent, or White blood in both of the parents, are likely to be those which involve the greater participation in White civilization with its superior hygiene and medicinal care, and with improved standards of living. On the other hand, it is impossible to maintain, in the face of these data, that the hybrids are inferior in fertility or in vitality.

The results of intelligence tests (whatever they mean) suggest that the mixed-bloods surpass the full-bloods at this sort of game. For example, Professor T. R. Garth reported that in the United States Indians of the Southwest the mixed-bloods scored higher than any of the various tribes of full-blood Indians, and that they were also superior to the Mexicans.* Here again the significance of the findings is not unequivocal. The mixed-blood children may have had the advantage of hearing English in their homes, and it is very difficult in such tests to eliminate the language factor. Nevertheless, the burden of the proof lies with those who assert that the hybrids are *not* superior in intelligence to pure-blood Indians.

The most complete and satisfactory study of race mixture between Whites and Indians is that made by Dr. George D. Williams upon Maya-Spanish crosses in Yucatan.† Race mixture in this area has taken place for more than 350 years, so that it is impossible to secure information as to the genetic composition of individuals studied or pedigrees indicating the proportions of blood from the respective parent races. Williams secured a series of 880 men and 694 women of varying degrees of mixture of Maya and Spanish strains. He then divided his series into five subgroups on the basis of their variations in

* Garth, T. R., "The Intelligence of Indians," *Science,* LVI, 1922, pp. 635-636.

† Williams, George D., *Maya-Spanish Crosses in Yucatan,* Papers of the Peabody Museum of American Archaeology and Ethnology, Harvard University, Vol. XIII, No. 1, pp. 1-256. Cambridge, Mass., 1931.

certain nonadaptive and nonmensurable characters which are of value as racial criteria for the American Indian stock. The characters used were hair form, hair texture, beard quantity, hair color, eye color, skin color, freckles, nasal profile, form of nasal wings, chin prominence, form of eye folds, frontal and lateral nostril visibility, amount of nasal tip depression. He defined Group A according to the combination of variations of these 14 characters which would, on the basis of anthropological experience, approximate most closely to a pure Maya Indian type. Group B consisted of those who lacked but one of the 14 typical Maya variations of head and face. Groups D and E were selected on the basis of their possession to a greater or less degree of five traits which are characteristic of Spanish Whites as contrasted with Maya Indians. Group E manifested lighter pigmentation than Group D. Group C was the residue of intermediates between the composite groups AB and DE. Thus Williams secured five subgroups, putatively grading from a nearly pure Maya type toward increasingly European types. He then set out to ascertain whether these five subgroups differed significantly from the total series in metric characters and in morphological traits other than those used as a basis for the group sortings. All of his subgroups were found to be overwhelmingly differentiated from the total series.

Only a few of the numerous clear-cut results of Williams' work can be summarized here. In these subgroups stature increases with assumed increments of White blood. Stature in the mixed-bloods seems to be intermediate between the low means of the Maya Indians and the higher averages of Whites. No hybrid vigor is observable after so many generations of crossing. The more Indian types have squarer shoulders and relatively longer arms; the shoulders of the Whiter women are relatively narrower than those who have more Indian blood. The Whiter subgroups have somewhat smaller chests than the more nearly Maya groups. The Whiter types, nevertheless, appear to have the more robust body builds and are heavier. Temperature, pulse rate, and blood pressure show no significant differences between the subgroups. The Maya Indians have a somewhat higher basal metabolism than northern Whites, as suggested by the study of a very small number of cases; but those Yucatecans who possess distinctly White physical characteristics do not deviate from White standards.

Head length increases with increments of White blood, and the cephalic index (which is very high in pure Mayas) tends to diminish. Head height and head breadth do not vary significantly in the several groups. Forehead width tends to increase with White blood and facial breadth to diminish. The breadth of the nose decreases with accretions of White blood. Wavy hair increases. The data on pigmentation are, of course, affected by the fact that hair color, skin color, and eye color were involved in the criteria by which the groups were distinguished.

In the blood groups Group O diminishes with increase of White blood and Groups A and B increase. This finding is in accordance with previous work in which it has been demonstrated that pure American Indians tend to be predominantly, although not exclusively, of Group O, which lacks the agglutinogens A and B.

Dr. Williams' superb study did not neglect the sociological aspects of race mixture in Yucatan. He showed that occupationally the status of his subgroups improved as they became Whiter in their physical characteristics, and that the more Indian groups are village or *hacienda* born, whereas the Whiter groups tend to be born to a greater extent in villages or in the larger towns. About one-quarter of the two Whitest groups are engaged in business or work at trades, against 6 per cent of the two most Indian groups. Some selective matings of the lighter-skinned persons with each other were demonstrated in the villages, but a much stronger tendency for matings to conform with skin pigmentation was found upon the *haciendas* or great plantations. As yet there is little progression toward the formation of a homogeneous type in these Maya-Spanish. Such homogeneity would result from random matings.

Statistics relative to number of offspring, et cetera, were derived from a study of 305 families. It was found that women belonging to the Whiter subgroups begin childbearing at a somewhat later age than the more nearly Indian mothers. Without regard to duration of marriages, an average of five children is born to each family. Infant and childhood mortality is high. Transmissible diseases—malaria, whooping cough, pneumonia and influenza, and diarrhea—are largely responsible for the infant mortality. Measles, convulsions, and general debility are also important. Williams does not distinguish between his different racially graded subgroups in regard to vital statistics. He thinks it highly probable that the strong and hardy constitutions of adult Yucatecans (of all degrees of mixture) may be attributable to the rigorous selection to which they have been subjected from their earliest childhood.

THE INTERMIXTURE OF WHITE RACES AND THE FORMATION OF NATIONAL BREEDS

We have already seen that a number of secondary subraces have been formed from the crossing of primary White races. Such subraces are the Armenoid, Dinaric, East Baltic, and Keltic. Local and national types are continually arising also from protracted inbreeding of certain racial elements within a restricted area. In a recent survey of the anthropological characteristics of criminals in ten states of this country I had an opportunity to ascertain the extent to which such local physical types have developed. My series of native-born White criminals of native parentage included some 4200 adult males from nine states. Most of these individuals were of British or German ancestry, and the majority were unquestionably sprung from stock of several generations of residence in the United States. With the exception of the inmates of prisons of Arizona, Colorado, and New Mexico, a great majority of these convicts were incarcerated in the states of their birth. In Massachusetts, Tennessee, Kentucky, Wisconsin, North Carolina, Texas, and the three combined states of the Southwest, I had seven distinct groups of Old American criminals. Each of these groups was found to be anthropometrically distinct from the total series of which it formed a part, and overwhelmingly so. This means that the various racial and ethnic elements inbreeding in the separate state areas have formed anthropologically different populations. It is impossible at the moment to determine to what extent climatic and other environmental factors have influenced the formation of these state types, as contrasted with differences in the ethnic composition of the original settlers and of the later immigrant stocks. There is no doubt that if we were to erect state barriers and limit free migration from one state to another, we should rapidly establish new and comparatively homogeneous racial subtypes.

A similar process has been going on in Europe and elsewhere for thousands of years. Within the British Isles, for example, several different White races and subraces have inbred since the Norman conquest without any vast increment of foreign blood. The result is a comparative physical homogeneity which almost justifies the statement that a British "race" or subrace is in process of formation.

Whatever may be the arguments raised against the desirability of racial mixtures which involve races of radically diverse physical characters, there can be little or no valid evidence presented to show that crossings between allied races are biologically or sociologically detrimental.

As a matter of fact, the question is rarely raised, except in so far as it involves mixtures of Jews with non-Jews. The Jews, of course, are not a race, but only a rather rigidly selected blend of a number of different racial elements. They have received some accretions of blood from all of the populations among whom they have dwelt. Nevertheless, they represent mainly an inbred product of the ancient blending of several allied White racial stocks in the Near East. No fair-minded anthropologist or geneticist can doubt that the Jews as a group are physically distinctive and, to some extent, homogeneous. No one but a fool or a fanatic can question their extraordinary intelligence and worldly capability. While they exemplify, without doubt, the benefits which may be derived from rigorous selection in connection with inbreeding, it seems probable that a new policy of continued outbreeding of Jews with non-Jews would result in a wide manifestation of hybrid vigor in the offspring of the matings.

Virtually no studies of the results of race mixtures between allied races have been made, because these are not generally regarded as race mixtures. The physical differentiae of allied races are not sufficiently marked to make the offspring of their crossings physically distinctive and sociologically anomalous groups. Such mixtures have gone on from prehistoric times, so that it is now almost impossible to isolate pure racial stocks. They survive, if anywhere, only in out-of-the-way places. Most individuals of an apparently pure racial type are probably the result of the resegregation of combinations of racial characters which once went into the melting pot.

If we look at the course of prehistory and of history from the point of view of the physical anthropologist, we must recognize that most of the sudden efflorescences of civilization can be synchronized with new racial infusions, followed by inbreeding and a hybrid vigor which is certainly cultural, and quite probably biological. I have not time here to cover the world in such an attempt to correlate race mixture with great advances of civilization. I can, however, refer to several of the European phenomena. The first budding of art in Europe took place toward the end of the glacial period when the Aurignacian cave-dwellers carved figurines in the round, and their Magdalenian successors executed realistic engravings of animals on bones and polychrome paintings on the walls of dark caverns. These artists were men of a modern type anatomically, but, in my opinion, definitely hybrid in their physical features. The tall Cro-Magnons may have been the result of an early cross between a round-headed, short, and broad-faced race, and a long-headed race with a rather narrow face of medium length. That is my view, but the matter is controversial.

No such dispute can arise in the case of the incomparable Greek civilization. It began with the transplantation to the mainland of the Late Minoan civilization of Greece, itself due to Egyptian and Near Eastern elements blended together in an original fashion by the racially Mediterranean inhabitants of Crete. The mainland graft of this culture was modified by the presence of indigenous Helladic elements, the result of migrations from the Black Earth region of peoples bringing painted pottery. Nordic and Alpine invaders mixed with the primitive Mediterraneans. At the beginning of the Iron Age new hordes of invaders (possibly of a Dinaric type) swept down from central Europe. There was superadded a strong racial and cultural element from Asia Minor. After the dark ages of the Geometric period, the Greek civilization burst forth. It is probable that we shall never see its like again. The racial elements which blended to produce this genius of all human cultures were Mediterranean, Alpine, Nordic, and Dinaric, or Armenoid.

The Classic Greek physical type, idealized by the ancient sculptors, may be dissected into its heterogeneous racial components. The blue eyes and blond hair come from the Nordics, the curl of the hair from the Mediterraneans, the round, globular head from the Alpines, the continuity of forehead and nasal bridge from the Armenoids or some other Near Eastern stock.

Italy in the Neolithic period was inhabited by an apparently Mediterranean race people with a shabby culture. New stocks came in bringing the Bronze Age from central Europe. Whatever these were racially, they were not Mediterranean. More invaders, probably mixed Nordic and Alpine, came from the same region, in the Early Iron Age, and around Bologna and the north of the peninsula the first Italian efflorescence of culture began. Shortly afterwards there landed from Asia Minor the seafaring Etruscan invaders, whom we suspect to have been rather Armenoid. After these stocks had inbred and stewed in their own juices for a few centuries, there emerged the glory of Rome, enhanced no little by cultural borrowings from the decaying civilization of Greece and not devoid of actual increments of blood from the Hellenic peninsula.

The Late Keltic, or La Tene, civilization of the Early Iron Age was the first real cultural blooming in central Europe. It resulted, on the racial side, from the impact of Illyrian (probably Dinaric) stocks upon the mixed Alpines and Nordics of the Upper Rhine region. It spread to the most westerly of the British Isles, there achieving an art of considerable beauty and originality.

Civilizations which have inbred to the extent of sterility and decay usually fall victim to the inroads of crude but vigorous barbarians. There follows a period of chaos and destruction when everything of merit seems to have been destroyed. Meanwhile the new and savage blood is mingling with the sluggish currents of the effete civilized stocks. Ultimately there is a revival of biological strength and even, perhaps, evidence of hybrid vigor. Then comes the Renaissance. I suspect the Italian Renaissance to be due in part to the assimilation of the Nordic barbarians.

There is no use in multiplying instances. Biologically, race mixture between radically different races brings increased fertility with no apparent impairment of vitality or longevity. Commonly the hybrids present mosaics of characters derived from both parental stocks, set together by a complicated type of Mendelian inheritance. On the whole, the hybrid presents intermediate features and does not invariably show heterosis, except in fecundity. But there is no biological deterioration. If the races are culturally unequal, with the one advanced and the other very primitive, the cultural result is a not very satisfactory compromise, because radical hybrids are socially stigmatized and usually thrust down toward the simpler culture and inferior political status of the aboriginal, suppressed race. The achievement of the hybrids is then restricted by their physical separateness and by racial and class prejudice. Only a complete amalgamation of the parent stocks eradicates this obstacle to hybrid progress.

On the other hand, if two physically allied but culturally dissimilar races interbreed, hybrid vigor in biological characteristics is the most usual result of the crossing. If each race has its own distinctive abilities and its own moderately or highly developed cultural and social tradition, there is likely to result that brilliance of civilization which is analogous to the fortunate combination of genes which produces the superman in individual crossings. In rare instances, such as the epochal case of the ancient Greeks, a whole nation replete with men of genius may spring into existence, flourish, and decay.

Sooner or later inbred races and inbred cultures deteriorate. They rot from within, become sterile, and degenerate. Material prosperity encourages the preservation, pampering, and reproduction of the biologically inferior elements which are parasitical upon any rich civilization. Then some cleaner-blooded, and culturally crude stock crashes in and wipes clean the slate. Out of apparent evil comes eventual good, because the cultural and biological dross is destroyed so that man and civilization can rebuild themselves. Evolution, if it is to be progressive, demands the selection of the unfit and the culturally obsolete for extirpation. We can either prune off our own rotten branches or submit to a ruthless cutting down and thinning out by more vigorous conquering stocks.

VII

CHANGE AND DECAY IN AMERICANS

A PLAIN TALK TO COLLEGE STUDENTS*

ALTHOUGH I have borrowed in my subject a phrase from a somewhat lugubrious hymn, oftenest sung at funerals, I assure you that I come neither to bury the American people, nor yet to praise them. The word "change" need not imply a shift from better to worse, even to one who is aware of the insidious approach of senile decrepitude to his own organism. Only those who have lost their adaptability with the onset of old age resent *progressive* changes.

It is the established educational custom to subject hapless children to dreary years of the study of the history of their own country, which includes no information whatsoever concerning the biological characteristics of the past or present inhabitants, almost nothing about racial origins and the relation of various national strains to cultural development and change, nothing at all about the development of local physical types and specific forms of culture in the different environments of that country. It is considered sufficient to love "rocks and rills, woods, and templed hills" and to have our hearts with rapture thrill, "like that above" (which is presumably the empty air) at the mere enumeration of geographical features. For the rest, there is the Declaration of Independence, the Louisiana Purchase, that al-

* Delivered to the students of the University of Iowa, June 24, 1938.

ternation of massacre and fraud which is called the Winning of the West, and an endless succession of stupid wars, insignificant politicians, and irrational legislative enactments. History is principally the inaccurate narration of events which ought not to have happened, precipitated by persons who ought to be forgotten, and written by arid pedants who deserve to be condemned to the perpetual torment of reading their own works. This is, of course, willful hyperbole, emitted without restraint in order to throw into bolder relief the stark truth that the memorizing of dates, the recitation of events, and the naming of dead personages teach us very little that contributes to our understanding of the characters and personalities and problems of our ancestors, and nothing at all about the physiques, mentalities, social behavior, and personal crises of ourselves and our contemporaries.

It is the business of the anthropologist to study man himself, and to interpret what man does in terms of relationship to the human organism. I submit that this is "big business," although it does not pay financial dividends which would bloat any bank account. (That, at least, is my experience.) Anthropology, or the study of man, is not a vested interest of education; but if we can only succeed in divesting uneducated educators of their ignorance of the nature of man himself, anthropology will reanimate the mummified tissues of history, transfuse new blood into the anemic circulation of medical science, and awaken mankind to the realization that its future depends not upon New Deals and the promulgation of political and moral platitudes, but upon the maintenance of high qualities in human organisms. Progressive evolution of an animal organism is a biological phenomenon; it is not a product of politics, industry, labor, economics, nor even of medical science. Man, as Bernard Shaw once said, is "only an ape with acquirements"; but that animal can retain its acquirements only if its organism progresses, since organisms are never stationary; there is always change—either improvement or deterioration.

It is my present privilege to address an audience mainly composed of Americans in whom the processes of bodily and mental growth have not yet terminated. The tide of vitality in the male man begins to ebb at twenty-five years of age, and, in the female, somewhat earlier but less rapidly. Mental development lags perhaps a decade behind; its flow and ebb depend, indeed, to some extent upon the growth and decay of the organism, but more upon its quality. In many there is no flood tide of mentality; but only a shallow and muddied pool which gradually evaporates. I assume that none of you is suffering from that premature mental desiccation which results from insufficient natural resources.

You are young; most of you are strong; many of you are beautiful; and some of you are intelligent. In fact, I fear that you do not adequately represent the youth of America, because you are too intelligent. At any rate, I hope so. Now, those of you who are approximately normal in mind and body have intense interests and preoccupations. What are they? If you are weighed down by anxiety concerning your economic present and future, it is the fault of the dull old men who run the world by political chicanery and by specious economic theory and practice, unmindful that man is an animal, with a tendency to become nastier as he ages. If you are entirely absorbed in the study of history, economics, science, literature, or even in the words of wisdom which I emit, you are either abnormal or deluded by false standards of educational value. But I think that you are interested principally in yourself and in each other, because you are primarily human animals and only secondarily cultural beings, and in some even more remote degree students.

What is it in yourself and others which arouses and sustains your natural, healthy interest? It is bodily form and the function of the organism, first in their purely animalistic manifestations, secondly in those less tangible processes which we crudely label with such terms as psychology, emotions, temperament, mentality, and the like. You are, in short, interested in human biology, and in culture only so far as a knowledge and utilization of it enables you to live your animal life to the full, including the reproduction of your own kind, or the procreation of offspring superior to yourselves, who will fulfill an even richer and more abundant biological destiny. Why then do we insistently put the cart before the horse and stuff our young human animals with all sorts of irrelevant knowledge about institutions, things, and abstract ideas, withholding, in prudery or perversion, the few scraps of useful information about man himself, which we have gleaned from centuries of fatuous and wasteful WPA-like education and investigation?

I am going to tell you a little about man, the animal which has forgotten itself, and particularly about some of those millions of the American people who have not been forgotten by presidents, statesmen, educators, scientists, and by themselves, because they have never been known at all. I am going to draw upon our scanty knowledge of the racial and national compositions and characteristics of the early White settlers in these United States, upon our somewhat more ample but still insufficient information about the changes which have taken place in the descendants of these Old Americans. I propose to deal briefly with the newcomers to our country and the modifications in physique which their offspring have undergone. I shall touch also upon the relation of racial and individual physique and heredity to culture and to social behavior, and shall refer to the inseparable association of pathology, degeneration, and crime.

PHYSICAL CHARACTERS OF COLONIAL AMERICANS AS RELATED TO NATIONAL DEVELOPMENT

Since anthropology, as an organized study of man, is not yet eighty years old, there are no contemporary studies of the physical characteristics of early Colonial Americans, except a few scanty data in old records concerning soldiers and sailors, generally limited to height, weight, and color of hair and eyes.

Casual descriptions of the physical appearance of individuals have been scattered through literature, but never to my knowledge assembled and analyzed.

Anthropologists can secure considerable information about the physiques, racial characteristics, age and sex composition, and pathology of extinct peoples by studying their skeletal remains. Unfortunately there is a violent prejudice on the part of our highly civilized population against the digging up of their ancestors by scientists for the purpose of study. There are even laws against this type of activity; and, of course, anthropologists are law-abiding persons. We know incomparably more about the physical and racial characteristics of the ancient North American Indians than about our own ancestors, because the American Indian is much more liberal about these mortuary matters, and further because no consideration has been given to his opinion, whatever it may be. So we have in our museum collections thousands of Indian skeletons recovered from archaeological excavations, but practically none representing the Colonial White population.

Recently there has been completed in Massachusetts a metropolitan water reservoir project which involved the flooding of a certain area and the abandonment of several old towns, together with the removal of their cemeteries. For a number of years we carried on a diplomatic drive to secure permission for a reverent anthropological study of these bones of old New Englanders in the interval between their excavation and reburying, but the authorities dared not allow it. I suppose that the public believes that caliper measurements of the bones of the dead might impede their carnal resurrection. Yet virtually all visitors to the anthropological museum of Harvard University morbidly demand to see the mummies and the shrunken human heads.

My friend Dr. Harry L. Shapiro, of the American Museum of Natural History, was more successful in securing permission to make a very brief study (in the rain) of some Old American skeletal material in New York City, when an ancient burying-ground was being removed in order to extend the rapid transit system. Perhaps the modern inhabitants of New York City feel themselves no more closely related to the Colonial Whites than the rest of us are to the American Indians, and hence are equally indifferent to their chances of resurrection. At any rate, Dr. Shapiro was able to study the remains of some twenty individuals, presumably of mainly British origin with some Dutch admixture, and dating from the eighteenth century.* He found that his series of Old New Yorkers appeared to be "a sampling from a population typified by three seventeenth century London groups and one from the Lowlands of Scotland." The evidence warranted the tentative conclusion that the generalized Colonial type found in New York just prior to the revolution was essentially similar to that of the average Englishman of the period, and that the English immigrants to this country were not a selected group. The mean stature of the Old New York males was about 168.6 centimeters (66.4 inches), which exceeded the London stature by about 3 centimeters. Dr. Gordon T. Bowles, however, has uncovered records of 315 Revolutionary War soldiers from New Hampshire with a mean age of 24.5 years and a mean stature of 172.51 centimeters (67.9 inches); and of 225 Peabody, Massachusetts, seamen, enlisted between the years 1811 and 1815, who had the same average age, but a mean stature of only 169.21 centimeters (66.6 inches).† The general suggestion from these few records is that the Old Americans of the Colonial period were somewhat taller than their English cousins, but otherwise little different. They were considerably shorter than modern Americans of British stock and long residence in this country.

That is about all which can be offered here about the early

* Shapiro, Harry Lionel, "Old New Yorkers. A series of crania from the Nagel Burying Ground, New York City," *American Journal Physical Anthropology*, Vol. 14, No. 3, 1930, pp. 379-404.

† Bowles, Gordon Townsend, *New Types of Old Americans at Harvard*, p. 30. Cambridge, 1932.

Americans except the fact that both Revolutionary soldiers and Peabody seamen seem to have been lighter in complexion, hair color, and eye color, than contemporary Old Americans, if we can trust the historical records. Now, it is perfectly certain that these data are practically nothing in comparison with what can be dug out of existing historical records and cemeteries, if only we are permitted to make investigations. I myself have had one or two chances to peek into tombs of an old Colonial bury-ing-ground near Cambridge, when the cemetery was tidied up for the financial benefit of our unemployed contemporaries. Unfortunately, ancient Cantabridgians do not last well. Their bones are, in fact, nothing but mush. I could go into further detail, but will refrain.

It is possible, of course, to study the records concerning the nationality and provenience of the successive groups of pioneers and immigrants which first settled or subsequently occupied each of the states of our country. Then from the present physical characteristics of these races and nationalities in their home-lands one may reconstruct the probable racial and general phys-ical composition of the Old Americans. However, such a process involves the assumption that, for example, the Ulster Scotch in Tennessee in early Colonial days were physically identical with the same stock in Ireland today. That is merely weaving a web of possibilities.

Now, I do not want to start any epidemic of grave-robbing, but I suggest that if our ancestors have to be dug up in the interest of the enlargement of the Public Utilities—an undoubt-edly sacred cause—anthropologists might at least be allowed to study them.

THE PRESENT OLD AMERICANS

There is a fair amount of information available concerning the physical characteristics of the living population of the United States, although the greater portion of it pertains to school children and to college students rather than to adults. Some extremely valuable material was gathered at the close of the World War in the measurement of troops in process of demobilization. This work was due to the diplomacy and persistence of Dr. Charles B. Davenport, who managed its accomplishment under the utilitarian pretext of getting the range and distribution of uniform sizes for the Quartermaster Department, after the Medical Department of the Army had refused, characteristically, to interest itself in the matter.* Unfortunately, tailor's measurements do not adequately describe a population from the anthropological point of view. Dr. Aleš Hrdlička of the United States National Museum has studied many hundreds of Americans, all of whose parents and grandparents were born in the United States. He calls these "Old Americans" and has written upon them a valuable and fascinating book.† The material which I shall deal with here has been gathered by the Harvard Anthropometric Laboratory. It includes more than 23,000 complete anthropometric records of adults. The larger part of it was gathered in a criminal survey of ten states during the years 1927-1928, but by no means all of the materials of the criminals' survey pertain to criminals, because it is necessary to compare the criminals with law-abiding citizens in order to find out whether they differ from each other in any anthropological way. Also, during the two summers of the Century of Progress Exposition in Chicago, Harvard maintained an anthropometric laboratory in the Hall of Social Sciences and made anthropometric records of some 6,000 adults, including rather more female schoolteachers than are representative of the American Population.

* Davenport, Charles B., and Love, Albert G., *Army Anthropology.* Washington, 1921.
† Hrdlička, Aleš, *The Old Americans.* Baltimore, 1925.

"If our ancestors have to be dug up in the interests of the public utilities, anthropologists might be allowed to study them."

"Racial Types"

First of all, I shall discuss the physical types which are distinguished by taking individual combinations of hair color, eye color, shape of the head, and sometimes also proportions of the nose and stature. I call these types "racial types," because they have been selected to conform to the combinations of hereditary features which are supposed to define the various physical races of the European Whites. It seems probable that the members of a single group with identical or similar combinations of physical characters are more closely related to each other than in general they are to members of other racial type groups. Of course, on account of variation and intermixture, children of the same parents might easily be assigned to several different racial groups, because in mixed families racial characteristics are swapped about and combined in the children in a variety of ways. The data here discussed pertain to adult males, unless females are specified.

The leading American type is Nordic-Mediterranean—longheaded (breadth of head under 80 per cent of its length), with dark hair and mixed or medium-pigmented eyes, or light hair and dark eyes, or red hair and mixed eyes (when stature falls below 170 cm.). We name it Nordic-Mediterranean because the long-headed Nordic race is supposed to have light hair and light eyes, the long-headed Mediterranean race dark hair and dark eyes; and when the two are mixed in matings they are likely to produce long-headed offspring of intermediate or mixed pigmentation. This Nordic-Mediterranean type constitutes about one-fourth of our combined American series, native-born and foreign-born, criminals and civilians, insane and sane, schoolteachers, their pupils, and what have you. This type ranks numerically somewhat higher among criminals than among civilians, and is strongest in native-born of native parentage of whatever series, less well represented in first-generation Americans, and still rarer in the foreign-born. Among the criminals it is especially numerous in Kentucky and North Carolina, and among the Exposition visitors it is perhaps unduly strong in those from the South Atlantic states. This type seems to be predominantly of British ancestry—English, Scotch, Welsh, and Irish. The criminals of the Nordic-Mediterranean group go in very strongly for murder and seem averse to burglary and larceny. They are very poorly educated and are rarely engaged in clerical occupations. On the other hand, the civilians of this type are frequently well schooled. In the Century of Progress series, 64.32 per cent of the men of the Nordic-Mediterranean group have attended college or professional school. In both civilians and criminals this type is particularly found in skilled trades and transportation workers. Of course, if you belong to this extremely common type, there is no implication that you commit murder, drive a truck, come from Kentucky, or have gone to college. It merely means that if the police send out a call for you, giving only these items of physical description, they may drag in a quarter of the whole White population of the United States of appropriate age and sex. The Nordic-Mediterranean type, then, enjoys the safety that is found in numbers.

The second commonest type in Americans is the Nordic-Alpine type. It is round-headed (breadth of head 80 per cent or more of head length). It has a moderately short and broad nose (nose breadth more than 63 per cent of nose length), and has the same mixed combinations of hair color and eye color described in the preceding type. It constitutes 23 per cent of our combined series; in fact, it runs a very close second to the Nordic-Mediterranean type. This Nordic-Alpine type is very strong in Massachusetts among criminals, and among those not yet convicted of felonies it includes myself and many others. It seems to be common in Wisconsin, Tennessee, and Texas, but weak in Kentucky. Among the Century of Progress civilians it is fairly evenly distributed over the various census districts.

The Nordic-Alpine type is not essentially an Old American or British type, although it is not devoid, by any means, of persons of British descent. It has excesses of individuals of Polish-Austrian, Russian, Teutonic, French, and Jewish birth or parentage. Criminologically it is high in robbery and low in burglary and larceny. It is not a rural, farming type, but is often engaged in transportation. In Boston this type leads in public service (mostly policemen and firemen) and in personal service (barbers, waiters, porters, bootblacks, domestic servants, et cetera). It is not common in factory workers, and is rather poorly educated in all of our series.

The third physical type in numerical strength is the one which I call Predominantly Nordic. It constitutes about 17 per cent of our combined series and includes all long-headed near-blonds (persons who do not qualify for "Simon pure" blondness, because their hair is a little off the ash-blond and golden shades, or because their eyes are not pure blue or gray). It probably includes most of the chemical, Hollywood, or platinum varieties of blonds who have the appropriate head shape. This Predominantly Nordic type is most strongly represented among the native-born of Old American ancestry, especially among criminals. Among the ten states studied in the criminal survey, the Predominantly Nordic type is strong in Tennessee, Kentucky, North Carolina, Colorado, and Arizona, but weak in Massachusetts and Wisconsin. In the Century of Progress series it perhaps is disproportionately numerous in the West North Central census district (Minnesota, Iowa, Missouri, North and South Dakota, Nebraska, and Kansas). It also seems largely British and Scandinavian in national origin.

Of the criminal propensities of this Predominantly Nordic type, little need be said except that it is decidedly disinclined to rape, less restrained than average in its indulgence in murder, and highly addicted to forgery, fraud, and bootlegging. In criminals and in Century of Progress civilians this type is particularly engaged in extractive occupations (farming, cattle-raising, mining) and in the cities it goes in for clerical work, skilled trades, and the professions. It includes few personal servants and unskilled laborers, and is about third or fourth of nine types in educational attainment. Among the exposition visitors it is only sixth in percentage of college men.

The fourth type is called Dinaric, from its European concentration in the Dinaric Alps. It is a round-headed, long narrow-nosed type, with a great many pigment combinations, mostly of the mixed varieties of hair color and eye color. It perhaps ought to be broken up into a number of subtypes. It comprises 13.3 per cent of our combined male series, but ranges from 11 to 23 per cent in the various different series of criminals and civilians, being particularly common in the civilian Bostonians of recent foreign extraction. On the whole, this group tends to be derived from the foreign-born and the native-born of foreign parentage. In the criminal series it is especially common in Massachusetts and Wisconsin, and rare in the Central Mountain and southeastern states. Polish-Austrian, French, Teutonic, Scotch, and Near Eastern extractions are typical of this Dinaric group.

Among criminals this type ranks second in forgery and fraud, in rape and in bootlegging. It seems little interested in other felonious pursuits. Criminals of this type seem mainly urban in residence and rank first in clerical and semiprofessional occupations, second in the professions and in public service, third in skilled trades. Manual laborers are few. The civilian ranking in occupation is similar in the Century of Progress series, but lower in the Boston civilian samples, which are composed largely of recent European immigrants. This Dinaric group is the best-educated criminal type, but varies greatly among the civilians, being the most poorly educated in Boston and fourth in the Century of Progress series. These round-headed, long and big-nosed men are rarely found among the Old Americans, and in the rural districts, but are common enough in jail.

The Keltic type is fifth in our combined series of males, with 8.48 per cent of the series. All of its members have long heads and either red or reddish hair with blue eyes, or dark hair with blue eyes. It is more common among criminals than among civilians, and much commoner in the older American stocks than in the foreign-born. It seems to occur especially in the eastern and southeastern states, and is largely of Irish and Scandinavian extraction. These Keltics are especially prone to commit assault with intent to do bodily harm, burglary, larceny, bootlegging, and sex offenses except rape. They appear to refrain from armed robbery. In the country they farm; in the city they go into public service and more skilled occupations. The Boston Keltic civilians are mostly Irish and are second in educational rank, as against sixth among the criminals of Keltic type.

The Pure Mediterranean type with long heads, dark eyes, and dark hair, ranks sixth of nine types, with only 4.38 per cent of the males of the combined series. In the Boston civilian series it is largely of foreign birth, but in the Century of Progress visitors it is found also among Old Americans and is probably taller and in other respects physically somewhat different. Among the criminals it is a type found excessively in Massachusetts, Colorado, and New Mexico. In the Century of Progress series it is common in the Middle Atlantic and East North Central districts, but rare in the West North Central district. The criminals of this type are largely of Portuguese, Spanish, and Italian descent. These criminals rank first in second degree murder, first in rape, second in assault and robbery, and third in first degree murder. They are low in most other offenses—last in burglary and larceny and next to last in forgery and fraud. I suppose that such crimes seem dull and tame to these hot-bloods. The Pure Mediterranean criminals are largely urban and rank high in unskilled laborers and personal servants, but low in education. The Century of Progress civilians of this type and the Boston civilians are better educated and higher in occupational status. One could make a good guess from the physical characteristics of a person of this description as to the kind of crime he may commit, the category of occupation to which he may belong, and even of his national origin.

The East Baltic type consists of all round-heads who are pure blonds and have relatively short and broad noses (nasal breadth 63 per cent or more of nasal length). This type is found in only 3 per cent of our male series and is commoner among civilians than among criminals. It occurs among Old Americans; and, in those of more recent European derivation, it is represented particularly in Teutonic, Russian, and Polish-Austrian strains. Undoubtedly it is most common among Finns and other East Baltic stocks, but very few of these happen to be included in any of our series. In the Century of Progress series this type is outstanding among natives of the West North Central census district and possibly among those of the Pacific and Mountain districts.

East Baltic types of criminals are very youthful and notable for their celibacy. They rank very high in burglary and larceny, and very low in every other offense except rape. This type, among criminals, is especially engaged in trade, but is also high in factory workers and unskilled laborers. It is found particularly in cities and is well educated. However, in none of the series does it include many professional men, perhaps on account of its tender age.

The Alpine type includes round-headed men with dark hair and dark eyes and relatively broad noses (nose breadth 63 per cent or more of nose length). It is found in only 2.68 per cent of our total male series. This is essentially a foreign-born type, or native-born of foreign parentage. It is very rare in all native Whites of native parentage. It occurs most frequently in the states which have received recent foreign immigrants. The Alpine type has its greatest ethnic representation among Italians, but is also strong in French Canadians, Balkan peoples, Spanish, Portuguese, Polish-Austrians, and those of Near Eastern descent. Very few of this type occurred in the sample of visitors to the anthropometric laboratory in the Century of Progress Exposition. Among criminals this Alpine group leads in robbery, and is last in forgery and fraud. It is high in assault, low in murder and rape, but high in sex offenses other than rape. In the criminals it is an urban type, high in unskilled laborers, but first in professional men and in personal service. Since it is the most poorly educated type in criminals and in Boston civilians, but in the Century of Progress series the highest in college-trained men, it seems to have been drawn from both the lowest and the upper ranks of the urban population. It is of some interest, but possibly of no significance, that the physical type which, in its antisocial exponents, specializes in robbery, should show, in prosocial activities, a preference for law and medicine.

The Pure Nordic type is the rarest in our population, with only 2.44 per cent of the total males. It is characterized by long heads, ash-blond or golden hair, and pure blue or pure gray eyes. It is a great deal more common among civilians than among criminals and is a strongly Old American type. Foreign antecedents when traceable are usually British or Scandinavian. Among the criminals it occurs excessively in New Mexico, Kentucky, and Colorado. Among civilians of the Century of Progress series, it is strongest in the West North Central census area. This is a very youthful and celibate type among convicts, and a very gentle, peaceable type, since it is last in murder, assault, robbery with violence, and next to last in sex offenses other than rape. But it is an easy leader in forgery and fraud, and a close second in burglary and larceny. Thus the virile Nordics specialize in the surreptitious and sneaky offenses. The Pure Nordic type, whether criminal or civilian, ranks first in the extractive occupations (farming, cattle-breeding, mining). In the city it apparently engages in clerical occupations, skilled trades, and transportation. It seems to be almost devoid of professional men, and is somewhat above the average in education.

I have said nothing about the American females in this sketch

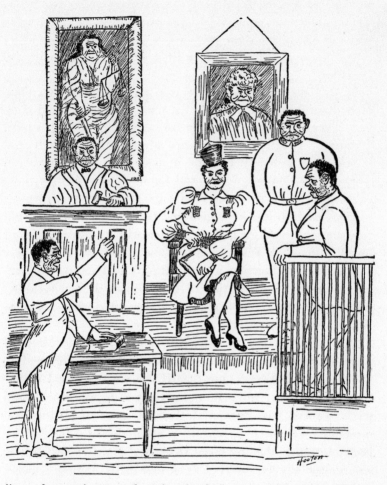

"... of some interest that the physical type which specializes in robbery should, in prosocial activities, show preference for the law."

of racial types. In the criminal series there are too few women to consider and in the Century of Progress series too many. They fall into the same racial types as the men, and these types occur in nearly the same proportions, but include a few more round-heads, and are perhaps a little darker in hair color and eye color.

Now, I do not wish to give you the impression that these nine physical types are exactly the same in criminals and civilians. They are found roughly in the same order of proportional frequency, but the criminals are always much shorter and lighter, and generally inferior in body size to the civilians. They are also more ignorant and far lower down in the occupational scale. I have every reason for supposing that they are in general much less intelligent and represent, in each physical type, those selected for biological inferiority, or those depressed by an unfavorable environment, or more probably both. There is a vicious conjunction of bad heredity and unfavorable environment in the production of the criminal. It is notoriously difficult to make a silk purse out of a sow's ear, but it is impossible to do it in a pigsty.

If your physical type conforms to our Pure Nordic combination, you need not conclude that you are condemned to bookkeeping or forgery; nor that, if you are a Nordic Mediterranean, your marriage mate may expect to be murdered. Each physical racial type certainly includes a range of abilities and disabilities in individuals which is determined by familial inheritance rather than by racial stock, and limited somewhat by environmental opportunity. I think that there is ample evidence for the supposition that with racial physical type are associated certain temperaments and sociological tendencies, but there is no such thing as racial predestination to success or failure, genius or mediocrity, at least in a truly democratic country. There is no reason, other than an aesthetic one, for gentlemen to prefer blonds, unless gentlemen are particularly interested in the achievements of modern chemistry. Kissing and choosing racial types are alike a matter of individual tastes, for which notoriously there is no accounting.

State Types

I am now going to tell you a little about the development of state physical types in our native White Americans of native parentage who are largely of remotely British ancestry, with here and there considerable strains of German admixture. In 1927 I began a study of the anthropological characteristics of criminals of ten selected states (Massachusetts, North Carolina, Kentucky, Tennessee, Wisconsin, Missouri, Texas, Colorado, New Mexico, and Arizona). It was thought that these states would afford adequate samples of all the races and nationalities represented in the United States. I assumed that the native White stock of native parentage could be treated as a single anthropological group, irrespective of state of incarceration, residence, or birth, because I knew this stock to have been derived principally from English, Welsh, Scotch, Irish, and German ancestry. After an enormous amount of data had been gathered and analyzed and the manuscript of one ponderous volume had been virtually completed, I awoke to the realization of a palpable Ethiopian in the nicely stacked woodpile. For I had divided up my native Whites of native parentage into groups according to the types of crimes that they had committed, in order to ascertain the presence or absence of offense of physical types, and I found that my first degree murder subgroup was not only physically distinct, but also crammed with Kentucky and Tennessee criminals. So I began to suspect that I had not isolated a murderer type, but only a hill-billy type addicted to that pastime. Therefore, with extreme reluctance and moderate blasphemy, I tore the entire series apart and reanalyzed it by separate states—lumping, however, Colorado, Arizona, and New Mexico. (Missouri was not included in the study of White criminals, because the Missouri prison authorities became tired of my field-worker before he had finished studying the Negro criminals.)

The result of this reanalysis was to establish the fact that the older American population of this country has differentiated into distinct state physical types. I shall give you a few samples illustrating how the Old American criminals of various states are distinguishable in anthropological and sociological features.

Massachusetts native-born criminals of native parentage differ significantly from total criminals in 25 of 33 measured characters. They are the second shortest, the lightest, the narrowest in shoulder and chest, the smallest in sitting height and in face breadth of all state groups. They have relatively the longest and narrowest faces and are the second youngest. They are also notable in qualitative characters: for thick beards, red-brown hair, certain shades of eye color, external and median folds of the upper eyelids, broad, high noses with concave profiles and thick tips, nasal septa skewed to the right, thin upper and thick lower lips, facial protrusion, pointed chins, bad teeth, poorly developed ear lobes, and lopsided faces—not to mention other peculiarities.

Texas has 28 dependable metric divergences from the total series of native White American criminals of native parentage. The Texans are tallest, heaviest, and attain the maximum in face breadth and nose breadth. They have relatively the shortest and broadest faces of all of these criminals. They are also remarkable for heavy beard and body hair; excess of red hair, red-brown, and black hair; gray-brown eyes, thick and depressed nasal tips, square chins, pronounced cheekbones, full cheeks, upper front teeth biting in front of the lowers, hollow temples, long ear lobes, and many other features.

Wisconsin criminals are the oldest, the shortest, the second lightest, and have the broadest heads, the longest upper faces, the longest and narrowest noses, and the greatest sitting height relative to stature. They are not only distinguished by heavy beards but by sparse body hair, straight hair, with frequency of dark brown and gray or white hair color, blue-gray and dark brown eyes, vertical foreheads, narrow nasal bridges with thin tips, and nasal septa frequently skewed, thin lips, pointed chins, loss of many teeth, presence of Darwin's point (remnant of the free tip of the animal ear), and other anatomical minutiae.

We cannot labor through an anthropological catalogue of the distinctive features of more state types. These examples must suffice. They show that several generations of residence within a state environment have worked upon the original national and racial strains which compose the population of that state, to produce by inbreeding and selection anthropological state types which are peculiar and recognizable. With these physical types are associated occupational and other sociological tendencies, doubtless due in part to the climate and natural resources of the state, but also dependent upon the physical and racial constitution of the people who have differentiated through residence in that state. There are vast differences between the criminals of the several states in education, occupation, prevalent offense, and in nearly every character investigated. Ranked on a ratio which divides the proportion of well-educated men by those who have had no education at all, Massachusetts criminals are 149 times as well educated as those from Kentucky, and Wisconsin criminals 81 times better schooled than those from North Carolina. First degree murder is an offense group packed with Kentuckians; offenses against public welfare (mostly bootlegging) are overloaded with Texans; rape and other sex offenses are the favorite crimes in my own natal state, Wisconsin. Now, of course, there are environmental factors which are involved in the determination of the sociological idiosyncrasies of any state, but certainly the constitutional proclivities of the native inhabitants should not be overlooked in the appraisal of behavior. I can see no present prospect of persuading stultified social scientists that they must study and understand the variations of the human organism which produces behavior before they can interpret that behavior, but I shall continue to insist that you must know people before you can intelligently reform their institutions.

CHANGES IN BODILY FORM OF THE OLD AMERICANS

Perhaps the most publicized of information on the physical characteristics of the American population pertains to the steady increase in size of college students observed during the past few decades. The physical examinations of entering classes almost invariably include height and weight, and the observation that these dimensions have increased substantially in the respective clienteles of Vassar, Stanford, Minnesota, or some other institution, evokes vast enthusiasm, presumably on the assumption that the bigger the dinosaur eggs the better. Let us examine this pleasing phenomenon—with, of course, the optimistic expectation that we shall uncover evidence of progressive evolution.

I shall use for this purpose the data compiled and analyzed by Dr. Gordon Bowles relating to Harvard students and to the attendants at certain eastern women's colleges. My choice is not due to provincialism, acquired during a quarter-century's acclimitization in New England, but rather to the genetic continuity of the older eastern college populations. Most data on physical changes in college students merely deal with successive generations composed of individuals who may be unrelated to the earlier groups studied in the same institutions. However, in the possibly effete East, owing to considerations of family tradition, social prestige, loyalty, or sheer inertia, parents commonly send their offspring, or try to send them, to the educational institutions which they themselves have graced or disgraced. Thus Bowles was able to study in the records of the Harvard gymnasium the measurements of Harvard sons, those of their fathers taken at the same ages, and, in a fair number of cases, those of their grandfathers—the bearded undergraduates of the seventies and eighties. I remember during the first year

of my teaching at Harvard my surprise at the pride with which
an undergraduate told me that he represented the sixth generation of Harvard men in his family, and his astonishment when
I remarked that he must find it very monotonous. At Vassar,
Wellesley, Smith, and Mount Holyoke colleges, Dr. Bowles
was able to secure physical data upon large samples of mothers
and daughters, but these institutions were in 1930 too young to
have accommodated the grandmothers of the period when
literacy was not ladylike.

It is, of course, unfortunate that the genetic continuity of the
material presented in these studies is confined to one or other
side of the family. The Harvard lines are exclusively patrilineal,
and the physical descent of the women is reckoned only matri-
lineally. Thus the pedigrees contain 50 per cent of dark horses
or night mares, as the case may be.

We may first deal with the men of Harvard. Increase in body
size has been steady for the past three generations. Sons have
increased 3½ centimeters in stature over their fathers, and
more than 10 pounds in weight. The filial increase is greatest in
the leg length, especially in the thigh; next in the trunk, especially in the lower segment. The increase in arm length of the
sons is greater in the forearm than in the upper arm. The hips
have increased in girth but diminished in breadth, and the upper
sections of trunk and extremities have increased in circumference more than the lower. Head breadth has decreased, and head
length has probably increased by way of compensation—a phenomenon expected with greater stature. When stature increases,
the volume of the brain usually does not grow proportionately
and the head becomes longer relative to its breadth. Economy
requires a spherical receptacle for the brains, but if the body
length is long, the skull length is likely to be great and there is
no need of distending the skull breadth by the bulge of excess
brains. An egg-shaped container then does nicely. The skull fits
the brain and the latter does not rattle round in a partial void,
however hard to believe it may be in certain individual cases.

Generally speaking, the proportional increase of son's measurements over father's is about 2 per cent. There are suggestions also that the sons have darker hair, but lighter eyes, than their fathers.

In the case of the girls similar increases over maternal measurements may be noted. The total increment of daughter stature is 2.93 centimeters, and of weight about 4 pounds. The daughters are more slender than their mothers, since breadth measurements have increased very slightly (with actual decrease in breadth of hips) in proportion to length and circumferences. Daughters have bigger chest girths and lung capacities than their mothers, possibly because of the obsolescence of the hourglass figure. The girls have been emancipated from the wasplike waist, artificially produced in their mothers by patient husbands tugging at the lacings of rigid corsets reinforced with steel and whalebone. The girls have much narrower hips than their mothers and about the same shoulder breadth. But hip and arm girth have increased. Unfortunately, measurements of the lower extremities seem not to have been included in the college daughters, though amply represented in the maternal data. This omission may be the result of decreased interest in an appendage previously concealed but now abundantly visible, although more probably it is due to the decline of anthropometry in educational institutions, owing to the increasing influence of the medical profession in physical education. My particular regret is for the absence of any basis of comparison between the size of feet of mothers and daughters, since it seems probable that this member has shown a phenomenal growth in the younger generation of American females.

Changes in the males and females have been much the same. Stature has increased; weight has increased; but pelvic breadth has decreased, although fleshy deposits in this region have not diminished. While shoulder breadth has become greater in both sexes, this increment has been at the sacrifice of chest depth, since in both sexes chest expansion has decreased. The young

1910　　　　　*1939*

"As the education of women has become broader, their figures have become narrower."

women of today, in comparison with the men, have become proportionately smaller in most measurements. While relative stature has remained about the same, there has been a 3 per cent drop in female weight relative to male weight, and a very signal loss in breadth of hips. The hip breadth of today's young women is much less relative to that of their potential mates than was the case in their parental generation. However, the modern girl has a waist considerably larger relative to the male waist girth than her mother had. Perhaps this increase may be correlated with the elongation of the arm in the younger male generation.

On the whole, differences between measurements of the males and females have apparently increased. As the education of women has become broader, their figures have become narrower. There is a suggestion, nevertheless, that in their narrower hips, bigger waists, broader shoulders, and more elongated legs, the females of today are converging somewhat upon the masculine type of body build. This reminds me of the possibly apocryphal tale which is related of Sir Arthur Keith, the famous British anthropologist, on an occasion when he was addressing an audience of workingmen in London on the subject of the Future Man. Sir Arthur is alleged to have declared, "Between the man and the woman of the future there will be but little difference." Whereupon some ribald soul from the gallery shouted, "Three cheers for that little difference!"

CHANGES IN THE BODILY FORM OF THE NEW AMERICANS

Many years ago Professor Franz Boas announced changes in the bodily form of children born in this country to immigrant parents. In many instances the progeny were considerably taller than their parents. If the parents belonged to very round-headed stocks, the cephalic index was likely to diminish somewhat in the offspring native to America, and *vice versa*. A considerable number of correlated changes were noted. These findings aroused a storm of controversy which has not yet died down. Professor Boas did not commit himself definitely to any causal interpretation, although he ruled out illegitimacy and the effect of abandoning the practice of flattening the back of the head caused by certain methods of cradling babies in some of the very round-headed peoples of Europe and the Near East. He seemed, on the whole, to favor the idea that it was the radical change in environment which brought about this moderate or marked alteration in the physique of first-generation Americans.

The Harvard Criminal Survey has yielded data bearing upon this subject, since the American-born of certain nationalities can be compared with the foreign-born of the same national origin. For this purpose we can utilize paired groups of criminals, including British (English, Scotch, Welsh, and British Canadian), Scandinavian, Irish, Teutonic, French (mostly French Canadian), Mexican-Portuguese, Italian, Polish-Austrian, and a somewhat composite pair of eastern European and Near Eastern peoples. We may select one of these nine pairs of groups to exemplify here the changes which the American-born exhibit when compared with the foreign-born.

The American-born Teutonic group differs significantly from its foreign-born cousins in 6 of 25 measurements and in 7 of 16 indices (or ratios of one bodily measurement to another). The Americans are younger, taller, narrower in head and face, shorter in nose and ear, more long-headed; have narrower faces relative to their head breadth, proportionately longer and narrow faces, broader foreheads relative to face breadth, and relatively narrower jaws.

The general trend of changes of the native-born from the foreign-born can be ascertained by noting the number of times the same alterations occur in the nine different ethnic pairs. All of the nine native-born groups are younger than the foreign-born (which is, of course, a circumstance and not a change); five of the nine native-born groups are taller; seven have shallower chests; five have narrower faces; six have narrower noses; five have shorter ears; seven have relatively narrower shoulders; five have diminished sitting height; five have narrower faces relative to head breadth; five have longer faces relative to face breadth; and five have broader foreheads relative to face breadth. The British Americans are undifferentiated from the foreign-born of the same stock; and the Irish, Scandinavian, and French have changed only slightly. The other five pairs of groups deviate widely, each from its foreign-born mate.

These changes in the native-born of immigrant parents are apparently virtually the same as those which the Old Americans of the present generation manifest in comparison with their parents, the latter also born in this country. Hence the modifications of the first-generation Americans cannot be ascribed merely to the fact that their parents have emigrated from Europe or from some other region to the United States.

There are also certain morphological changes (changes in form of nonmeasurable features) which seem to take place consistently in the American-born of foreign parentage when they are compared with the foreign-born of the same nationality. I shall mention only a few of these. In the New Americans there are fewer sloping foreheads, less depression of the nasal root, narrower and higher noses, thinner integumental lips (the part of the mouth covered by the mustache or the goatee), less facial protrusion, less prominence of cheekbones and jaw angles, fewer "buck teeth," or pronounced overbites, fewer Darwin's points on the ear, less lopsidedness, or asymmetry, of the face. One gains the impression that the squat build of the parent, associated with a broad short face, has been transformed into a more weedy, linear body type, in which horizontal dimensions have been compressed and vertical diameters stretched. These changes are probably not confined to the peoples of the United States, since similar increases of stature have been observed also in several countries of Europe and even in Japan.

It is now pertinent to inquire whether these bodily modifications of the younger generation constitute an evolutionary improvement or the reverse. Very few observers have raised this point seriously, and the public seems to assume with fatuous optimism that animals which are bigger are, as a matter of course, also better. One may as well argue that big mistakes are preferable to small mistakes. My own opinion is that the trend of these variations is, on the whole, unfavorable. I think that these big-footed, long-shanked individuals with short torsos, flat chests, narrow pelves, pinched noses, and lantern jaws are probably constitutionally inferior to their broader, shorter, and more compact parents. Since the study of body build in relation to health and disease has not progressed very far as yet, these impressions have not been scientifically verified so that they can be stated as facts. Some of the medical profession and some physical anthropologists have begun to awaken to the importance of investigating the relation of body type to pathology, to psychology, and to social behavior. But most are still sound asleep and snoring, with their eyes closed, their ears closed, and their minds closed, but with their mouths open.

Perhaps if the medical profession knew more of the evolutionary and biological implications of these common changes in the body build of recent generations, it would be less ready to arrogate to itself the credit and responsibility for these modern somatic trends. As it is, one has only to mention the fact that children are outgrowing their parents to evoke from the physician a complacent smile, an expansion of the chest, and a patronizing remark that it is all on account of improved methods of infant care, modern sanitation and hygiene, vitamins, orange juice, and spinach. This recalls the immortal remark in the *New Yorker,* of the modern child who refuses to eat broccoli: "I say that it's spinach, and I say, to hell with it!"

If medicine, particularly the specialty of pediatrics, is to take the credit for this rank overgrowth of youth, it must also accept in part the responsibility for the proliferation of dental decay and malocclusions, which are caused in part by unbal-

anced artificial diets. We of the older generation, who break-
fasted on oatmeal, beefsteak, and fried potatoes, walked to
school on our stumpy legs, studied Greek, Latin, and mathe-
matics, or accepted upon our more ample posteriors the painful
penalties of not studying, and then walked home again, and
were licked by our parents for having been licked at school.
But we could usually get a draught through our noses, and
were as innocent of adenoids as the modern youngster is of
Greek roots. Some of our teeth had holes in them and ached;
but, as the darkey said, whom someone pitied because he had
only two teeth, "Bress de Lawd, dey *hit!*" Now the attenuated
pupil is chauffered to school by his long-suffering mother, while
he slumps upon his meager buttocks and cramps his elongated
shanks between the seats of the machine which has superseded
pedal locomotion. In school he is offered learning, but no lick-
ing; he is allowed to develop an untrammeled personality. But
his teeth are restrained by wire bands, and he has to wear elas-
tics to help him keep his mouth shut. He loses his tonsils and
his adenoids before he loses his milk teeth, and wears spectacles
before he wears pants.

I cannot cite statistics here to prove that dental caries (tooth
decay) and dental malocclusion (crooked and distorted growth
of the teeth) have greatly increased among the populations
of the United States during the past two generations, but I do
not know any careful dental student or practitioner who
doubts this to be the case. Dr. Weston Price, of Cleveland, has
collected information pertaining to many races over the world
which suggests that increase of dental caries, malocclusions of
the teeth, facial pinching and elongation, and other defects are
brought about in large measure by the adoption of a civilized
but stupid diet of processed, manufactured foods too high in
energy-producing materials and too low in bone- and tissue-
forming constituents. In many primitive peoples Dr. Price has
been able to show a horrible change from the well-developed
faces, perfect dental arches, and sound teeth of the parents

Going to School 1900—1939

raised upon primitive diets to the unfortunate offspring who have acquired, coincidently with store food, rotten teeth so irregularly and crookedly erupted that they are scarcely usable, set in obviously malformed faces, and often accompanied by other bodily defects. Of course, these distressing conditions are not to be charged to the account of the medical profession, and they are not necessarily associated with the changes in body build which I have described. But it is very reckless to assume that modernization in bodily build is attributable to better environmental conditions and superior medical care without first making sure that these bodily modifications are accompanied by a general improvement in health and a decrease in the incidence of bodily defects.

I have suggested on a number of occasions that increase in the proportion of the population which is tall and narrow may be due indeed to the well-intentioned and skillful activities of the medical profession in reducing infant mortality. According to this theory, the long, skinny babies are constitutionally inferior to those of shorter, more compact build. Under the old crude conditions hordes of these weedy infants were eliminated early in life by the process which is called natural selection. Now, by artificial feeding and the extension and application of medical knowledge, many of them are saved to grow to excessive stature at maturity and to acquire, with their long legs, flat feet, varicose veins, and haemorrhoids. However, I cannot offer any proof of this theory, which may be quite wrong.

Actually, the steady increase of stature and the transformation in body build have been going on for much too long a time to be ascribed to the comparatively recent and still-limited extension of modern medical care to the populations affected. Some of the tallest stocks in this country live in areas where diet is insufficient and veritably atrocious, and where doctors are almost nonexistent, but many kinds of constitutional and infectious diseases run riot. These southern mountaineers have evidently grown tall and thin, not through the benefits of medicine, but through sheer hereditary cussedness. There are some reasons for believing that in areas and countries unaffected by so-called modern civilization, including especially indiscriminate diets of manufactured foods and advanced medical care, stature and body build have not undergone any marked change in recent times. The old equilibrium, established as a resultant of hereditary tendencies and a stabilized environment, whether favorable or unfavorable, has been maintained. Peoples in these benighted areas tend to be short and broad, or tall and thin, or medium in build, as they have been for centuries. Whether there are general evolutionary trends of body build or pendulumlike oscillations occurring in cycles, I am unable to say. However, it is possible to state unequivocally that no steady rise in stature has been observed as a general phenomenon in the races of man from the end of the glacial period, perhaps twenty thousands of years ago, up to now. I cannot point to any bodily feature in man which, within that considerable span of years, can be declared to show evolutionary change for the better.

In point of fact, if we are on the road which leads to physical deterioration and eventual extinction, it is not yet too late to turn back. In any case we can doubtless shuffle along on our flat feet for many thousands of years, and transmit our weakened organic tendencies to generations of unborn offspring destined to live their lives in an atmosphere of organic decay. But no doubt they will be convinced, as each generation is convinced, of their general and specific superiority to all of their predecessors and to their immediate successors. Hope springs eternal in the human breast even if the latter is completely flat; and the appetite for living is large, although the alimentary canal may be far advanced in morbidity.

Really, the only reason for worrying about man's physical status is that it affects his mentality and his intelligence. It does not matter one whit whether you lack wisdom teeth if you only possess wisdom. But if your wisdom teeth are impacted, that physical disturbance creates an impact upon your mind. If you cannot digest food in your stomach, you cannot assimilate food for thought. I think it may be said that for many thousands of years man's mind has outstripped his body in evolutionary advance, and brain evolution has proceeded at the expense of a symmetrical and healthy development of other organs of the body. But man has "got by" with a makeshift body, because of the keenness of his mind, which has grown partly through hereditary momentum, but largely through active function. Yet natural selection, on the physical side, has always established a lower boundary of organic fitness beyond which the human creature cannot descend and live.

Now, there are many artificial conditions of civilization, which we call benefits, most of which tend to foster, preserve, and perpetuate those weak and unfit in body and in mind. The mentally and the physically incapable breed like rabbits, and cannot be exterminated as mere animal pests, because we have developed certain humanitarian principles by which we must abide, and according to which we must act, if we do not wish to revert to the tooth-and-nail struggle for survival whereby man emerged from apedom. Evidently we must support, tolerate, and shelter the economic, social, and mental ineffectuals until we can learn to eliminate them by some method less drastic than massacre or starvation.

Science cannot, as yet, suggest any practicable means of halting physical decline with its horrible concomitant of mental deterioration. Sterilization and birth control might help a little, but neither is altogether efficient nor entirely practicable for the attainment of the ends we seek—the production of human types which are better in mind and body. There is but one clear course indicated—the immediate and intensive study of human biology in its relation to human behavior. We cannot legislate ourselves into evolutionary progress, nor hope to perfect social institutions which will be operated satisfactorily by an unintelligent population. The millennium for morons is here, but not even the morons enjoy it.

We undoubtedly know a great deal about our culture, but we know very little about ourselves. There exist no substantial fund of accurate knowledge concerning the precise effects of physical environment upon man, and almost nothing at all is known of human heredity. Animal husbandmen know that they can improve their stocks by breeding and by feeding. But the better animals must be bred before they can be fed. I am utterly convinced that education has built its house upon the sand, when it has concentrated upon the social sciences, the humanities, and the physical sciences, leaving general biology to concern itself exclusively with lower animals, and medical science to preoccupy itself with human diseases, but not with man.

What the world must know, and what your generation must find out and teach to it, is the organic basis of human behavior. It is your task and that of your successors to discover man's animal organism, not only in its structure, in its functions, and in its manner of reproduction, but in the correlates of these aspects with the life of the individual animal in society. I would make biology a basic part of elementary education and lay in the earlier years of schooling a foundation for the comprehension of man's organic variation as it relates to his culture. The higher education could then be devoted to the very utiliarian problem of fitting each type of the varying human organism to the cultural task for which it is best adapted and to the far more difficult and important problem of finding out how to breed better men. Let us stop this futile tinkering with moribund social institutions. In so doing we treat the symptom and not the cause. When better human institutions are built, better men will build them.

VIII

NOSES, KNOWLEDGE, AND NOSTALGIA—THE MARKS OF A CHOSEN PEOPLE

HISTORY OF THE AUTHOR'S RELATIONS WITH JEWS

BECAUSE MY father was a Methodist minister, I was brought up in a considerable number of Wisconsin small towns. We had plenty of contacts with Germans, Swedes, Norwegians, and Czechs (usually then called Bohemians), because we attended the public schools. No one went to private schools except the incorrigible sons of the rich, who were frequently committed to military academies. In my boyhood and youth I scarcely recall knowing anyone as a Jew. The German Jews were generally undistinguished from the rest of the population of Germanic origin. There were a few Jews, probably of Polish or Russian origin, who were junk dealers or peddlers; and I think that when we identified Jews at all, it was by the practice of these occupations. Of course we read the *Merchant of Venice* in high school, and it always seemed to me that Shylock was the recipient of a particularly dirty deal. I could reconcile the approbation of the treatment which he received from that female shyster, Portia, only by reflecting that, after all, the characters of the play were mostly Italians. I had a very thorough education in the Bible, not only because I was compelled to attend every religious service which was held in the church, but also because I used to read the juicier bits of the Bible when I was

227

supposed to be listening to my father's sermons. One of the things which used to puzzle me as a child was the fact that we were taught to regard the children of Israel as a wholly magnificent people up to the time of the birth of Christ, and thereafter as a thoroughly ornery lot. My mother got round this by explaining that the Jews were not really bad at heart, but were dominated by the Pharisees, a group of religious snobs who prayed on the street corners instead of going into their closets. This really did not clarify matters very much, since my father prayed all over the place, mostly *coram publico;* and, what was worse, he forced us to do likewise. I also had a sneaking sympathy for the Sadducees because I always thought one of them got decidedly the better of Jesus in a certain argument. Perhaps you remember that the Sadducees did not believe in the resurrection, and one of them asked Christ whose wife a woman would be at the resurrection if she had married successively seven brothers. He replied that those who get to heaven "neither marry nor are given in marriage." This seemed to me the most pitiful kind of an evasion, although reported in the King James Version under the chapter subheading "He confuteth the Sadducees." On the whole, I was not brought up to hate Jews; and, in point of fact, I did not know any, or did not know that I knew any.

Even in the pre-war days at Oxford we were pretty generally blissfully ignorant of the presence of Jews. Most of the English Jews were thoroughly assimilated and unrecognizable. They talked with the same adenoidal public-school accent and guffawed as loudly over the "frightfully amusing" jokes in *Punch* as did the undergraduates of simple faith and Norman blood. It was not until I began to teach at Harvard that I really encountered the Jewish question.

There was a sufficient number of Jewish boys attending Harvard before the war so that they formed a distinguishable group. Since most of them lived in Greater Boston and commuted, they had restricted opportunities for participating in undergraduate activities. After the war there seemed to be a considerable rise in the proportion of Jewish students, and there was some discussion as to the desirability of establishing a quota. The great majority of the faculty was strongly opposed to any such action, and the matter was dropped. I remember walking home from a faculty meeting with Leo Wiener, the famous professor of Slavic languages, after a session in which the limitation of Jewish students had been discussed. Professor Wiener, who was of Russian origin, remarked that he had never really made up his mind whether or not he was a Jew, because he had been persecuted by Jews and Gentiles alike. I began to feel more or less that way about it myself recently after I had written an article about the Jews for one of our national weeklies.

A good many Jewish undergraduates were usually enrolled in my courses in anthropology, especially those dealing with physical anthropology, race mixture, and criminal anthropology. Perhaps the greater number of these were intending to enter the medical profession. Anthropology in most of its branches is a field which has aroused the active interest of American Jews, and a high proportion of the leading anthropologists of the country were and are of Jewish or partially Jewish origin. Most of these were not Harvard-trained, because Harvard anthropology specialized in American archaeology, whereas linguistics and ethnology were the branches most favored by Jewish students. However, I was impressed early in my teaching career by the frequency with which Jewish names appeared among the lists of the higher-ranking students of my courses. I have always found it difficult not to like students who are keen upon the subject which is my life work and who are extraordinarily able in that subject. I received a great deal of inspiration and encouragement in those early days from Jewish students who did not choose anthropology as a gentlemanly field of concentration, but really believed it to be worth studying and put their backs into it. Yet the Jews in anthropological courses at Harvard constituted a small minority, and we had plenty of brilliant

non-Jewish students. I never had to like Jews because they were
the only students who would listen to my lectures. In any event,
the person who categorizes his likes and dislikes by ethnic or
racial groups is indiscriminating and stupid.

I do not pretend to have had any extensive experience in the
world of commerce and industry or in any walks of life other
than those which may be called academic, professional, or scientific. But I suspect that the same frailties and the same virtues
are distributed throughout all the social and occupational ranks.
It is quite incredible to me that the honesty, dependability, and
loyalty which I have found in my Jewish colleagues and students
is peculiar to Jews of any particular social or economic class.

I do not aspire to champion any group, however virtuous and
oppressed it may be. I have written and talked about the Jews
because their problem is in part anthropological and I am an
anthropologist. What I have written about them here and elsewhere has won approbation neither from the Jews nor from the
Gentiles. I receive many letters from unsolicited correspondents,
frequently abusive, generally condemnatory, and rarely approv-
ing. One whole-hearted anti-Semitist from Minnesota wrote me
that he had read my book *Up from the Ape* when he was at the
University, and had supposed that I was a respectable if not
intelligent anthropologist; but now he realized that I had sold
out to the Jews. He ended his epistle with the not altogether
original reflection that "every man has his price." However
low my price may be, I must admit that I have had no Jewish
bidders.

For some reason or other, people have the same attitude toward supposed racial mixture as toward syphilis. We have to
pretend that no one whom we know has it. In the course of the
history of the Jewish people a considerable proportion of their
racial blend must have lost its identity by intermarriage with
non-Jews. Such amalgamation does not constitute biological
extinction, but many Jews evidently regard it in this light and
are infuriated at the suggestion of intermarriage as a solution

of their social problems. Rabid anti-Semitists are equally opposed to it. Nevertheless, the process goes merrily on, as it has
in the past.

Because I have remarked that I could "do" with a little
Jewish intelligence and that a Jewish strain in my ancestry
might, at any rate, have improved the shape of my nose, correspondents have inferred that I have been frustrated in my
desire to marry a Jewish woman. I cannot imagine how one's
wife could affect the shape of one's nose except by pulling it,
as in the case of the Elephant's Child, or by smashing it. Any
wife could do either.

Nearly everyone who encounters social difficulties wishes to
resolve them by changing the rest of the world. It seems to me
altogether futile for the Jews to hope to extricate themselves
from their predicament by complaining, standing on the Bill
of Rights, and emitting counterpropaganda. Their oppressors
are amenable neither to reason nor to moral suasion. There are
mannerisms and types of behavior which anti-Semitists and
even sympathetic Gentiles commonly attribute to Jews. Many
of these attributions are doubtless incorrect, and many of the
"Jewish" characteristics are meritorious, however objectionable
they may be to prejudiced non-Jews. Now, I do not believe that
any deeply aggrieved group is likely to study its situation with
the purpose of ascertaining how far its own idiosyncrasies may
have aroused dislike. It is much easier to assume one's own complete virtue and to complain of the other fellow. Conceivably
the Jews might educate themselves in social behavior so as to
mitigate their unpopularity; thousands of them individually
have succeeded in achieving general esteem in spite of prejudice.
But no large ethnic or social group is willing to reform its own
mores so that they will be acceptable to those of other groups.
That is why it seems to me that assimilation offers the only
chance of life, liberty, and the pursuit of happiness to this able
but unbeloved stock.

AN ANTHROPOLOGICAL APPRAISAL OF THE JEWISH PEOPLE*

Although I am somewhat inured to public speaking, an ineradicable aversion to such performance, together with an inherent meanness of disposition, usually impels me to select a controversial subject and to deal with it in such a brutal and inept way as to alienate all parties. I differ from the man in Aesop's fable who tried to please everybody, but pleased nobody and lost his jackass in the bargain, only in that I do not try to please anybody, yet succeed equally in pleasing nobody and have no personal property to lose. So I am going to discuss the anthropological and sociological status of the Jewish people, neither offering an apologetic nor delivering a polemic, but in a cold-blooded, unemotional mood of inquiry. I shall not resort to the puerile artifice of flattering statement, nor to any demogogic attempt to win favor by denouncing those ignorant and stupid nations or individuals who wreak their inferiority complexes upon a gifted and successful minority people. The time has come, I think, for an interpretation of the problem of the Jew by one who does not pretend to be a passionate lover of Justice but, at most, a platonic friend.

Perhaps my prime qualifications for this task are the facts that I do not participate in the heritage of Jewish blood and culture, and a certain British obtusity prevents envy of those with whose superiorities I am unable to compete. The study of the physical characteristics of groups of men is the business of the physical anthropologist, in which I have been engaged for the past quarter century. The interpretation of the relationship of physical features, or of the human organism as a whole, to man's psychological processes and to his behavior in society, seems to be regarded as nobody's business, and is generally ignored or denied. Sociologists and social anthropologists do

* Delivered at the opening program of Jewish Book Week, at the Boston Public Library, May 15, 1938.

indeed concern themselves with human behavior and human institutions, but it is convenient for them to believe that these social phenomena have nothing to do with human biology, because they know nothing about the latter.

I do not claim to be a specialist upon either the social or the physical anthropology of the Jew, but I have long had an interest in their interrelations, and I think that I can discuss them with a certain detachment and without any emotional involvement. My contacts with the Jewish people have been sufficiently numerous, though restricted for the most part to a university environment. I do not think that I have developed any prejudices from these associations. An anthropologist should school himself to refrain from generalized attitudes toward ethnic and racial groups, and must not carry over his dislikes or likes of individuals to the physical or social units to which they belong. Thus, I insist upon basing my feelings of friendship, admiration, and the opposite upon the personal qualities of individuals, and restrict my antipathies or affinities to individuals, although I pronounce judgments with respect to the characteristics of groups.

The topics which present themselves for treatment in this anthropological appraisal of the Jewish people are physical distinctiveness, social separateness, psychological differentiae, contribution to civilization, and the genetic basis of success, assimilation, and future prospects. None of these can be exhausted within the limits of allotted space and knowledge possessed by me.

The Physical Distinctiveness of the Jew

The term race means to a physical anthropologist a large body of mankind, the members of which present similar combinations of physical features which they owe to their common heredity. Members of the same race resemble each other physically in such mainly inherited variations as shape and proportions of the head, face, and nose; color of skin, hair, and eyes; form and distribution of hair. Many details of anatomy—mostly trivial—contribute to such racial resemblances, and they are also expressed to a lesser extent in stature and body build. The more of these physical resemblances or identities found in groups of men, the closer are they related to each other in blood. Extremely detailed and far-reaching likenesses imply not only identical racial origin, but beyond that, local and familial blood relationship.

Now, for purposes of this discussion, I restrict the term Jew to members of the so-called White races of mankind who by virtue of familial tradition practice or are affiliated with the religion of Judaism.

Large samples of Jewish populations have been measured and observed by physical anthropologists in many parts of the world —the Near East, the various countries of Europe, North Africa, and the United States. These studies show very clearly that Jewish people, the world over, are by no means physically homogeneous and cannot be considered in any anthropological sense a unified and pure race. They tend to approximate the physical racial characteristics of the populations of which they are a part when they have been domiciled among them for several or many generations. Thus, in countries where round-headedness tends to prevail, such as in Russia and Poland, the Jewish people are generally brachycephalic; whereas in North Africa, among the long-headed Berbers and Arabs, the Jews are, as a rule, also long-headed. Again in the midst of brunet pigmented stocks, the Jewish peoples tend to have dark skin, hair, and eyes; while in the centers of blondism they swing toward light pigmentation.

There are two main reasons for the approximation of Jewish physique to the modes and means of the racial and ethnic stocks within which they dwell. The first of these is the original participation of the various Jewish groups in the blood and race of the surrounding populations. The community of physical features between Jews and non-Jews in any country may be due to the fact that both are derived from similar blends of identical racial strains, such blends having been stabilized through centuries by selection in the same environment from the common reservoir of racial features. Such is the case in the Near East, where many Jewish groups are almost indistinguishable anthropologically from certain of their neighbors. The second and predominant cause of resemblance between Jews and non-Jews in areas in which the former dwell as immigrants, comparatively recent or of long standing, is actual interbreeding between the stocks. A third, but slender, possibility of explaining the physical resemblance of Jews to non-Jews in the same area lies in the theory that identical environmental conditions, such as temperature, moisture, and available food supply, may mold diverse racial stocks into similar types. In general, it seems certain that the physical convergence of Jews and non-Jews is mainly attributable to the actual commingling of their bloods, and not to postulated common environmental influences.

Now, in spite of the fact that the Jews are not a unified race and that they resemble their neighbors more or less closely in any area in which they have resided for a long period, they are usually, none the less, physically distinguishable from the latter. It is common knowledge that the Jew can be recognized by his physical appearance—not, of course, invariably, but at any rate in the majority of individual cases.

The two causes of physical distinctiveness of the Jew are the dominance of certain anatomical features due to the relatively constant presence of a specific racial strain, and Jewish inbreeding, which intensifies certain physical resemblances in interrelated family lines. The racial strain which is generally persistent through Jewish peoples is probably the recently distinguished Iranian Plateau race. This race is brunet White, with black or dark-brown wavy head hair, abundant beard and body hair, and moderate to short stature. Heads are very long and narrow; faces long and with prominent bony structure. However, the outstanding feature of this race is nasality. The nasal skeleton is always highly arched and strongly jutting. The nasal profile may be straight, but it is oftener convex or concavo-convex. The tip of the nose is usually depressed, but not especially thick, the wings of the nose of moderate development. This prominent nose, often hawklike, is a very advanced evolutionary character and seems to show many details which are dominant in inheritance—that is, they persist at the expense of other variations when racial strains are mixed. Seemingly, this dominant type of nose does not originate with Semitic-speaking peoples.

Now, in the Armenians it has been demonstrated by the recent and as yet unpublished work of Dr. Byron Hughes, of the University of Michigan, that we have not a pure race but a type of dominants blended from this convex-nosed, long-headed Iranian Plateau race, and a round-headed, globular, brunet Alpine stock with a broad short face and a fleshy, straight, or concave nose. The composite result is a high, short, pointed head with a somewhat flat back, a sloping forehead with a long, high, straight, or convex nose, the tip of which is depressed and somewhat heavy, and a face terminating in a not too prominent chin. This Armenoid nose is slightly different from the same feature in the so-called Ashkenazic Jews, as it has a somewhat flatter, more oblong tip, and thicker wings. Many of the round-headed Eastern Jews show head form and nose form very similar to the characteristic Armenoid type; but there is usually a subtle difference in the tip of the nose, which is not quite so fleshy and oblong, and in the wings of the nostrils, which curve back from the depressed tip and septum of the nose along its side walls at the juncture of the face in a very characteristic but almost indescribable fashion.

Many of the Jews of Iran and Iraq can scarcely be differentiated from the Iranian Plateau type except in the details of nasal tip and wings, especially the recurvation of the latter, which is apparently absent from the Iranian Plateau stock, and

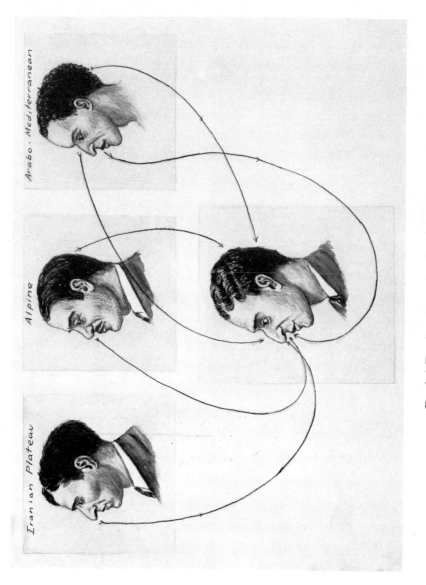

Racial Derivation of a Jewish Type

in the tip, which is a little fleshier in the Jews without reaching the Armenoid grossness.

In the Near East and through North Africa and Spain there are many very dark brunet Mediterranean race types in which the contours of head and face are smoothly oval, the hair very wavy with a tendency to curl, the lips rather full and everted, the chin pointed, and the body build slender. When the Iranian Plateau strain gets mixed with this fundamental Mediterranean type, the nose becomes convex and hawklike, with a thin, depressed tip and compressed wings instead of a straighter, shorter, lower, and blunter type of nose. In many Arabs and Jews alike, especially Sephardic Jews, these noses are practically indistinguishable; but I fancy that the Jewish variant usually shows a little more fleshiness of the tip and that curious recurvation, or setting back of the alae or wings, not so often seen in non-Jews of mainly Mediterranean stock.

Now, we have from the Iranian Plateau race the dominant feature of nasal convexity with a depressed nasal tip, from the Mediterranean race a certain fullness and eversion of the lips, and also from that stock a tendency to deep, short-waved hair. It is possible that this peculiarity of hair form may derive from still another racial strain. However that may be, all of these features tend to persist in Jews when mixed with other White racial stocks, such as blond long-heads—so-called Nordics—blond round-heads, called East Baltics, et cetera. All of them do not necessarily present themselves in combination in each individual, but of them the characteristics of depressed nasal tip and recurved alae are by far the most persistent individual features and occur irrespective of pigmentation (skin color, hair color, and eye color) and shape of the head or face. The Jew, if physically recognizable—and by no means all are so distinguishable—is generally identified subconsciously by these features of nasal tip and wings (high-bridged, convex noses not in themselves being diagnostic), and the recognition is made more readily when with that nasal tip there occurs a certain deep concavity of the integumental upper lip (the part which grows a mustache in males) and a certain fullness and eversion of the membranous lips, or lips proper, and, finally, a deep wave of the hair.

To these morphological minutiae, the Jews, being on the whole an inbred group, add some quite indescribable nuances of what are, broadly speaking, family resemblances, due to the fact that they are more closely inbred and more nearly related to each other than are the very mixed European stocks or other populations within which they reside. There are also some features in connection with the fullness of the eye and the high biconvex opening of the lids which are not so generally characteristic, but are very common in certain Jewish peoples.

Without going into excessive detail, these are then my impressions of the cause of the physical distinctiveness of many Jewish individuals. I may be wrong. This subject has not been completely or scientifically explored, and I am recording impressions rather than the results of detailed surveys.

Now I come to the sociological effect of physical distinctiveness of groups. If you meet a stranger in a public place and he jostles you rudely or performs some pleasingly courteous act in that casual meeting, you are either annoyed or gratified. If that stranger in his physiognomy presents an indescribable hash of features, such as occur in most mixed Europeans, and such as I have, you either recall his act as an individual manifestation to be associated with that single person, or more likely you forget it and him entirely. If, however, that fortuitous stranger is identifiable as a member of some physically distinguishable ethnic or racial group, you charge his kindness or misdemeanor to his whole group, and remember the act for or against that group. This is particularly true in the case of physically distinct groups which are minorities in one's own population. Thus, in the crudest exemplification, any act performed in Boston by a Chinese or a Negro has a group significance which the same act does not possess when it is committed, for example, by an Irishman, who is both commoner and not so easily distinguishable.

I do not think that I need labor this point, which is, however, of very great importance in the problem we are discussing.

The situation is accentuated in group gatherings. When fifty Americans of mixed northwest, north, and central European descent gather together, they are so heterogeneous physically that they do not create an impression of type unity. They are simply a group or a crowd. When a similar number of Jewish people assemble, there are just enough points of physical resemblance in the individuals of the aggregate to promote a judgment of likeness.

Now, it is unfortunately the case that men in general are still so stupid and brutish that they react unfavorably to physical features which are dissimilar to their own, especially when these are manifested by groups of persons. The lone physically dissimilar individual in a crowd feels strange and a little afraid. The crowd of like individuals feels somewhat resentful and scornful of the physical dissimilarity of that single unlike person. He is an ugly duckling. Hence it may be seen that any minority group which is physically identifiable has to encounter primitive antagonisms, simply because it is different in trivial anatomical details. Such feelings of physical difference promote social separateness. It is easy enough to understand this fact when one recalls the unwelcome general attention which is bestowed upon a man who dares to wear a straw hat before the open season. If he *has* to wear a certain kind of nose or an unusual skin color, he is thereby permanently marked.

The Social Separateness of the Jew

There are very potent social factors which in the past have contributed to the social segregation of the Jewish people. The first of these is their religion. Of course, there are a great many sophisticated people in modern society who do not care a straw what the religion of a person may be, or whether he has any at all. But these, I think, are still a very small minority. It is also a curious phenomenon of human nature that the less inclined people are to practice the ethical codes which belong to their religions, the more bitterly they resent the different rituals and beliefs to which other persons adhere. Religious tolerance is perhaps oftener a manifestation of indifference to religion than devotion to the latter. Now, when a religion is highly ritualistic and exclusive, as in the case of the Jewish religion, and when it involves deviations from the ordinary calendar of work days and holy days; when it further requires dietetic restrictions, peculiar forms of dress, and the preservation of an alien tongue in the procedure of worship, it necessarily sets its worshipers apart. Add to this the fact that in European and American countries Christianity, the general form of organized religion, is actually an illegitimate and disowned offspring of Judaism, and that professed Christians therefore have the hypersensitiveness of those who carry the bar sinister, and it becomes all too easy to explain the historical and present basis of much of the antagonism which obtains between the less intelligent of both religions. If there are two religions, each of which professes as its creed peace and good will toward all men, and if these two religions differ otherwise slightly or markedly in ritual and belief, there will result inevitably not peace and good will, but no end of a scrap to determine which brand of peace and good will is better and who shall dispense it. Man is made that way.

I cannot enter here into the historical causes of Jewish dispersion and into the obvious sociological consequences of the Diaspora. An originally single people, of a more or less unified and stabilized physical blend, with a highly formalized, nonproselytizing type of religion and a language which is morphologically and genetically far removed from Indo-European tongues, has established itself in isolated colonies in foreign nations of many different kinds. The survival of Jewish physical and social distinctiveness through many centuries in scores of countries and amid diverse races is the demographic miracle of human history.

This consideration leads to the suggestion that within the Jewish peoples themselves there have been operative factors which make for exclusiveness and for social cohesion, which are in part bound up in their religion, but must be in a measure independent of it. Religion, after all, is the outgrowth of the mentality, temperament, and social institutions of a group. In the beginning the group creates its religious beliefs and practices, and not the reverse.

Since I am not a student of Jewish institutions and in fact know less of them than perhaps any of the audience which I address, it would be folly for me to draw upon the vast thesaurus of my ignorance. But it appears to me that the biological family and the kin are far more closely integrated among Jews than among most non-Jews of western European countries. Parental authority, and perhaps especially the reverence for the matriarch, seem to me to be much more potent factors in Jewish family life than is commonly the case in peoples of other faiths and customs—within, of course, the circle of so-called European civilizations. Such a condition, if it is a fact, carries with it a stronger tendency for married children to live in the households or in the immediate vicinity of their parents and relations. It implies a closer reckoning of blood relationship and marriage kinship. It involves a more rigid selection of marriage mates—in fact, stricter endogamy and closer inbreeding. This maintenance of a strong type of family, as contrasted with a weak and rapidly disintegrating family among non-Jews, makes for the retention of Jewish uniformity, both physical and social, in a modern world of unstable and fluid institutions. It also emphasizes and reinforces the general distinctions between Jews and non-Jews.

Now, I am confident that I am right when I attribute this extraordinary social cohesiveness of the Jewish people to initial qualities of temperament and mentality which are bound up with the specific biological blends which the Jews present. This cohesiveness, of course, has been enormously strengthened and increased by Jewish religion, Jewish custom, Jewish isolation, dispersion, and by the antagonisms of the populations within which Jewish groups have settled as immigrants. But the original cause lies in the bio-psychological constitution of Jews in their homeland, preserved and perpetuated elsewhere. In other words, the Jews have considered themselves a chosen people, and have elected to remain separate and different from their neighbors. To put it even more bluntly, the Jews have never wanted to have any dealings with the Samaritans, not because the Samaritans disliked them and regarded them as inferiors, but precisely for the reverse reason. I think that we need not pretend that, as a general rule, Jews as a group have been popular in the nations of non-Jews among whom they have lived. The mutual dislikes may well have been simultaneous, but I am much inclined to doubt that the priority of antipathy and of the exclusive tendency, if there was any priority, lay with the non-Jews. I hope that you will recognize that in this matter I am attempting to allocate neither praise nor blame. I am quite as able to understand the feeling of superiority which Jews entertain toward Gentiles as the dislike the latter may have for the former. I sympathize with neither.

Before I leave the subject of social separateness I must comment upon the apparently individualistic character of the Jewish mentality. While the Jew exhibits a very high degree of emotional regard for his kin and a very strong attachment to his familial and broader social institutions, he seems on the whole to be disinclined to uniformity of political belief and is strongly eclectic in his adherence to systems of thought and patterns of behavior. He is averse to regimentation. This highly evolved mental individualism results from intensive inbreeding and selection, and it is quite the opposite extreme from the undifferentiated state of gregariousness and sheep-through-the-gapishness out of which fanatically nationalistic parties are molded from more naïve and primitive human material. Nationalism is, of course, a fairly crude and barbaric manifestation of men who have not outgrown the herd instinct, if there is such a thing.

However, this very individualism sets the Jews apart as possibly superior, yet relatively helpless and much preyed upon, minorities in populations which are so unintelligent as to allow themselves to be excessively governed and to like it. Here in the United States it is suggestive of Jewish individuality that Jews have not established to any extent separate Jewish institutions of higher learning, whereas Jewish hospitals are to be found in most large cities. I interpret this situation to mean that the Jew is devoted to the acquisition and dissemination of knowledge, irrespective of its connection with his religion and his own social group, but that the physical and medical care of his own people is regarded as peculiarly a religious and family matter. In so saying, I recognize that Jewish hospitals offer their facilities as freely and readily to non-Jews as to those of their own people.

Psychological Distinctiveness

It is, of course, rash to generalize concerning the psychological qualities of an entire people, and such generalizations inevitably carry us beyond the bounds of scientific observation into the realms of impression and conjecture. Nevertheless, it is undesirable to limit one's self to the mere statement of proven facts simply because one is a scientist and is reluctant to indulge in that precarious pastime vulgarly described as "sticking out your neck." That psychological qualities are bound up with individual, ethnic, and racial physical organization I have no doubt, although it must be repeated that satisfactory scientific demonstrations of such associations are lacking, partly because of the crudity of available techniques of observation and experimentation.

However, it would be very hard for anyone who is familiar with the results of psychological studies, or even for anyone who is able to survey with impartiality the course of human history, to deny that superior intelligence is pre-eminently the possession of the Jewish people. If there have existed within the limits of historical record peoples who may be said to have been endowed with such a high degree of individual intelligence as to cause them to bring forth at frequent intervals that supreme manifestation of ability which we call genius, only two peoples, in my opinion, can aspire for recognition as of that primal rank. The first of these is the ancient Greeks, during the five centuries preceding the birth of Christ. The second is the Hebrew people. I have no intention of comparing and contrasting the achievements of these two lone peoples of genius —they are familiar to all of you.

However, I must insist that genius is a matter of hereditary endowment of supreme mentality, that men of genius are produced by a fortuitously favorable combination of the superior genes in their parents' germ plasms. Even more important is the undeniable fact that the production of individual genius is at a maximum in peoples of high average intelligence and sinks to virtually nil in low-grade populations. Of course, genius can be made manifest only under environmental circumstances which favor its development and exercise.

It is this high mean of individual intelligence among the Jews which has enabled them to produce genius with such a frequency that it becomes monotonous and irksome to less gifted peoples. Now, I am not disposed to accord to Jews credit for conscious and purposive breeding for genius, nor to praise them for transmitting the superior genes which are their hereditary endowment. If you are a genius, it is not a matter which may be credited to you as a virtue of your own individual achievement; and if you are an idiot, it is certainly not your own fault. I am interested here only in the explanation of that maintenance of high intelligence in a group century after century which has permitted the production of the occasional genius, to whose individual efforts, for the most part, I believe that progress in civilization must be assigned.

Added to the primary requisite of an originally superior mental endowment, which is indispensable, there have been many factors in Jewish history and Jewish custom which have promoted the preservation of that heritage and have tended to improve it. The first of these is inbreeding caused by Jewish consciousness of superiority (induced partly by their religion) and by the hatred and persecution of the non-Jewish peoples among whom they have lived. This inbreeding has brought forth repeatedly doubly and triply distilled abilities in certain lines. There has been little diffusion and loss of mental superiority by interbreeding with less gifted stocks. The second factor is the extremely severe social selection and, as it were, natural selection, to which the Jews have been subjected century after century, because they have been as a rule disliked and envied by their neighbors. Inbreeding makes for the segregation in some individuals of the inferior qualities of the stock and in others of the superior qualities. Long continued, it produces organisms which are, on the one hand, combinations of the best hereditary characters, or at least those which have the most biological survival value; on the other, those which are the least fit to survive. Now, in the Jews this process of inbreeding and segregation has resulted in a most stringent selection of the superior, since other peoples have generally seen to it that Jewish survival is made exceedingly difficult. Competition with non-Jews has always been bitter and bloody.

Lest you begin to feel flattered and complacent at my analysis of this situation, I wish to add at once, and perhaps unpleasantly, that men of genius are not usually likable individuals, nor persons with whom it is easy to live, and that stocks of the nervous quality which is likely to produce genius also breed in great numbers decidedly neurotic and mentally unstable individuals. They are, from the point of view of the less highly organized in the nervous system, decidedly uncomfortable people. They are not without consciousness of their own mental superiority and may manifest their feeling of it in arrogance, or attempt to conceal it under the guise of a false humility or a mien of submissiveness, which neither convinces nor pleases. In general, people with superior mentalities find it difficult to make social adjustments of a satisfactory nature to the run-of-the-mill of humanity. They are likely to be socially inept.

Success in worldly competition, whether intellectual or economic, requires not only ability but excessive determination and pertinacity, often accompanied by a certain aggressiveness and ruthlessness. Sympathetic personalities are perhaps commoner among men of mediocre or inferior ability. One does not have to be an anthropologist to realize that any group which is physically and socially distinct is sure to arouse envy and hatred among outsiders with whom the members of that segregated group continually and successfully compete. It is deplorable that human nature is so constituted that losers do not love winners, and that the less intelligent have not a whole-hearted admiration and liking for the brilliant; but it is very naïve to expect such generosity and self-abnegation in a type of animal which has emerged comparatively recently from apedom, and is by nature both predacious and competitive. The successful individual will continue to arouse in his fellows jealousy and the desire to "get even."

There are also certain temperamental incompatabilities which aggravate relationships which have been strained by competition, whether between individuals or between groups. If one person is phlegmatic, inarticulate, and repressed by nature, he is likely to be unsympathetic with another who is ebullient, excitable, voluble, and gesticulatory. Very frequently—though not, of course, invariably—the Jew possesses as a part of his heritage, perhaps reinforced by the traditions of his people, a certain emotional intensity which expresses itself in modes of behavior alien to certain northwestern European stocks—especially perhaps to Anglo-Saxons. The Anglo-Saxon, who is bitterly ashamed of showing his emotions and has been schooled to conceal and to repress them, is mystified, shocked, and re-

volted by the exuberance of emotional expression which he encounters not only in Jews, but in many other peoples. If he is
capable of self-analysis, he may find that he envies Latin or
eastern European peoples for the ease with which they secure
outlets for emotions which in himself are bottled up until they
burst him. Such temperamental contrasts are not so trivial as
they may appear in adding to the antagonisms which spring
up between competing groups.

Assimilation and the Future of the Jewish People

Now let us sum up the situation, not as it exists in countries
where a population debased in intelligence by the dysgenic effect
of a disastrous war and in desperate economic straits deliberately sets up the Jewish minority as a sort of national scape-
goat to suffer for the sins of all, but in democratic countries
such as Great Britain and the United States, which have not
as yet succumbed to the virulent infections of fascism or communism.

The Jewish people are set apart socially by the exclusiveness
of their religion and other institutions; they are distinguished
physically by a few minor characteristics which they owe in
part to certain racial strains and in part to their intensive inbreeding; they are palpably superior in intelligence and breed
a disproportionately large number of men of genius in many
fields of activity. With the factors of environment consistently
adverse, they nevertheless succeed in economic and intellectual
competition to such an extent as to arouse the envy and dislike
of those whom they surpass. They are often sufficiently distinct in temperament and in social behavior from those who are
able to compete with them on equal terms, so that they are un-
congenial to the latter, although feelings of inferiority may
be absent.

What is to be done about this situation? We can let it run
on, as it has for centuries, hoping perhaps to ameliorate it by
appealing to such humanitarian ideals as those of justice,

mercy, and pity—the so-called higher sentiments of man. Perhaps we can educate human beings, of a generally low intelligence and brutish disposition, to tolerance, and teach them to refrain from laying violent hands upon the property and persons of those who have when they themselves have not, and who are yet numerically weaker and an easy prey to superior force. However, since I take what I consider to be a realistic view of the present status of man—a view which you may regard as pessimistic—I think that this policy of dependence upon the broken reed of educational enlightenment and humanitarianism is altogether fatuous. For it is my opinion that, owing to a number of factors, in part sociological, but basically biological, average human intelligence is diminishing. We may therefore expect (and we are getting) more and more frequent, violent, and general manifestations of predatory brute behavior. The disease is not irremediable; it can be ameliorated and perhaps cured by a realignment of educational policy and by the concentration of scientific attention upon the problems of human biology.

But we cannot wait for the intellectual redemption of mankind and the revival of human intelligence if we are to take precautions against the occurrence of such national sadism and sheer suicidal lunacy as impels the present German government to destroy that minority element which has been responsible for some of its most brilliant cultural achievements. Since we can do little with the mass of so-called civilized humanity in its present state of mental debasement, the issue must be put up to the Jews themselves, who, as a people of high intelligence and apparently endless patience, have doubtless foreseen and deliberated the several possibilities of solving their own social problems.

Jewish intellectual pre-eminence, the hothouse flower of Jewish genius, the virtues of Jewish religion, the peculiar merits of essentially Jewish culture can be preserved only through a maintenance of the traditional policy of inbreeding and social exclusiveness. The continuance of such a policy in Jews domiciled among non-Jewish populations is likely to result in cruel and unjust oppression of the minority in the future as in the past, since there is no present prospect of eradicating from mankind the deplorable motives from which it springs.

There is, of course, the recent and bright realization of a purely Jewish state established in the original homeland, which will serve not only as a refuge for persecuted Jewish peoples from all nations, but also as a focus for Jewish culture and for the achievements which may be expected from an untrammeled development of Jewish ability in an environment of social equality and political liberty.* While this state will undoubtedly serve as the symbol and embodiment of Jewish nationalism, it will hardly attract to itself the majority of Jewish peoples long domiciled in countries of whose culture and economy they form an integral part. Such a wholesale migration of the Jews back to Palestine from the United States could only result from an infection of madness which would overthrow our democracy and make this country intolerable to all liberty-loving persons, Jew or Gentile.

Another possible solution is the merging of the Jewish peoples into surrounding populations by outmarriage and by the abandonment of peculiarly Jewish institutions. It is apparent, however, that no partial or halfway assimilation measures would be efficacious, since the preservation of a purely Jewish nucleus as a segregated minority identifies the mixed and intermediate class with the original stock, against which the majority discriminates. But a complete assimilation of the Jewish stock by intermarriage presents not the slightest biological difficulty. There is no radical difference of a physical nature between the Jew and the non-Jew, such as would create an obvious class of physical hybrids stigmatized by anatomical separateness. No dysgenic effects may be anticipated from such intermarriages, which, as a matter of fact, have always taken

* This paper was written before the British sold the Jews down the river.

place in sufficient quantity to modify the character of Jewish groups long resident in non-Jewish populations. The effect upon the absorbing populations could be nothing more startling from an anthropological point of view than a somewhat higher incidence of convex noses, deep-waved hair, and other anatomical trivialities. Such an assimilation would distribute the superiorities of the Jewish mind through a much larger proportion of mankind and would also diffuse Jewish qualities of temperament. On the mental side, such a merging would have some slight effect, no doubt, in elevating the general intelligence at the expense of diluting the Jewish concentrate, and at the sacrifice, almost certainly, of occasional peculiarly Jewish manifestations of genius.

Now, I am not here to advocate this policy or any other; I am only discussing a subject of mutual interest and, I believe, of great importance. I imagine myself to have discussed it without prejudice. I confess, however, that I entertain a great respect and admiration for Jewish achievement and more especially for men of genius, so copiously bred by that people. I admit also in my numerous and, in some cases, very intimate Jewish friends a quality of loyalty and a depth of sympathy which are rare and precious. However, I revert to my introductory statement and reiterate that, as a physical anthropologist, I neither like nor dislike groups, peoples, or races, but only individuals.

IX

THE ANTHROPOLOGICAL PROSPECT OF THE
SURVIVAL OF HUMAN LIBERTY*

As DEMOCRATIC observers of fascism and communism, which
are chasing each other around Robin Hood's barn, I think that
we ought to emulate the philosophical detachment of a certain
hardy American pioneer. This individual returned from the
hunt one day to find his wife running round and round their
log cabin pursued by a bear. With characteristic Anglo-Saxon
chivalry and resourcefulness, the husband mounted to the roof
of the cabin, seated himself upon the ridgepole, and shouted,
"Go it wife! Go it ba'ar!" I suppose that he figured that the
odds against the maintenance of his own personal liberty were
equally long in either outcome.

Let us also view the prospect of the survival of human liberty without the morbid fatalism of those who sally forth to

* The subject of a lecture delivered before a discussion group in the
Harvard Club of New York, January 25, 1938. I was invited to speak
specifically upon this subject. I did not like the subject, but rather fancied
my treatment of it. With the discussion group, so far as I could judge, it
was the other way round. In the course of the discussion a man got up and
asked me whether I could reconcile with my view of the biological deterioration of modern man the fact that contemporaneous marriages were often
blessed by numerous offspring (e.g. the Dionne family). I replied that I
could, because only lower animals have litters. This rather feeble sally
evoked an altogether disproportionate roar of laughter. In fact, it nearly
broke up the meeting. I was perplexed until someone explained to me that
my questioner was an unusually fecund parent who had just added twins to
an already sizable brood.

witness "death in the afternoon." There is still a sporting chance for liberty, if you regard its existence as anything in the nature of a biological or social reality.

ORGANIC LIBERTY DEFINED

Liberty is usually a somewhat vague political or sociological concept, but I intend here to discuss mainly its biological basis and implications, which are nearly always ignored. Perhaps a first crude definition of biological liberty would be: the freedom of the animal organism to behave more or less in accordance with its instinctive tendencies. It is immediately apparent that such biological liberty is not synonymous with independence, since animal life inevitably exists by virtue of other life and subsists upon it. Animals live upon other animals and upon plants, whereas the latter possess exclusively the ability to transform inanimate matter into living substance. But even plants are not independent. It is then clear that, for profitable discussion, the concept of liberty as applied to animal organisms must be restricted. Possibly it may be stated that animal liberty implies the behavior of the individual organism unimpeded by the dominance of other organisms, either of the same species or of different species; but subject, of course, to competition in the struggle for survival. Within these limitations it may be conceded that all wild animals enjoy freedom of a sort, and that all animals domesticated by man have been deprived of liberty, since their existence is controlled and their behavior restricted by another species.

However, it at once becomes obvious that the existence of higher animals is necessarily social and cannot be completely individual and solitary, and that life in the social group inevitably diminishes the freedom of action of the individual. Social liberty can only be achieved by the subordination of individual freedom to the will, or to the aggregate of instincts, of the total group. Collective liberty necessarily involves some sacrifice of individual liberty. However, in lower animal societies it may be presumed that behavior is largely instinctive or reflex, more or less unconditioned; and that, individual variability being slight, the tendency for the single animal to diverge from his fellows in wants and actions is feeble. Unanimity depends upon lack of organic differentiation in the individuals and produces a socal freedom which is nearly coincident with individual freedom, both existing on a mainly instinctive level.

But surely we have little interest in social or individual liberty which is merely the unhampered exercise of instinctive activity. It therefore becomes necessary to differentiate human biological liberty from that of lower animals. Higher animals are distinguished in general from their inferiors by the greater elaboration of their structure and the added complexity of their functions. In particular, differences in form and in pattern of behavior seem to be connected with the evolutionary status of the nervous system. Now, I think it may be asserted that the only really fundamental biological distinction between man and his nearest infrahuman relatives, the anthropoid apes, is based upon the fact that the human central nervous system (especially the cortex of the brain) has achieved such a high development that it dominates the structure and behavior of the animal, both in a different manner and to a higher degree. The enormous development in the brain of the areas of pictured movements and of the association tracts is correlated with the fact that a considerable part of human behavior is volitional rather than automatic, intelligent rather than instinctive.

At this point it seems necessary to attempt a definition of intelligence, with no vain hope of satisfying the psychologist or the philosopher, but with the simple purpose of trying to make clear the meaning of the term as used in this discussion. One might say that an animal behaves intelligently when it knows and understands what it is doing. I am afraid that such a statement is largely a transfer of ambiguity from one word to two others. Perhaps I come closer to the mark when I say that intelligence is the ability of the animals to cope with new situations by utilizing associations and memories of past experiences in a conscious effort to solve a problem. It is more than mere learning ability; it is the manifestation of insight—the habit of surveying the whole layout of a situation and then proceeding to work out a rational solution.

But the transition from purely instinctive behavior to rational or intelligent behavior is not direct. There is the middle ground of the conditioned reflex—of habitual actions which are learned through experience, practice, and custom, but are not in their origin instinctive. These conditioned reflexes eventually are performed without conscious deliberation, without the intervention of reasoning processes. Behavior of this kind is characteristic not only of animals, but also of human beings. Indeed, perhaps the greater part of habitual human behavior is of this variety. Such behavior is not, of course, on the instinctive level; but it is not highly intelligent in the sense in which I am defining intelligence for purposes of my argument.

Human liberty from the biological point of view consists in the more or less complete emancipation of behavior from the automatic mechanism of the reflex, by which a sensation is conveyed to some part of the central nervous system which instantaneously directs a motor response without deliberation or conscious choice on the part of the animal. Thus, after some fumbling, we have laid hold of a definition of human liberty. It is the ability of the animal man to exist within society under such conditions that individual behavior, directed by conditioned response or by reason rather than by instinct, is permitted to vary widely, with a minimum of compulsion exerted upon it by the group as a whole or by any aggregate of members of the group.

EVOLUTION OF HUMAN LIBERTY
Organic

I now propose to trace the evolution of liberty—organic and sociological—from subhuman times through savagery and the earlier stages of civilization. The achievement of organic liberty presupposes a relative emancipation of the animal from his environment and from his instinctive behavior. We shall see how the first is an outgrowth of the second.

Environmental emancipation begins when an animal ceases to adapt itself to an environment and starts adapting the environment to itself. It is completed to as full an extent as may be when a single species is able to command an adequate food supply, to survive and to perpetuate its kind in any area of the earth's surface which is capable of sustaining plant and animal life. While it is possible that such a mastery of environment has been gained also by certain insects and micro-organisms, it is certain that, among the highly organized vertebrates, man alone can claim such supremacy. Let me describe the successive events in prehuman and human history which brought about this control of environment. First there was the abandonment of tree life by our ape ancestors and with it the relinquishing of a mainly frugivorous diet consisting of leaves, shoots, nuts, and fruits—relatively unnutritious, demanding the mastication and digestion of a vast bulk of food with the elimination of great quantities of roughage. Next there came the assumption of the erect posture and biped gait on the ground, the emancipation of the fore limbs from locomotor duty, so that they could be used for feeding, feeling, grasping, and—most important—for fabricating and wielding tools and weapons. The commitment to terrestrial life greatly enlarged the range of the subhuman species, since there is more ground than forest. It permitted the shift to an omnivorous diet. Roots, vegetables, and cereals were added to fruits and salads; fish and meat provided concentrated, energy-producing foods which gave the animal respite from the incessant feeding necessitated by an arboreal diet of greenery. For the first time there was offered a wide choice of foods, with the best meal awaiting the swiftest, the most courageous, and the most adept in the use of weapons. Man became a carnivore, not by developing claws and specialized teeth, but by levying upon his physical environment for the raw materials of tools and weapons whereby he could kill and eat. Thus he avoided limiting his evolutionary prospects by bodily adaptation and specialization. Relatively late in human prehistory man achieved the culminating stage in his environmental emancipation when he succeeded in domesticating plants and animals, breeding them for his own purposes—thus forcing them to perform his own work. His subsequent attempts to control natural forces and to harness the elements are a natural outgrowth of previous successes. Observe that man became emancipated from his physical environment only by subjugating a large part of that environment, and that biological liberty in this sense is gained always and only at the expense of taking it away from some other animate or inanimate objects.

This whole process of gaining control over physical environment has been due to the growth and exercise of intelligence. The transition from tree to ground could not have been forced by some radical environmental change such as a deforestation of the anthropoid habitat, because our ancestors could have migrated as did their relatives who remained apes. It was a matter of choice and willingness to risk safety in order to secure a fuller existence. This, at any rate, is my interpretation, although some may find it possible to regard the phenomenon as a purely chance resultant of environmental circumstance and hereditary trend. The assumption of the erect posture was not an inevitable consequence of previous bodily adaptations; it was achieved only by the persistent efforts of animals whose nascent intelligence made them realize, however dimly, that an upright stance and a bipedal form of locomotion would enable them to get their noses off the ground, enlarge their horizons, and set free their upper limbs for prehension and for the use of tools. These were indeed organic adaptations—and I have stated that the superior animal adapts its environment rather than itself—but I do not think that they can be considered as merely passive responsives of the organism to environmental requirements. They were the result of protracted learning processes in which the mind directed the body in the acquisition of difficult, but exceedingly advantageous, motor habits, and ultimately succeeded in warping the inherited organic pattern into a new and superior mold. It was literally a victory of mind over body, a suppression of instinct by intelligence.

The apes with human destiny actually crossed the Rubicon when they began to contrive and to use tools. More than two decades of methodical scientific experimentation with apes and monkeys have made it certain that the only reason why our primate relatives do not make and use tools is because they lack the intelligence (in my sense of the word) which would stimulate them to such types of behavior. There is no anatomical deficiency which prevents the chimpanzee from achieving humanity, except in the region above the ears. A full belly and an empty head are, however, a bodily combination which is incompatible with progress, whether in culture or in organic evolution. On the contrary, a full head and an empty belly stimulate the animal to activity; things begin to happen. When the nutritional needs are easily supplied and an excess of energy is available for a brain which is definitely "on the make" in a functional and evolutionary sense, there originates the practice of setting aside a reserve of surplus food, which connotes a probably exclusively human mental faculty—foresight. We are then at the beginning of a realization of property in things and of a cumulative transmission of material culture.

But this is not all. The solution of the food problem, with its concomitant assurance of continued existence and satisfaction of the reproductive urge of the organism, releases the animal from a previously incessant subjugation to basic needs. Instincts are now more easily satisfied, and there is available an excess of nervous energy for contemplation, for constructive thinking, for the initiation of an immaterial culture—language and social institutions. Thus it appears that man, partly by the exercise of intelligence, but aided perhaps by natural selection and a few environmental breaks, lifted himself by his bootstraps from the status of ape to humanity. By mastering and remaking an obsolete bodily inheritance, he succeeded in becoming a tool-user and achieved a relative emancipation from environment. This latter facilitated the acquisition of biological liberty in the exclusively human sense of a substitution of intelligent for instinctive behavior. I have now completed my outline of the *organic* evolution of human liberty.

Social

Within the biological family, the natural group of parents and offspring, behavior is likely to vary least from old instinctive patterns, because the family is the focus and center of the ancient mammalian method of reproduction and the rearing of offspring which insures the perpetuation of the species. For each zoological group family behavior has been evolved through an enormously long period, during which it has been sifted and refined by natural selection. The end product is capable of very little volitional alteration or modification if the species is to survive. Hence, whether we belong in a savage society or in a civilized society, we behave most naturally when in the bosom of our families. This means that the exercise of intelligence is at a minimum and adherence to automatic or instinctively directed behavior is very close. It also means that such artificially evolved ideas as that of personal liberty are largely in abeyance. There is very definite subordination and superordination. The male parent is dominant, if he can manage it, over his mate and his young. If he cannot manage it, she generally does. I am not aware that there are any constant differences between savage

"The male parent is dominant, if he can manage it, over his mate and his young. If he cannot manage it, she generally does."

and civilized families in this respect. Parental care and affection equally are manifest; if anything, savages are more lenient with their children than are civilized parents; husbands and wives quarrel as incessantly and ferociously until one or other gets the upper hand. In some societies the weight of custom bears down the balance in favor of maternal dominance; in more cases the rule of the male is the established fact, probably because of his superior strength. In any event, ideas of personal liberty and self-expression are not, so to speak, indigenous in the family soil, but when present are late transplantations from the larger social group and tend as such to be tares among the wheat.

The aggregation of family units into nomadic hordes or into sedentary social groups necessarily implies further restriction of individual and family liberty, since concessions to the wishes and prejudices of the majority are demanded in the interests of group cohesion. As long as the group existence is maintained at an instinctive level little above that of the brute primates, one might suppose that a good deal of freedom of action might be enjoyed by the individual, merely because individual variation, differences in initiative, and divergence in tastes and in wants ought to be at a minimum. However, liberty of action and unanimity are by no means implicit in a common sharing of wants and needs. For, when everybody wants the same thing, it frequently happens that there is not enough of that thing to go round. Take, for example, the two most fundamental needs —food and women. It may be instructive to contrast in these regards the relative amounts of liberty enjoyed in an infra-human society—that of baboons—with that of one of the lowest-grade human groups—the native Australians. If we may judge from Zuckerman's observations upon a colony of captive baboons in the London zoo, no baboon gets anything to eat if his wife, children, friends, and relations can help it, and *vice versa,* although a baboon may allow his wife some food if she is in a certain interesting condition. Baboon society is ruled by dominant and aggressive males, each of which has his own following of females, young, and bachelors. The latter are unmated adult and subadult males, and enjoy about the same measure of privilege and the same degree of freedom as businessmen under the New Deal. They are allowed to hang around, providing that they make themselves useful to the overlord by fighting his battles, and providing that they keep their hands off his property—which is food and a harem—and concede him the major share of theirs, which consists of food only, if they can get it. Under these conditions, which we may call the Baboon New Deal, what becomes of the property—namely, the females and the food? What actually did happen on Monkey Hill in the London zoo was that the females were literally torn limb from limb and most of the food was spoiled. Under natural conditions—the Baboon Old Deal—as opposed to the artificial restrictions of captive life in the zoo, it seems probable that some sort of social equilibrium would have been established, in that the unreconstructed bachelors would have been driven out of the group by the economic royalists.

This illustration seems to indicate that, in a subhuman primate society, mainly instinctive behavior and community of wants do not insure individual liberty. On the contrary, sex competition and the struggle to obtain food result in a situation in which the only freedom of choice and behavior ordinarily granted to the individual is the option of fighting or running away.

A generalized description of Australian hunting society (not applicable in every detail to any specific tribe) will indicate the extent of individual and social liberty under very primitive human cultural conditions. The social group consists of perhaps a score or more of natural families of parents and children, aggregating possibly a hundred individuals of all ages. This group ranges over a more or less defined territory within which it conceives itself to possess proprietary hunting and collecting rights. Within the group certain individuals have special property rights in restricted areas by virtue of their membership in specified totemic clans. Nevertheless, there is usually a communal sharing of food according to fixed rules which prescribe the exact disposition of the various parts of the body of a game animal. If, for example, you have killed a kangaroo, the man who helped you carry it home may be entitled to the left hind leg and your father to the spareribs; your mother-in-law may get the neck; and so on through your relations. For each individual in the group stands in a specific relationship of blood or of convention to every other member of the group. Practically the entire conduct of the individual is dictated by the rules prescribing the approved types of behavior between kinship relations of various grades. The residuum of his life is largely consumed in participation in certain religious rituals and in formalized types of behavior determined by his sex and his age grade. His choice of a mate is narrowly restricted by an elaborate system of marriage classes, which determines the few individuals he may marry and the many he may not and is incomprehensible to all but native Australians and some social anthropologists. A man is, of course, free to indulge in quarrels with his wife, in sex rivalries involving recriminations and bloodshed, and in the general communal fights which seem to arise from sheer animal spirits. He has also a certain liberty in his methods of hunting and food collecting and in his use of the implements and weapons which he makes for himself. If he is an old man, he has a voice in the government and in the enforcement of the rules designed to hold the group together and to keep the women in hand; he has his part in initiating, directing, and performing traditional ceremonies. There is no anarchy; there is comparatively little disorder; there seems to be some scope for the exercise of individual initiative; but on the whole behavior is stereotyped and formalized. If a person deviates from prescribed patterns sanctified by custom and tradition, somebody sticks a spear into him, or bashes in his head, or otherwise signifies to him that he is the object of social disapprobation. Under these conditions each individual enjoys

Baboon New Deal

complete personal liberty only as long as he elects to behave exactly the way society thinks he should behave. There is practical unanimity upon these matters, and the social group may be stated to enjoy a high degree of liberty, which is limited only by their contacts, of a hostile and competitive nature, with similar neighboring groups.

Evidently, in such a society there are certain factors or conditions making for simplicity, which at the same time promote social liberty and, to some extent, individual liberty. The first of these is isolation. Savage hunters and food collectors usually have to range in small groups over wide expanses of territory, because the natural yield of food is small. Encounters with other groups are relatively infrequent; and incentives for warfare, such as overpopulation and the desire to acquire booty and additional territory, are not strongly developed, partly because hunting and collecting groups must be small, partly because there is little accumulation of property. The members of the group scatter during the daytime and return to a camping rendezvous only at night. Lack of cohesiveness in daily activity favors individual freedom and initiative. Each person is on his own for the most of his waking hours.

Because there is very little in the way of material property which can be acquired and stored, inequalities in the distribution of wealth are insignificant. Apart from certain intangibles and a few personal possessions, property rights in general tend to be vested in the group rather than in the individual. The absence of well-developed economic and political systems— which are, of course, incompatible with a low state of material culture and scanty populations—permits a minimum of interference on the part of the group with the livelihood-gaining activities of its members. In these respects primitiveness makes for the development and maintenance of liberty.

But there are other factors which prevent the realization of this beatific and idyllic state. First of all, there is authority, without which the group disintegrates. This authority among the Australians is not so much vested in individuals as in the will of the group as a whole, crystallized into custom. Of course, the elders tend to be the repositories of the folk custom, its enunciators and the executors, to some extent, of its dictates. But the force of custom is none the less compulsory, in spite of lack of differentiation into social ranks. The phrase "Custom is King" (title of a recent volume of essays in honor of R. R. Marett, the veteran social anthropologist of Oxford University) sums up the situation. The savage is literally enslaved by convention. If he rebels and violates it, he is sometimes ostracized, sometimes banished, but usually exterminated. The antisocial individual receives short shrift. There is no coddling of criminals.

Religion, which is merely the social attitude toward the supernatural and the practice of the group in dealing with phenomena which are beyond human understanding and the power of human control, cramps the freedom of the individual as well as the social group. Peoples who live very close to nature, and with the scantest margin between existence and starvation, naturally take their religion seriously. They try to utilize it in making their livings by propitiating the powers which, if favorably disposed, yield them a subsistence. Primitive religion is based upon fear and awe more than upon love and confidence; it is in general a pretty grim business. Under these circumstances, it is very dangerous to tamper with belief and ritual, and there is no room for the skeptic and the nonconformist.

Custom, then, clasps each individual of the group with rigid tentacles. It prescribes and enforces his manner of behavior under almost every conceivable set of circumstances and in nearly every relationship. Where he manages to wriggle free in some few situations which call for actions more or less of the instinctive type, such as sex relations, he still has to encounter the competition of his fellows, which is more than likely to result in restriction of his personal liberty of action.

In short, then, it would appear that human societies at the primitive status we have been considering do indeed achieve a large measure of what may be called collective liberty, in that the group does in general behave unrestrictedly according to its customary pattern. This pattern is the result of an attempt on the part of generally low intelligences to work out some sort of *modus vivendi* in intra-group relations and with the spiritual and material environment. Every individual's life has to be cut out according to the particular size and style of that inflexible pattern, which is varied only according to age and sex. Thus, it seems that the liberty of the individual savage is practically nonexistent, and that the social liberty which is shackled by ignorance to the dead weight of its own traditional customs is nothing to enthuse about.

As compared with the baboon society in the London zoo, the sort of human society which I have sketched represents a considerable advance. Instead of a perpetual tooth-and-nail fight, we have a social order, arising no doubt out of the cumulative efforts of human intelligences to contrive a method of emancipating their lives from instinctive behavior and of adjusting themselves to their physical environments. The conception of society has originated; but social tradition, the original product of active intelligences, has already petrified. Law, religion, and order are important fabricators of civilization; but they breed lawyers, priests, and politicians.

At the level of Australian society, liberty, as a social or individual ideal, is almost certainly absent. There is perhaps a realization that the organically unfit person is incapable of performing his proper function as a unit of the group. It is improbable, however, that such measures as infanticide, senicide, and abandonment of the infirm are practiced as social policies. As yet there exists no conception of organic or biological liberty as a prerequisite of social well-being and group progress.

I have long held the opinion that the most significant difference between the savage and the civilized man is that the former is a gentleman of leisure and the latter is a manual laborer. One can observe this difference in their skeletal structure, for the bones of the savage tend to be more gracile, those of the civilized man more sturdy and with the ridges for muscular attachments more strongly developed. Especially the contrast is marked in their hands and feet, those of the working man being larger, broader, with the articular facets much more developed and sharper in definition. I think that it can be deduced that civilizations have been built up principally because the members of the societies which have produced them have been made to work—to go on performing manual labor beyond the point where they have enough food to go round.

Now, I do not believe that the habit of incessant labor is natural to animals of the primate order, nor that it arises from any instinct or innate psycho-physical disposition. It may be different with ants and termites. The natural man resembles rather the grasshopper. On the other hand, it *is* perfectly natural for man to try to get somebody or something to do work for him. Even an incorrigibly lazy animal is willing to do that. So our ancestors achieved their first successes in this effort by inventing tools, and a signal triumph in domesticating animals and putting them to work. But civilization really began to accelerate only when the more clever and more powerful individuals contrived to hold the noses of their fellows to the grindstone. I think that it was the Dutch ethnographer, Nieboer, who made the statement: "The economic regime of every high civilization has been built upon slavery." This is not a very pleasant generalization, but it is probably true. When one contemplates the vast monuments of antiquity—the pyramids and temples of Egypt; the palaces and cities of Crete, Mesopotamia, and the Indus Valley; the colossal fortifications and religious edifices of Peru; and even the great rough stone erections of western Europe—he has to be very naïve to convince himself that these were the products of willing hands. There is plenty of archaeological and historical evidence to the contrary.

Slavery presupposes war, and the principal objectives of warfare among ancient civilized nations were to obtain the territory and property of other peoples and (by no means the least important) to force them to work for their conquerors. Rank and authority are gained in the most primitive levels of society by those who are more intelligent, more capable, or physically stronger and more courageous than their fellows. In the higher grades of barbarism and in most civilizations these positions of authority, which enable their occupants to force others to labor, have generally arisen from conquest, amalgamation, and the foundation of ruling military classes. It is still possible to discern in most of the savage states and in many of the civilized nations evidences of the persistence of physical differences between the various social classes, which are due not alone to inbreeding and lack of social mobility, but initially to ethnic and racial differences. The ruling groups are descendants of alien invaders who have been only partially absorbed. Because of the social inertia which is common to mankind, these ruling classes, which first established and exercised their overlordship by force of arms, were enabled to substitute largely therefor the weight of custom, tradition, artificial concepts of loyalty, patriotism, and other sentiments. Thus rank tended to become hereditary, and people were taught to be content with the "situation in life to which God had called them." So it appears that the early stages of civilization began with a reversion to the Baboon New Deal, in which certain individuals ruled by dint of physical strength and dominance, and forced the conquered to work. Then came a reversion to the Australian system whereby authority rested upon customary and traditional rule, with the difference that civilized custom was not in itself king, but worked through the divinely appointed human agents of the upper classes.

Under these conditions there could have been little individual or social liberty. Although presumably man had emancipated himself to some extent from instinctive behavior, the actions of the multitude were largely prescribed by custom and law enforced by rank and privilege. It should be noted, however, that even when civilization develops under rigid class restrictions which deprive the majority of the people of every vestige of liberty, there is nevertheless considerable scope for the exercise of individual intelligence and capacity within class limits. The very piling up and elaborating of material culture and social institutions tend to start within each social class the selection of the more intelligent and capable persons for leadership, the apportionment of various types of occupation according to individual abilities and skill, and the gravitation toward the bottom of those who are least gifted. The division and diversification of labor inevitably accentuate differences in capacity, whether due to training or to inbreeding under a caste or class system in which occupations tend to be hereditary in social groups. Dissatisfaction with the limitations of opportunity and the unequal distribution of privilege is most acute in the more intelligent members of each ironbound class. Consciousness of social injustice and of lack of liberty develops in the mentally superior of the depressed strata. There is still, however, no realization of an organic basis of liberty, nor any comprehension that social and individual liberty arise from conditions other than the absence of dominance.

It is the task of the historian, the sociologist, and the philosopher to trace the evolution of the intellectual concept of liberty. A physical anthropologist, such as I, is properly concerned only with the relation of the human organism to behavior, and I have already ventured upon ground which is not my own, where I am likely to lose myself or to get bogged down in my own ignorance.

I have forgotten whether it was one of the Sophists or one of the more reputable Greek philosophers who enunciated the paradox "None but the slave is free." At any rate, it illustrates the fact that academic discussion of liberty is no modern phenomenon and that even in antiquity there was some doubt as to the meaning of liberty. I am not sure that anyone has found it out up to this day. I am quite incompetent to deal with the development of political theory and with the effect of the growth and dissemination of liberal ideas in precipitating such events as the French and American revolutions. The conception that human beings not only have the right to exist, but also to pursue happiness and to enjoy equality of opportunity, and that the object of government is to insure these rights, represents almost the most ambitious effort of man to depart from instinctive, animalistic behavior and to govern his existence by reason. At the same time it seems to me that the abrupt substitution of government based upon ideals of democracy for the old system of grab-and-hold, with the devil taking the hindmost, involves an overconfidence in the ability of practice to keep pace with theory. It also neglects the fact that man is still a predatory animal organism which has fought its way upward in the evolutionary struggle, always at the expense of other species.

But, in my opinion, the failure to observe the dependence of social liberty upon the organic liberty of the individual has been, up to now, virtually total. Of course, inferior zoological status and low mentality of the subjugated have frequently been urged as excuses for slavery and oppression. But an effort of the protagonists of liberty to promote organic fitness in the entire population as the means of acquiring and maintaining liberty is yet to seek. Liberty has been dissociated from the capacity of individual men to enjoy it and to accord it to others. How to maintain a system of human relations thus based upon a set of idealistic and intelligent conceptions which are opposed to both instinctive animal behavior and also to unenlightened conditional response, is the difficult question which we are asked to consider. The degree of individual and social liberty which has been enjoyed in this country and in one or two other places in the past suggests that the approximate realization of such an ideal system, however contrary to nature it may seem to a physical anthropologist, is within the bounds of possibility. I think there can be no argument as to its desirability. I, at any rate, am in favor of democracy, providing that the *demos* is intelligent.

REQUISITES FOR SURVIVAL OF LIBERTY

Before it is possible to discuss the anthropological prospect of the *survival* of human liberty, it is necessary to define the ecological and anthropological conditions under which it may exist. Liberty, you will recall, I have defined as the ability of man to exist in society under such conditions that individual behavior, directed by intelligence rather than by instinct, is permitted to vary widely, with a minimum of compulsion exerted upon it either by the group as a whole or by any of its members.

In the first place, it seems necessary for the existence of human liberty that there be a favorable balance of food supply in relation to the size of the human population. As soon as the available amount of food is insufficient to supply the wants of all the members of a society, its members tend to revert to the instinctive level of behavior, at which the strong seize what they need and the weak must go without. I doubt that it is possible to inculcate altruistic teachings and the principle of communal sharing into any large group of human beings to such an extent that the majority of its members are content to starve and starve alike. If you are optimistic enough to believe that such self-abnegation can be bred into the stock or otherwise substituted for its instinct of self-preservation, you will, at any rate, admit that social and individual liberty under such conditions would be uncommonly difficult to realize.

Granting that this indispensable ecological condition—a sufficiency of food—is fulfilled, the existence and maintenance of liberty then depend upon the anthropological character of the population, since the organism makes its own behavior, and liberty is only the realization in human behavior of an artificial and abstract ideal of social conduct.

The anthropological characteristics which have to be considered are: race, or the inheritance of physical features in large related groups; the physical state of health, disease, strength or weakness, as exhibited by the majority of the human units in the society; the corresponding mental fitness or unfitness, and the individual and group level of intelligence.

Some of these anthropological characteristics may seem to bear no relation to the concept of liberty, but lack of recognition of such relationship is just another example of the superficiality with which man studies his own institutions as abstractions. However, we need not concern ourselves at length with the relation of race, anthropologically speaking, to the idea and practice of liberty. Race is a term used anthropologically to denote the broad similarities of anatomy and physiology which large groups of common ancestry present. It is the inheritance of certain morphological and metrical features, such as pigmentation, hair form, head shape, et cetera. We do not know that such physical features when inherited are linked with mental traits; or, if they are, the precise nature and range of these psychological racial characters. It would be possible, of course, to argue from observation of the various societies in different racial groups that this or that race seems to manifest a stronger tendency toward the exercise of individual and social liberty. However, so many environmental factors and so many historical circumstances condition the appraisal of the status of liberty in any society that I think that a generalization concerning its racial connotation would be most unsound. I therefore dismiss race in its relation to liberty with the mere statement that some races seem to have contrived to enjoy more liberty than others.

The relationship of individual physical fitness to the existence and maintenance of human liberty is, however, by no means remote. By physical fitness I mean an adequately nourished organism which functions vigorously, unimpaired by chronic or infectious disease. In most human groups one may observe a range of physical condition from complete decrepitude to virtual perfection. Unless an organism is free from disease, it cannot ordinarily be free in any other respect. Of course, I grant you the cases of the rare individuals in whom mind has triumphed over matter to such an extent that they are able to enjoy intellectual freedom, serenity of spirit, and unimpaired mental function in spite of general bodily debility. I believe, however, that the number of such persons has always been negligible, and always will be, and that there has been no little sentimental exaggeration in accounts of mental efflorescence from bodily putrefaction.

Let us revert for a moment to savage and primitive society. Here the manifestations of human infirmity are less frequent than among the civilized, because the rigors of savage existence do not permit invalids and very weak persons to survive. There is, furthermore, a disposition in many savage groups to rid themselves of the unfit and the diseased by methods which we may politely call "euthanasia." Our previous discussion has indicated that a savage is not necessarily free merely because he is a healthy animal, granted that he is that. On the other hand, it is evident that the debilitated savage cannot enter into competition with those who are fit, except at the expense of having to knuckle under, to accept their leavings, and to survive upon sufferance. Where individual and social freedom can be secured only by physical competition, the bodily unfit are out of luck in the handout of liberty. If an entire savage group is physically inferior, it is destroyed, enslaved, or driven out and forced to seek survival in the most remote and undesirable parts of the world.

Now let us return to civilized society. The puny individual suffers less from his physical inferiority than in primitive society, partly because we have developed sentiments in favor of protecting the weak, and partly because our minute division of labor affords some opportunity for self-support in occupations which require little physical exertion. On the whole, however, the unfit person is a dependent and unable to assert his liberty or to enjoy it. Societies made up of a majority of the weak and diseased are likely to fall victims to the aggressions of stronger groups.

However, the most serious effects of physical inferiority are in the impairment of mentality, initiative, ambition, courage, and constructive thinking which follow in the train of disease or of constitutional weakness. Neither sound minds nor intelligent actions are compatible with unsound bodies. Thus we are led to the consideration of the relation of intelligence to liberty, which is at the root of the whole matter.

According to our definition, man has raised himself above the level of the brute and achieved organic liberty by controlling his behavior through intelligence, reason, and volition—or at least through some complicated type of conditioned response—rather than mainly by instinct. The less intelligent the group as a whole, the farther it misses this organic emancipation. Yet in a primitive culture some degree of social and even of individual liberty may be maintained because of the very homogeneity of stupidity which narrows the range of behavioral variation. But in a complex industrialized society, involving a much larger population, the range of individual variation in intelligence and ability is necessarily great, and increased by occupational selection, by rank, by government, and by other factors. Where the dominance of groups of individuals is secured by hereditary rank or by militarism there is, of course, little or no liberty for the masses. When these repressions are absent, individuals rise in the economic and social scale by their own intelligence and competitive ability; the mentally inferior remain at the bottom, sunk by the weight of their stupidity.

In such a putatively free society, where each organism enjoys freedom according to its ability to rise above the instinctive and conditioned response levels and to grasp environmental op-

"... disposition in many savage groups to practice euthanasia."

portunities, there develops the political and social concept of liberty. This idea is indubitably the sublimated product of very high intelligences, in the sense of those intelligences which most completely dominate their own organic behavior by the employment of thought as a determiner of action. For the social ideal of liberty presupposes not only the ability of the individual to behave somewhat rationally and hence to enjoy organic liberty, but also to adjust that free behavior so delicately as to permit all other members of the society to achieve similar liberty. As a concept and theory of behavior it is as far removed from animalistic survival in evolution by natural selection or by combat as it is possible to imagine.

Closely allied to this concept of social and individual liberty is a general group of sentiments, very slowly developed in human society, which we may call humanitarianism. Here are included such ideas as that the strong should protect the weak, that human life is sacred, that each individual should be allowed to pursue happiness, that those who have should share with those who have not, that equality of opportunity should be accorded to all members of a society, that government should exist for the benefit of the governed. In short, we have the whole theory of the Declaration of Independence and the full-blown ideal of democratic government.

It should be apparent by this time that this entire altruistic scheme of social and individual behavior is practicable, if at all, only in a society whose human constituents are individually and collectively of relatively high intelligence. For the amount of self-restraint, of reason, of recognition of the necessity of voluntary concession to the rights of others, is far outside the range of realization in mainly instinctive human animals—i.e., those of low intelligence. This humanitarian theory of behavior, if you will, is contrary to nature and to evolution. It is none the less noble, even if virtually superhuman.

Let us now examine the case in which society, consisting of a mainly unintelligent populace, attempts to practice idealistic humanitarian behavior, including the full extension of liberty. Immediately the originally intelligent conception of individual liberty graduated to the varying mentalities of different human organisms is warped into a dogma that all men should be equally free, irrespective of their capacities to enjoy liberty and to accord it to others. At once there is added to the proposition that all men are born free the false corollary that they are born equal. But the intelligent, who have invented the political and social theory of liberty, have generally risen by virtue of that same intelligence, exerted along more practical lines, to positions of economic and social superiority. It then follows that theories of liberty inculcated on inferior minds tend to relegate the original teachers and proponents of liberty to the ranks of those who are alleged to have taken it away from the masses. For the more intelligent have acquired property and authority and the responsibility of directing the behavior of the less gifted. The signers of the declaration have become tyrants and economic royalists. This situation is not altogether imaginary.

Liberty now becomes the exclusive prerogative of the economically and socially depressed majority. The first exercise of this liberty is to deny it to all save their own class. But within this class we are postulating, purely for the sake of argument, behavior not greatly above the instinctive level. We then find ourselves immediately back in the old evolutionary bear garden with its survival of the fittest by wits and by combat, and with no quarter given. For within this social and economic stratum which arrogates to itself the exercise of liberty, there arise cunning, selfish, and ambitious individuals of somewhat superior intelligence who dominate the group and become dictators, having none of the altruistic ideals of intelligent humanitarianism, but, in the name of social liberty, operating with all of the ruthlessness of the overlords of the Baboon New Deal. Undigested theories of liberty sit heavily upon the stomachs of the unintelligent and eructate proletarian despots who establish militaristic regimes. The moronic masses are unified and controlled by a skillful utilization of the primitive appeal of symbols—shirts, swastikas, or whatnot—and by national and class slogans which evoke fanaticism rather than thought. The individuals who manifest humanitarianism and aspirations for liberty are promptly liquidated.

We may now assert flatly that organic liberty depends upon intelligence (the capacity for dealing rationally with novel situations), and that social and individual liberty is a concept arising from superior intelligence. In order to realize liberty the majority of the population must be physically sound and must possess a measure of mentality which will permit both a full comprehension of this idealistic conception and a disposition to put it into practice.

PROSPECTS OF SURVIVAL

Thus we finally approach the prospect of the survival of human liberty. I maintain that the lowering of the intelligence of a population diminishes the amount of social and individual liberty enjoyed. How can such a mental deterioration take place? A most active agency in producing such an effect is the ill-considered and stupid practice of the originally wise and intelligent sentiments of humanitarianism. We have seen that in savage society only the strong survive because there is little or no succor for the weak in body, in mind, or in both. This ruthless extermination of the unfit does not in itself insure liberty for the survivors. That late development is dependent upon many artificial factors including high intelligence and humanitarianism.

But a policy of unenlightened humanitariansm multiplies the physically unfit and establishes population ratios in which the denominator of inferiors increases much more rapidly than the small numerator of the fit. For humanitarianism assumes that the strong can look after themselves and devotes its attention to the preservation and succor of the weak. It operates through the socialization of medical science, through private and public charity, and through the toleration of antisocial individuals and their maintenance at the expense of the law-abiding.

Medical science is continually decreasing infant mortality by saving the lives of the young who in earlier times would have succumbed through constitutional weakness or by infectious disease. It cannot be denied that it has operated to preserve more of the weak than of the strong, the majority of whom would have "got by" in any event. Medicine has also extended the lives of the aged, without, however, eliminating the physical and mental decrepitude of senility. It has alleviated human suffering, but has also prolonged it. It has insured the continued existence of countless individuals who through its ministrations "carry on" in society under the handicap of physiological malfunction and organic deterioration. These unfit, rescued by medicine, not only live, but breed, and that right abundantly. Only the most incorrigible optimist can regard with satisfaction the quality and numbers of the resulting offspring, even if we insist that few diseases are heritable. Up to now I have been talking about the effect of socialized medicine in preserving the physically unfit, but this salvaged human material presumably functions on a lower level of mentality because of its deteriorated organism. The patched-up sick, by and large, cannot behave with the vigorous intelligence of the healthy.

Mental disease and mental defect are frequently compatible with the retention of fair health, moderate bodily vigor, and an unimpaired reproductive capacity. This statement is undeniable, although I myself have found the criminal and civil insane of different nationalities much smaller, apparently weaker, and biologically inferior to the sane criminals and to the sane civilians of similar ethnic origin. Medical science can do very little to cure the insane and nothing at all to supply brains to the mentally deficient. But humanitarianism does support and shelter the mentally inferior, and moreover turns them loose to reproduce their kind. Only the intelligent have developed that social and economic responsibility which induces them to limit the number of their offspring to those which they can rear under tolerable environmental conditions. The moron breeds without taking thought for the morrow.

Humanitarianism rightly regards the criminal as a more or less innocent victim of heredity, or of environment, or of both, and therefore tries to effect a cure rather than to administer a punishment. It has directed almost exclusive attention, thus far, to the prevention of crime and to the rehabilitation of criminals by education and by attempts to improve the environment or to adjust the individual to the latter. No one can deny that these efforts have resulted in complete failure and that toleration of the antisocial individual and sheltering him in institutions have been tantamount to the establishment of factories for the mass production of crime. The thousands of criminals operating at large, incarcerated in institutions, and in the making wherever inferior human stock exists in an unfavorable environment, do nothing to add to the mean intelligence of the population nor to further the maintenance of human liberty.

Of public and private charity and of the subvention and support of the needy, whether by voluntary contributions or by government levy, I have little to say. Charity is necessary, and many of its beneficiaries are deserving. Its less encouraging result is to relieve the least capable of the population of the necessity of supporting themselves, and to permit them to live and breed copiously in idleness and in discomfort. Nor does it bring them content and an increasing disposition to improve their lot by intelligent labor—the only efficacious way. Much charity fosters human stock of inferior intelligence, which is willing to take liberty but not to grant it to others.

Scientific warfare and the organization of modern civilized nations for it are more convincing demonstrations of the low level and depreciated quality of human intelligence than would be thousands of tables of statistics relating to increase of crime, insanity, and mental defect and to the lowering of average intelligence quotients. Modern war does its own bit in decreasing the proportionate numbers of the physically fit in populations by selecting as active combatants the healthy and vigorous males and leaving the diseased, the constitutionally inferior, and the senile to remain at home to direct war and to plan more of it. Of course, it seems clear that future wars will involve the destruction of the civilian populations, as well as active combatants; and, if this gives comfort to anyone, he is welcome to it.

Against all of these inroads into the physical health and mental fitness of modern populations—the well-meant activities of medical science and of indiscriminate humanitarianism, and the sheer insanity of war—we have nothing to pit except education and the never-ceasing efforts of the socially minded to adjust human institutions, which imply intelligence and co-operation, to a population which does not possess the former and does not want the latter.

I do not come before you to suggest that we abandon education, but to remind you that the success of this paramount social measure depends not only upon the extent and intensity of its application, but also upon the educability of the human material, which varies with its degree of intelligence. I do not advocate the restriction of medical science except in its efforts to save lives which are predestined to social uselessness by constitutional defect or by incurable disease. Humanitarianism is a term which I apply to the loftiest aggregate of human sentiments, from which has arisen in part the concept of human liberty. But these sentiments, divorced from reason and applied without judgment to those who lack the intelligence to comprehend them and to reciprocate them, nourish vipers. That humanitarianism which presided at the birth of liberty bids fair to destroy it.

How long are we to continue in the belief that the accumulation of knowledge implies a proportionate increase in the intelligence of the human beings who contribute to that knowledge not one iota? How long shall we delude ourselves with the idea that we can remake man himself by infinite education and skillful readjustment of human institutions? How long must we pretend that representative government is intelligent when it is chosen to represent an unintelligent majority?

I have tried to show that social liberty springs from organic liberty which implies a relative emancipation of human behavior from animal instinct—or, in short, its control by intelligence. Then liberty can survive only by the maintenance of a high degree of intelligence in the human units of populations which seek to exercise it. Liberty cannot survive if that intelligence, whether inherited or acquired, is concentrated in a small minority. I have not attempted to prove a decline in the intelligence of modern civilized populations by the presentation of factual data. You may believe, on the contrary, that the mean of intelligence has increased. If you do adhere to this belief, you need not worry about the maintenance of human liberty, because it will not be throttled by the development of better brains in common men nor by any other agency when the quality of human thought and judgment is improving.

If human organisms are deteriorating, what can we do about it? I cannot write a prescription for the cure of all human ills. I can only suggest that we study the biology of man in relation to his intelligence and to his behavior. We can apply the vast resources of intelligent science to the investigation of that great unknown, human heredity. We may be able to learn to breed better human beings before "the night cometh when no man can work." We can at least use our common sense by restricting the reproduction of the insane, the criminals, and the feeble-minded; and we can permanently segregate the antisocial, however little they and fatuous humanitarians may like it. I have no other hope for the survival of human liberty. Yet, in turning our attention to the human organism and its improvement, we need not and must not relax our efforts to improve human institutions. We do not want less social science, but more biological science and the application of the results obtained by correlating research and endeavor in the two fields, which never should have been separated.

I have expounded the views and convictions of one very fallible physical anthropologist on the prospect of the maintenance of human liberty. I claim for these views no authority, no validity, beyond that of my own thought, experience, and study. I have not attempted to document these views by learned citations, nor do I pose as the official spokesman of any branch of science or any school of thought. If, in discussing liberty, I have talked only nonsense, I can plead but one extenuating circumstance. In the selection of my subject of this evening I was accorded no liberty of choice.

X

THE WAGES OF BIOLOGICAL SIN*

RELIGIOSITY, LIKE a predisposition to nervous disease, breaks out sporadically in the successive generations which carry the taint, manifesting itself in Protean forms. In my more detached or schizophrenic moments I contemplate with sardonic amusement what I must regard in myself as the late blooming of a perverted evangelism, probably a transmogrified biological equivalent of the gospel preached by my father, who was a Methodist minister, or perhaps even an atavistic legacy from a Wesleyan, circuit-riding grandfather. And so I have the temerity, in addressing this certainly intelligent and probably godless audience, to adapt a text from the Epistle of St. Paul to the Romans: "The wages of (biological) sin is (evolutionary) death." You will remember that the Devil was apt at quoting Scripture, and I am often regarded as the Devil's advocate, even when acquitted of the charge of genetic Mephistophelian relationship.

Biological sin is any want of conformity unto, or transgression of, the law of Nature—a definition achieved by a slight distortion of the meaning of plain sin given in the Century Dictionary. Further, like theological sin, biological sin falls into two classes: original sin and actual sin. Original sin is conceived to be that innate depravity and corruption of the

* Lecture delivered in the Columbia University Extension Course, February 11, 1939. Reprinted by permission of the *Atlantic Monthly*.

nature common to all mankind, or—in a more strictly biological sense—the inherent weakness of the human species accumulated and transmitted through the course of evolution. Actual sin, according to the theologians, is the voluntary, conscious act of the individual. In our sense actual biological sins are those committed either deliberately or ignorantly by man since he has reached a status of his intelligence and culture which has permitted him to bungle his own organic evolution.

In this biological sermon, then, I shall first expound original anthropological sin, since we must initially acquaint ourselves with the frailties of the human vessel, which is well known to be made of clay but is not always realized to be only half-baked and frequently cracked. We shall then proceed to discuss the actual sins whereby man himself has made a bad matter considerably worse.

ORIGINAL BIOLOGICAL SIN

Man is an animal organism which has been evolved by the impact of shifting environments upon a variable hereditary endowment. The intrinsic and extrinsic forces which have been involved in this process are variation, adaptation, and selection. Variation is the result of nature's inability to produce two organisms which are exactly alike, due to the imprecision of reproductive processes and to the instability of the essential germinal matter which clings to life through fluctuating environments. Adaptation is not mere organic plasticity; it is a process of adjustment which, although unconscious and involuntary, demands something which I call organic initiative—a quality notably displayed by all higher primates. Selection is not an intelligent process; environment does not pick and choose organisms for survival or for extinction. It merely sets up a series of barbed-wire entanglements placed without purpose. The animals or plants which continue to "get by" achieve survival as a result of their own adaptability or merely because they possess, by sheer chance, a combination of organic variations which maintains their equilibrium in an environment as long as the latter remains stable. The more highly evolved the organism, the more complex and manifold in its parts and functions, the more it has to depend upon its own organic resources in the continual struggle against an impersonal but hostile environment. It seems probable that evolutionary immortality—if there is such a thing—is more likely to be vouchsafed to very simple organisms, since these proliferate in such vast numbers that the odds are always against total extinction. Moreover, the fewer the parts, the rarer the weak spots and the less vulnerable is the organism. Yet man seems as little regardful of his evolutionary peril as were those nit-brained, colossal dinosaurs which trailed their ungainly bulks over the Mesozoic landscape until they bogged down into extinction through the organic stupidity of overspecialization upon unessentials and gross size. One can hardly expect the man in the street to develop an anxiety neurosis over the prospect of human extinction within the next thousand years. When altruism toward contemporaries is so rare, a vicarious foresightedness on behalf of the nth generation is unimaginable. Yet man is such a complicated organism and has built up so intricate a civilization that an evolutionary slump—a deterioration in the quality of the species—immediately upsets the delicate bio-sociological equilibrium and causes cultural ructions. Whether the present biological depression is the beginning of a fatal evolutionary decline or merely a temporary lapse, it threatens to bring about the downfall of our present civilization and the destruction of many or most of its human participants. Consequently, it behooves us to take stock of the situation.

A glance at the fragmentary record of primate evolution will orient us for our examination of original biological sin. Sixty millions of years ago the first primates developed from a group of primitive little mammals much like the present-day tree shrews. These were long-snouted, small-brained quadrupeds which climbed about the trees, eating everything which an arboreal life provides and grasping branches and picking food with their five-digited hands and feet. The modern lemurs of Madagascar are specialized descendants of these early primates. In the same fossil-bearing strata are found fragmentary remains of other small tree-dwelling primates whose feet have become specialized for hopping, whose arms have been shortened, whose snouts have receded. These were erect-sitting, hand-feeding tarsioids, relatively unchanged in modern representatives of the Malay Archipelago. They mark an evolutionary advance toward the monkey stage. Many millions of years were required to establish the larger-brained monkeys which possess stereoscopic vision, vastly increased intelligence, and a generally more complex bodily organization. These are still arboreal or ground-living quadrupeds with primitive pentadactyle hands and feet capable of skillful grasping movements, and with digestive systems still suitable for a generalized diet, although showing some tendency toward herbivorous or frugivorous specialization. The evidence of fossils suggests that the first small anthropoid apes emerged soon after the monkey stage had been reached. Unspecialized ancestors of the long-armed gibbon were probably the first on the scene. These animals may well have moved through the trees by swinging from their arms. Their viscera were probably hitched up in the body cavities so that they would not slump when the animal sat up; the external tail had degenerated and disappeared. The foot was still a grasping organ, after the pattern of all primates except eventual man. Probably not more than fifteen millions of years ago, in the Middle Miocene period, many primates of gigantic size came into being from small and primitive apes. These large apes ranged from the southern slopes of the Himalayas to western France and over the whole African continent. Living specialized descendants of some of these families are the African gorillas and chimpanzees and the Asiatic orangutan. Various genera and species, some of them much more manlike than the great apes of today, became extinct. One or more of these groups of generalized anthropoids took to the ground, adopted the erect posture, and attained human status. The development from ground apes to man must have taken place during the Pliocene period, which is estimated to have begun seven millions of years ago. By the beginning of the Pleistocene, or glacial, period, perhaps a million years back, the human animal had acquired most of its distinguishing anatomical features and was already making recognizable stone implements.

It is important to realize that the very remote Miocene period witnessed a proliferation of large anthropoid forms, some differentiating in a generally human direction and others toward the more conservative organic patterns found in the present great apes. Most of these succumbed in the struggle for existence. Nature is a prodigal experimenter, a waster of laboratory material.

Man in surviving these evolutionary vicissitudes has inherited weakness of every main division of his organism: skeletal framework, musculature, alimentary apparatus, nervous and circulatory systems, endocrines and reproductive organs, sense organs and integument.

The human skeleton has been modified from that of the generalized quadrupedal mammal. The most radical alterations have taken place between the hypothetical stage of the arm-swinging, arboreal protohuman ape and the erect, ground-walking human biped. We are concerned here only with those which have left the human organism vulnerable to disease and liable to trauma as a result of mechanical defect. These are concentrated in the spine, the pelvis, and the feet. Tilting the animal up on his hinder end has shifted the entire weight-transmitting and -supporting function of the skeleton to these bony parts. The head and the fore-quarters ride; the posterior half does all of the work. The primitive quadrupedal spine is roughly bow-shaped, with the concavity directed toward the ground and with the neck and tail ends slightly turned up. The spines of the vertebrae converge toward the central keystone of the arch—the anticlinal vertebra. The fore and hind limbs are the supporting pillars of this arch, the elements of which are separated by elastic pads of fibro-cartilage, like mortar between stones. This horizontal spinal arch is an admirable mechanical structure until it is tipped up on end. It then becomes S-shaped, because a forward bend just above the pelvis is required for the erection of the trunk. This lumbar curve is a weak point in the column, liable to overflexion under the weight-bearing strain, particularly as a result of faulty posture. The specialization in the use of the right hand for skilled movements causes hypertrophy of that half of the body, with consequent lateral skewing, or curvature, which compresses the vertebral disks on one side or other and possibly, as the osteopaths claim, pinches the spinal nerves as they emerge from the intervertebral foramina. At any rate, the unbraced lumbar column is a legacy of backaches, slipped vertebrae, and a promising prey for attacks of inflammatory disease.

The human pelvis is a makeshift contraption. Its worst feature is the articulation of the triangle of used vertebrae (called the sacrum) with the lateral parts of the pelvis or haunch bones. In man this central spinal element is like the keystone of an arch, but all of the weight of the upper portion of the body bears upon this keystone and transforms it into a wedge which tends to be driven downward through the arch. The human articulation of the sacrum with the pelvic bones is not mortised, or interlocked, as in the anthropoid apes, but is practically a bevel. Consequently it slips, with dire results. Appendicitis has yielded to sacroiliac trouble as the fashionable ailment of the day. The lowering of the front wall of the pelvis in man renders the male liable to extrusion of the abdominal viscera, or hernia, while the opening of the pelvic floor in the female, essential for child-bearing, also opens the door for slumping of the uterus and for other ailments resulting from the losing battle with gravity.

I need say little of the human feet except that they too are decidedly of clay. Ill-constructed and wobbly arches, vestigial and superfluous toes, the lack of an adequate protecting integument—all of these faults raise the question of the evolutionary advisability of warping an organ designed for grasping branches into one ill-suited for support and locomotion. Man has been footsore ever since his forebears took to the ground. Perhaps the real primate Garden of Eden was up a tree, and the expulsion was the descent therefrom.

As for the muscles of the body, they labor under the disadvantage of frequent shifts of their points of origin and insertion to mechanically disadvantageous positions, necessitated by man's unnatural erect posture. If we accept the conclusions of students of living anthropoid apes, we have to admit that pound for pound our muscles are much weaker than those of our poor relations, and probably less efficient.

The digestive tract of man, inherited ultimately from quadrupedal ancestors which lived upon leaves, shoots, fruits, and nuts, with occasional small additions of animal food, has also been embarrassed by man's assumption of the erect posture. The elongation of the legs, in connection with their increased function, has been accompanied by an abbreviation of the trunk —the pelvis, so to speak, having climbed up the spine. This change, together with the flexion of the backbone in the lumbar region, has shortened the body cavities and cramped the viscera. The enormous lengths of gut are subject to more snarling and twisting in the abdominal cavity of the erect animal than in the longer-bellied quadrupeds. In the latter they may rest upon the abdominal wall without compression from diaphragmatic breathing and in no danger of slumping into the cavity of the pelvis and jamming the pelvic organs. This well-intentioned gut has not kept pace with the evolutionary trend of the human organism as a whole and has remained inconveniently long. It was adapted in our quadrupedal ancestors for passage of large masses of coarse vegetable food which moved through it in a generally horizonal direction, keeping it physio-logically well-scoured. It is less suitable for the digestion and elimination of a small bulk of concentrated food consisting of meat and processed cereals with little or no roughage. Kinks, adhesions, and inflammations result from a comparative atrophy of function, together with the accumulation and decay of food waste in out-of-the-way corners. Without going further into indelicate detail, one may conclude that *Homo flatulens* would be a better name for our species than *Homo sapiens*.

The circulatory system of man also has to work against grav-ity because of the erect posture. This difficulty naturally affects most seriously the arterial supply to the brain above the heart and the return of venous blood from the regions below the heart. L. J. Henderson has pointed out that the maintenance of the upright posture involves an accumulation of lymph in the legs and a thickening of the blood, so that the military position of rigid attention is unsupportable to the average middle-aged man for as long as fifteen minutes. Hardening of the arteries and dilatation of the veins are almost inevitable consequences of erect posture in the aging human organism. Experiments carried out by the Harvard Fatigue Laboratory demonstrate all too clearly the vast inferiority of man to or-dinary domesticated quadrupeds, such as dogs and burros, in maintaining for protracted periods a moderate level of work without physiological prostration due to cumulative bio-chem-ical changes. The factors involved include particularly insuffi-cient intake and transportation of oxygen, loss of water and salts through perspiration, and disturbance of carbon dioxide balance. Thermostatic control of the human organism is also very imperfect.*

I am informed that the rhesus monkey, or macaque, is the only mammal of which the reproductive cycle is adequately known and understood by modern science. There exists, then,

* Dill, David B., *Life, Heat and Altitude, passim.* Cambridge, Harvard University Press, 1938.

no sufficient knowledge for comparing man with other animals in regard to the quality of the reproductive system. However, the exaggerated loss of blood which is a feature of the oestrous cycle in the human female of child-bearing age is equaled in no other mammal. It is barely perceptible in the great anthropoid apes, and discernible as a purely microscopic phenomenon in some of the monkeys. Surely this fact suggests wastage and lack of efficiency of the human reproductive system. The mechanical difficulties encountered by woman in the course of pregnancy and parturition and the disarrangements which are frequent after-effects of child-bearing are partially attributable to the unsatisfactory modifications of the female organisms for the erect posture, complicated further by the enormous size of the head of the human foetus. On the whole, however, I should be inclined to judge that the human reproductive system works altogether too well—especially in those who ought not to reproduce at all.

The normal processes of growth, development, and functioning of the human organism are governed by the secretions of the ductless glands or endocrines, and a delicate balance of these several glands is essential to the well-being of the individual. Something is also known of the dire effects of disease or abnormal functioning of the pituitary, the thyroid, the adrenals, and so on. Morphology, physiology, psychology, total personality, and, ultimately, social behavior are in the individual the resultant in a large measure of the endocrine forces operating within each of us. It seems improbable that anyone knows enough to offer an adequate appraisal of the merits and defects of the endocrine system in the light of comparative physiology. However, to the lay mind of the physical anthropologist, the available evidence suggests that man has altogether too complex and delicate a system of endocrines, which easily gets out of kilter and is likely to go mysteriously and wildly haywire not only in individuals, but possibly in whole groups, whether through hereditary or environmental causes, heaven knows.

There can be no doubt that the development of the central nervous system has dominated the evolution of the primate stock which gave rise to man. The enormous and, occasionally, magnificent brain of the human animal is responsible for man's unique cultural achievement and for his leadership of the parade of living organisms. I cannot enter here into certain unfavorable effects upon the rest of the organism exerted by the dictatorship of a predatory central nervous system. The excessive development of any part of the organism takes place at the expense of other parts. Enlargement, or hypertrophy, involves the necessity of an increased blood supply and of heavier draughts upon the store of vital energy, which in any organism at any time is strictly limited by the physiological capacity of the animal to ingest food and to convert it into energy. I wish here rather to emphasize as the heaviest evolutionary liability of man his inheritance of a preponderant brain mass which is terrible in its potentiality for malfunction. Evidently the increase of brain size in the protohuman stock was due to the selection of a favorable variational trend which promoted the survival of the species. I think it may be presumed (without taint of Lamarckianism) that this generous cerebral endowment was largely, if not fully, utilized in the struggle of an otherwise physically inferior animal to survive by its wits. Starting from scratch as a tree-dwelling animal which had outgrown the arboreal habitat, or had been forced to the ground through some environmental cataclysm, or (most probably) had been impelled by sheer organic initiative to pursue the more abundant opportunities of a terrestrial existence, man simply had to use his brain. "Dominion over the fish of the sea, and over the fowl of the air, and over everything that moveth upon the earth" was not achieved by morons carrying a dead weight of atrophied brain mass. Constant cerebration was necessary. However, with the accumulation of material culture and with the development of complicated social orders the rigors of natural selection were abated and the larger portion of mankind could survive and propagate its kind in the low status of domestic animals, kept and fed for the produce of their unthinking labors. The full effect of this survival of the mentally unfit, this stultification of man's cerebral endowment, was not felt until the advent of the modern industrial, mechanized age. I must emphasize the fact that an insufficiently exercised brain is not like an unused muscle. It does not merely shrivel and become weak, but either continues its activities in the irrational and unbalanced functioning which is called insanity, or, under the conditioning of vicious propaganda and the stimuli of "mob psychology," energizes its possessor to inhuman types of behavior of which lower animals are incapable. However stupid he may be, the human individual can draw upon the cerebral endowment transmitted through the inertia of heredity to reinforce his feeble muscular strength by a malevolent cunning and ingenuity in misbehavior which makes him infinitely more dangerous than an ape or any other lower animal of superior physical power.

ACTUAL SINS

Now, when we add together all of man's original or inherited sins, we arrive at a sum total of potentialities for an evolutionary mess which seems a trifle depressing, even to an incorrigible optimist like myself. Evidently the optimum functioning of all of the indifferently constructed parts of the organism is essential for a tolerable state of well-being. There is very small leeway for healthful or "normal" variation within the limits of the pathological and the defective. If the kinks of the spine are a trifle exaggerated, either through hereditary variation or through bad postural habits, this small defect initiates far-reaching organic disturbances which almost immediately affect the dominating nervous system and ultimately distort mental processes and pervert behavior. Man's behavior is rational, if ever, only when the entire organism is in tune.

Moreover, irrelevant and trivial difficulties of bodily origin, which under primitive cultural conditions affect only the individual, are likely to determine the fates of entire races and peoples under the integrated political and economic systems of modern congested civilizations.

Actual biological sin includes the practices and policies of man which accentuate his original hereditary weakness, or inflict upon his organism a biological regime for which it is not adapted, or, finally, interfere with those natural processes which, in lower animals, eliminate the unfit and prevent them from propagating their kind. We may consider the extent to which modern culture remedies or accentuates the evolutionary defects which I have described as our legacy of original biological sin.

First of all, we have that delicately adjusted, upright spine with its dangerous lumbar curve. Even before the infantile vertebrae are completely transformed from cartilage to bone, we begin to prop up the babies in a sitting posture which is likely to distort that plastic spine. Soon we thrust them into schools where they sit for hours acquiring rudimentary scholarship and advanced scoliosis, or lateral curvature of the spine. Meanwhile the shoulders are hunched, the chest contracted, and the organs of vision strained by a premature concentration upon the dubious wisdom of the printed word. The mysterious human predisposition to specialized use of the right hand is exaggerated into a physiological abnormality, and bilateral asymmetry advances to the threshold of deformity. The human foot is so radically modified for support and locomotion that it requires optimum physiological utilization if it is to do its work at all. Straightway we encase this delicate organ in rigid, ill-fitting shoes which cramp it, distort the already vestigial toes, and by artificial support destroy the strength of the makeshift arches which have been bestowed by a casual heredity. Then we lay hard and inelastic pavements and floors upon which the imprisoned feet are condemned to stand and walk during the remainder of their unnatural life. Before the child has cut his first permanent tooth, he is ripe for the ministrations of the orthopedist, because his spinal curves are askew, his foot arches flattened, and the entire muscular tone, essential for proper maintenance of the erect posture and for bipedal progression, has been destroyed. Then we cap the climax by substituting for the ordinary animal method of locomotion the conveyance of a stinking mechanical contraption, which more than any other invention of modern civilization is responsible for bodily and mental atrophy, the breakdown of social organization, and the decay of public and private morals. It is not strange that unaccustomed strains or sudden movements of the body result in sacroiliac slips and other joint difficulties when the flabby automobile addict attempts to indulge in exercise.

One look into the mouth of the civilized child reveals the havoc wrought by unbalanced diets of manufactured foods. Dental decay usually sets in before the milk teeth have been shed. Malerupted teeth and deformed arches are the concomitants of defective nutrition and loss of masticatory function. If we could look into the rest of the alimentary tract, we should probably see similar evidences of pathology and degeneration. In the upper economic levels of American society mother love may still survive, but mother's milk has vanished. The hapless infant is raised on synthetic substitutes for natural foods. His upbringing is not mammalian but chemical. The earliest tactile experience of the groping baby hand is not the warmth and softness of the maternal breast, but the vitreous surface of a fusion of silica with various bases—in short, a glass bottle.

For a long time it has been known that primitive hunters and food-gatherers the world over almost invariably have excellent teeth, practically immune from decay. But no one has had the common sense to go and find out why savages have good teeth except Dr. Weston Price, of Cleveland.* He has been all over

* Price, Weston A., *Nutrition and Physical Degeneration*, Hoeber, N. Y., 1939.

"Mother love may survive, but mother's milk has vanished."

the world inspecting mouths and recording diets, and he has found the answer. Primitive man is guided by instinct and by experience to seek a sufficient variety of all kinds of food, however coarse and unpalatable, to furnish all of the constituents necessary for bone- and tissue-building, as well as for the production of energy. The savage generally has to eat everything masticable within sight and reach; and, in so doing, by hook or by crook he achieves a balanced diet which keeps his teeth and his entire alimentary tract in healthy working order.

Civilized man, on the contrary, has a wide choice of cheap processed foods which have usually been deprived of vitamins and other essential constituents in the course of manufacture and preservation. He might better, like the prodigal son, fill his belly with the husks the swine eat, rather than stuff himself with these devitaminized, energy-producing foods which build neither bone nor muscle. His teeth decay, his digestive system goes sour, and he literally starves amid plenty. We grovel in admiration at the feet of the medical scientists who keep on discovering new vitamins until the alphabet bids fair to run out; yet it seems possible that the untutored savage who knows not Vitamins A to X, but nevertheless eats all of them, has the better of the bargain. Medical science is principally occupied with uncovering the needless actual biological sins which man has committed against his organism by developing an artificial civilization. But civilization moves forward at such a pace that the doctor is always a few laps behind. He chases on foot the ambulance of civilized ailments.

However, man has done a much more thorough job in deteriorating his nervous system and the working of his mind than he has accomplished in any other part of the organism. The statement may seem false and even silly when we consider the time and effort which have been lavished upon education and the stress laid upon intelligent planning for machines and measures which are supposed to promote material and social progress. Yet it is easy to demonstrate that vast majorities of the populations of civilized mankind are suffering from cerebral dry rot because they are supported by machines which not only produce for them, but actually think for them; and that the small minority which does cerebrate constructively is so overdeveloped and overstimulated on the nervous side of its organism that it is prevailingly neurotic and not infrequently psychotic.

I have expounded so often the mental atrophy which the use of ingenious gadgets has wrought upon the ungifted millions of human drones which swarm in the industrial hive that I am not going to inflict these banalities upon you, whom I persistently judge to be capable of thought. I wish rather to concentrate upon the imbecility of educational and social policies which are based upon mainly metaphysical conceptions of the nature of man and completely erroneous evaluations of the importance of culture. The mortal sin which has accelerated the deterioration of the human organism is man's stubborn refusal to recognize that he is an animal which has evolved from simpler forms and is subject to the same natural laws which govern the development and decline of other animal groups. It must have dawned upon human consciousness at a very early stage that man is more intelligent than any other animal, and that it is only by virtue of that excess of intelligence that he has achieved mastery of the animal kingdom and ability to shape for his own ends the material resources of nature. This recognition led to the three fundamentally erroneous human beliefs: that human intelligence is fixed and immortal, that man's lofty evolutionary status is permanent, and that the perfecting of human culture will provide a panacea for the ills of mankind.

The most cherished of human beliefs is the separability and immortality of man's soul. Since this belief arises from man's realization of his individual consciousness, it is firmly and naturally established. The transition to a conception that the human soul is a unique divine gift, inalienable and immutable, is easily made. It is unfortunate that our ideas about mind and intelligence have been mixed up with this belief in the immortal soul. From this confusion there arises the conviction that a godlike intelligence is also divinely implanted in each human being, irrespective of the quality of his animal organism, which is recognized to be a frail and corruptible thing. So we have persisted in the ancient error of divorcing mind from body, of perfuming the former without washing the latter. It is true that many schools of magico-religious therapeutics have recognized the inseparability of mind and body, but they have usually gone at the business backwards by attempting to treat the body through the mind.

There is one terribly vital fact which must be grasped by the small fraction of mankind which is concerned about the social present and the biological future, if our species is not to destroy itself. It is merely that the mind of man and his social behavior are essentially functions of his animal organism, although susceptible to considerable environmental modification. Defective anatomical structure and inferior physiological functioning are inseparable from stupidity, lack of educability, insanity, and generally antisocial behavior. This does not mean that an ingrowing toenail necessarily causes an ingrowing disposition, nor that a partial paralysis of the leg inevitably effects a partial paralysis of the mind, but only that enfeebled bodily structure, physiological malfunction, and inferior mentality are the indivisible and unholy trinity of the degenerate organism.

It should be sickeningly obvious to every person who is capable of an intelligent survey of past and present human affairs that no accretions of factual knowledge and no process of ethical education, moral suasion, or religious teaching can permanently improve human conduct which is the expression of low-grade mentality.

It is discouraging to reflect that, because of this persistent disregard of the animal nature of man, progress in the two noblest fields of human endeavor—humanitarianism and science—has contributed to man's organic delinquency. The ideal-

istic code of humanitarianism is wholly admirable in so far as
it insists upon the brotherhood of man, mutual help, and the
protection of the weak by the strong. It is wholly vicious when
it exalts the sanctity of human life above the welfare of society
and the value of that life to itself; when it insists upon human
equality to the extent of according the same rights and privileges to the feeble-minded, the insane, and the criminalistic, as
to the mentally and physically sound, the economically capable,
and the socially minded. When it prescribes that the resources
of those who work and earn should be used to an inordinate
extent for the support of those who will not or cannot work, it
penalizes human initiative and puts a premium upon inferior
human quality. It is true that, under a capitalistic regime, vast
wealth may accumulate in the hands of comparatively few individuals who may be adjudged to have taken toll of the earnings
of others without undue effort on their own part. No one denies
that some human beings have been exploited by others or that
huge unearned increments should be taxed for the public good.
But the extreme policies of humanitarianism apparently operate
under the theory that human beings earn copiously only by
depriving other equally deserving or more deserving human
beings of their just share in this world's goods. These errors
of humanitarianism are based upon the assumption that it is
underprivilege which makes the underdog, and that the potentialities for intellectual and cultural development are essentially
equal in all men—in short, upon the delusion that mind and
social capacity in man are independent of the organism and that
an equalization of opportunity will bring the millennium. The
only alternative explanation of the theory underlying this policy
is that the unproductive and inefficient human being either is a
desirable member of society or is possessed of some inalienable
human right to exist upon the labor of others. This policy results not only in the preservation and multiplication of degenerate human stocks; in a democratic country it also leads to
political and social domination by the inferior elements as soon

as their rapid proliferation makes them constitute the majority. But the worst is still to come, since dull and witless human beings are unduly suggestible and quickly become subjected to the rule of fanatics and lunatics of moderate to superior intellectual endowment who have become mentally unbalanced without losing their energy and their capacity for leadership.

The mechanical inventions of a few clever men have made it possible for millions to live comfortably and luxuriously without even understanding the machines which produce for them. The control of nature achieved by the cerebration of a few active minds has created delusions of grandeur in the otiose brains of countless morons. Others, even more numerous, have been dulled and crazed by the monotonous repetition of muscular movements which they must perform incessantly as human adjuncts to machine production. Worst of all, the natural forces which have been harnessed to do the will of man can be utilized for the destruction of human culture and human beings much more effectively than for their benefit. A nation possessed of a somewhat archaic Oriental culture is able, within the space of two generations, to borrow the techniques of science which have been developed elsewhere during many centuries and to convert them to devastating purposes of predacity. Another nation which is peculiarly gifted in mechanical invention repeatedly threatens the ruin of Western civilization, because this nation is composed of organic blends which, for some unknown genetic reasons, combine marvelous understanding of mechanical techniques with utter obtusity in human relations, and which are of a suggestibility so extreme that they are more easily possessed by devils than were the Gadarene swine.

Medicine today is an extension of the maternal instinct mixed up with scientific techniques. It operates in an odor of sanctity and formaldehyde. Any objective criticism of medical science is difficult, merely because everyone of us is, or has been, or hopes to be, a grateful patient. My remarks upon medicine do not constitute in any way a repudiation of the

personal debt of gratitude which I owe to the profession. However, the real question at issue is not what advantage you or I
individually may have enjoyed from medical science, but rather
the value of the cumulative effect of medical ministrations upon
the entire human species. Medicine has alleviated suffering and
prolonged life; but it has, in so doing, also prolonged suffering
and nullified the purging effect of natural selection. It has
saved hundreds of thousands of debilitated organisms which
are adding to the burden of society by reproducing more and
worse offspring. Medical science has committed this sin against
the species because its members are not sufficiently enlightened
or not courageous enough to declare their independence of the
dogma of the sanctity of human life. Although medical men
have arrogated to themselves the entire field of human biology,
although they pride themselves upon their professional code
of ethics and are unremitting in their efforts to elevate the
qualifications of their personnel, they seem to have no clear
conception of what they are doing to man, of what man is, or
of what he ought to be. They have hung back and let others
lead whenever unpopular biological measures are necessary.
I am not aware that they have taken any united professional
stand in favor of birth control, nor in the matter of sterilization
of the feeble-minded, the insane, and the criminalistic, nor even
in the establishment and enforcement of rigorous medical examinations for persons intending marriage. They have taken
almost no interest in the study of the normal anatomical and
physiological variations of man which should be the bases for
their investigations of pathology. Not only have they neglected
the study of man's biological evolution, but they have con-
tented themselves with a minimum of general biological
knowledge which would hardly suffice a practitioner of animal
husbandry. While they have accumulated vast files of medical
histories, they have not, for the most part, learned the elementary methods and principles of accurate scientific recording
and are usually incapable of analyzing massed data from which

valid general conclusions may be drawn. Although the social sciences and all other biological sciences have long relied upon mathematical statistics as the only dependable means of elucidating quantitative or qualitative data affected by a multiplicity of causes, medical science stands aloof in obdurate and selfsatisfied ignorance. There are, of course, individual exceptions to each one of these strictures, but I do not think that I am unfair when I state that they are only exceptions.

Yet I am the last to deny medical science credit for remarkable achievement in the conquest of disease and for disinterested devotion to human betterment. Actually, I think that medicine is doing its job admirably if that job is conceived to be only the care of the human organism, taken "as is," and the remission of venial biological sins which are consequent upon civilized man's abuse of his bodily inheritance.

I appeal to medicine because it is the one branch of applied science which might be expected to realize not only that human behavior is a function of the human organism, but that all animal organisms exist and transmit their qualities through the mechanism of heredity. The fundamental principle of organic evolution is improvement or retrogression through the selection of inherited anatomical features and physiological functions. And I reiterate the statement which I have bellowed up and down this country for years, until I am thoroughly sick of it and everyone else is equally sick of me. Our entire system of education is upside down because it studies only human behavior and not the human organism; we know virtually nothing at all of the most vital factor in human evolution— human heredity.

I ask whether medical science is prepared to accept the responsibility for the reckless deterioration of human stock which it promotes by lavishing its skill and care upon the preservation of the unfit, when it takes no measures whatsoever for beginning the study of human inheritance by which alone permanent improvement of the species can be anticipated. I call upon this profession which is actually directing the course of human evolution downward to reflect upon the wages of biological sin.

Human deterioration can be checked if we tincture our humanitarianism with biological common sense. Human conduct can be corrected through education if only we have sound organisms to develop and to instruct. We can actually improve the quality of the sound human organism if we are willing to devote biological attention and generous medical co-operation to the study of human inheritance through several consecutive generations. We must found institutes for the study of human heredity in which every pathological and normal variation is followed from birth through reproduction and on to death with the purpose of determining the physiological, psychological, and sociological correlates of each of these variations. This is not the task of the physician alone. It will require the services of the geneticist, the psychologist, the sociologist, and even of the anthropologist. It is, in my opinion, the most exigent need of the human species; for upon the acquisition and application of this knowledge of human heredity is staked not only the immediate fate of our probably evanescent civilization, but also the survival or extinction of man himself. "The wages of biological sin is evolutionary death."

INDEX

Adaptation (see Variation)
Ainu, 74, 80
Alpine, 78-79, 81
Americans, body build 221-223, college students 214-218, early 197-199, "New Americans" 218-221, racial types 202-208, state types 211-213
American Indian (see Race and Race mixture)
Apes, 34-35, relation to man 8-9
Armenoid (see Race and Race mixture)
Australian, 261-265 (see Race and Race mixture)

Baboon, 260-261
Body build, 214-218, 221-223
Brain, 20-21, 26, 34-35, 38-41, 293-294
Bushman-Hottentot, 99-104

Century of Progress, 200-208
Chimpanzee, 18-19
Christianity (see Religion)
Classification, zoological 133-134
College students (see Americans)
Culture, 43-44, 46

Democracy, 54
Digestive system, 39-40, 290-291
Dinaric, 123

East Baltic, 123-126
East Indian, 104-107
Education, 55
Endocrine, 127-128
Eskimo, 118
Eurasian (see Race and Race mixture)
Evolution, 12-15, 286-290
Eyes, development of 14, Mongoloid-White 152-153, Negro-White 145-146

Food, 296-298
Foot, 15

Genius, relation to progress 23-25, 33
Geographical isolation, 67-68
Gibbon, 16-17
Gorilla, 19

Hair, 40, 71, 74, 81, 91, 100, 144, 152
Hand, 13-14
Hawaii, 176-181
Hottentot (see Bushman-Hottentot)
Humanitarianism, 49-55, 280-281, 300-301

Implements (see Tools)
Inbreeding, 137-138
Indian (see Race and Race mixture)
Indonesian-Malay, 112-114